T0207492

Communications
in Computer and Information Science 1758

More information about this series at https://link.springer.com/bookseries/7899

Mariana González · Silvia Susana Reyes ·
Andrea Rodrigo · Max Silberztein (Eds.)

Formalizing Natural Languages: Applications to Natural Language Processing and Digital Humanities

16th International Conference, NooJ 2022
Rosario, Argentina, June 14–16, 2022
Revised Selected Papers

Springer

Editors
Mariana González
Universidad Nacional de Rosario
Rosario, Argentina

Andrea Rodrigo
Universidad Nacional de Rosario
Rosario, Argentina

Silvia Susana Reyes
Universidad Nacional de Rosario
Rosario, Argentina

Max Silberztein ⓘD
Université de Franche-Comté
Besancon, France

ISSN 1865-0929   ISSN 1865-0937   (electronic)
Communications in Computer and Information Science
ISBN 978-3-031-23316-6   ISBN 978-3-031-23317-3   (eBook)
https://doi.org/10.1007/978-3-031-23317-3

This Springer imprint is published by the registered company Springer Nature Switzerland AG
The registered company address is: Gewerbestrasse 11, 6330 Cham, Switzerland

Preface

NooJ is a linguistic development environment that provides tools for linguists to construct linguistic resources that formalize a large range of linguistic phenomena: typography; orthography; lexicons for simple words; multiword units and discontinuous expressions; inflectional, derivational, and agglutinative morphology; local, phrase-structure, and dependency grammars; and transformational and semantic grammars.

To describe each type of linguistic phenomenon, NooJ offers formalisms that cover the extent of Chomsky-Schützenberger's hierarchy: regular grammars, context-free grammars, context-sensitive grammars, and unrestricted grammars. Grammars can then be applied to corpora of texts automatically by NooJ's parsers, which range from very efficient finite-state automata and transducers to augmented recursive push-down automata that have the power of Turing Machines. This makes NooJ's approach different from most other computational linguistic tools that offer a unique formalism to their users and are not compatible with each other. NooJ contains a rich toolbox that allows linguists to construct, test, debug, maintain, accumulate, and share large linguistic resources.

NooJ provides parsers that can apply any set of linguistic resources to any corpus of texts, to extract examples or counterexamples, annotate matching sequences, perform statistical analyses, and so on. Because NooJ's linguistic resources are neutral, they can also be used by NooJ to generate texts automatically. By combining NooJ's parsers and generators, one can construct sophisticated natural language processing (NLP) applications, such as automatic machine translation and automatic paraphrasing software.

Since its first release in 2002, several private companies have used NooJ's linguistic engine to construct business applications in several domains, from business intelligence to opinion analysis. To date, there are NooJ modules available for over 50 languages and more than 140,000 copies of NooJ have been downloaded. In 2013, an open-source version for NooJ was released, based on the JAVA technology and available to all as a GPL project supported and distributed by the European Metashare platform. The NooJ platform is in constant evolution:

- NooJ has recently been enhanced with new features to respond to the needs of researchers who analyze texts in various domains of human and social sciences (history, literature and political studies, psychology, sociology, etc.), and more generally of all the professionals who need to explore their corpus of texts and perform some discourse analyses. An interface specifically designed for the digital humanities has been implemented in the ATISHS software: http://atishs.univ-fcomte.fr.
- The new linguistic engine for NooJ "RA" was presented to the participants of the NooJ 2022 conference. It is open-source (written in the Swift programming language), is available on the GitLab platform, and is compatible with the LINUX,

macOS, and Windows platforms. It can be downloaded from http://www.nooj4nlp. org/downloads.html.

The 16th International NooJ Conference was held at the Universidad Nacional de Rosario (UNR) in Argentina, during June 14–16, 2022. Because of the COVID-19 pandemic, the conference was organized as both an in-person and a virtual (video conference) event. However, this hindered neither the quality of the presentations nor the success of the conference, as over 70 participants were able to attend and participate in the thematic sessions.

Overall, the NooJ 2022 conference received 49 submissions; each submission was reviewed by at least 3 members of the Program Committee, following a blind review process. 40 submissions were accepted for full or short (posters) presentations at the conference. This volume contains the best 17 articles selected by the editors of the volume and by the members of the conference scientific committee for publication in this volume.

The following articles are organized into four parts: "Morphological and Lexical Resources" contains five articles, "Syntactic and Semantic Resources" contains four articles, "Corpus Linguistics and Discourse Analysis" contains four articles, and "Natural Language Processing Applications" contains four articles.

The articles in the first part involve the construction of electronic dictionaries and morphological grammars to formalize various linguistic phenomena, in several languages:

- In his article "The architecture of SANTI-morf's guesser module", Prihantoro presents the new morphological annotation system for Indonesian: SANTI-morf, which contains an annotator, an improver, a disambiguator, and a guessor. SANTI-morf applies various linguistic resources in a pipeline. Prihantoro discusses NooJ's system of priorities and proposes a new way of organizing linguistic rules.
- In "Formation and evolution of intensive adverbs ending in-mente derived from the adjectival class <causatives de feeling: fear> in Spanish and French", Rafael García Pérez and Xavier Blanco examine the history of some adverbs derived from adjectives in French and Spanish. They show that the paradigm of intensifiers in modern Spanish and French is the result of a grammaticalization process which began with one or two adverbs and extended to many other semantically linked ones.
- In "Formalizing the Ancient Greek participle inflection with NooJ", Silvia Susana Reyes presents a new formalization of the Ancient Greek present active and middle-passive participles based on the morphological grammars implemented by Lena Papadopoulou for Modern Greek. She applies her new resources to Aesop's fables.
- In "Automatic Analysis of Appreciative Morphology: The Case of Paronomasia in Colombian Spanish", Walter Koza, Viviana Román, and Constanza Suy analyze a group of Colombian Spanish nouns and their corresponding paronomastic variants to implement a set of morphological and syntactic grammars, and then apply them to a test corpus, proving the feasibility of performing automatic analyses of paromasia.
- In "Prosodic segmentation of Belarusian texts in NooJ", Yauheniya Zianouka, Yuras Hetsevich, Mikita Suprunchuk, and David Latyshevich present a set of

morpho-syntactic grammars that formalize prosodic boundaries in Belarusian. They tested these resources on a corpus of literary and medical texts and discuss the results.

The articles in the second part involve the construction of syntactic and transformational grammars:

- In "Zellig S. Harris' Transfer Grammar and its application with NooJ", Mario Monteleone discusses Zellig Harris' theoretical approach to automatic translation, discusses the limitations of current automatic translators such as Google Translate, and shows how Harris' Transfer Grammars could be implemented on the NooJ platform.
- In "Formalization of transformations of complex sentences in Quechua", Maximiliano Duran describes various transformations that produce subordinated sentences and relative clauses in Quechua and proceeds to implement them with NooJ's transformational grammars; some of them can automatically produce paraphrases for the sentences that contain adverbial subordinate clauses. Finally, Duran discusses how transformational grammars can be designed to implement an automatic Quechua to French translator.
- In "Automatic extraction of verbal phrasemes in the electrical energy field with NooJ", Tong Yang presents three grammars he developed to represent French phrasemes used in technical texts in the electricity domain. By applying these grammars to his corpus, he was able to automatically extract 1,389 phrase sequences that can be used to teach technical French language.
- In "A Linguistic Approach for Automatic Analysis, Recognition and Translation of Arabic Nominal Predicates", Hajer Cheikhrouhou and Imed Lahyani present a bilingual Arabic to French dictionary of nominal predicates and support verbs, classifying them into two classes: predicates in the category <خنِصَة> "advice" and in the category <نظرة> "look", before describing their linguistic characteristics.

The articles in the third part "Corpus Linguistics and Discourse Analysis" discuss the contruction and the exploration of large corpora of texts as well as the implementation of various discourse analyses:

- In "Processing the Discourse of Insecurity in Rosario with the NooJ Platform", Andrea Rodrigo, Silvia Reyes, and Mariana González chose to analyze a recurring topic in post-pandemic Argentina: insecurity. The authors aimed to record what impact insecurity had and still has on the linguistic domain. To do this, they built a corpus of journalistic texts published in December 2021 in the main newspapers in Rosario, Santa Fe, Argentina.
- In "Analyzing political discourse: finding the frames for Guilt and Responsibility", Krešimir Šojat and Kristina Kocijan study disagreement between political and/or ideological opponents. Specifically, they have implemented a set of grammar rules to detect the usage of the Croatian lexemes *odgovornost* [responsibility] and *krivnja* [guilt], with all their morphological variants, that they applied to the corpus of plenary debates from the Croatian Parliament (127 million tokens). They show that there are more occurrences of terms of responsibility than guilt in the corpus, and

that right-oriented party tend to use these terms more frequently than left-oriented parties.

– In "Creation of parallel medical and social domains corpora for the Machine Translation and Speech Synthesis systems", Mikita Suprunchuk, Nastassia Yarash, Yuras Hetsevich, Valery Varanovich, Siarhey Gaidurau, Yauheniya Zianouka, and Palina Sakava present the construction of a corpus of medical and social texts to study words' linguistic peculiarities (mainly morphological) that were not considered by NooJ's main Belarusian resources.

– In "Creation of a legal domain corpus for the Belarusian module in NooJ: texts, dictionaries, grammars", Valery Varanovich, Mikita Suprunchuk, Yauheniya Zianouka, Tsimafei Prakapenka, Anna Dolgova, and Yuras Hetsevich present the procedure of creating a corpus of legal texts that can be used to help NLP software compute prosodic characteristics and perform syntagmatic delimitation.

The last section, dedicated to the presentation of various NLP applications, contains the following articles:

– In "Construction of an educational game "CONJ_NooJ"", Héla Fehri and Nizar Jarray present a serious game that improves the player's level in languages by mastering the conjugation of Arabic, English, and French verbs on the one hand and the inflection of French nouns and adjectives on the other hand.

– In "Annotation of procedural questions in standard Arabic using syntactic grammars", Essia Bessaies, Slim Mesfar, and Henda Ben Ghzela present the construction of an automatic question-answering system and, more specifically, its processing of procedural questions. They show how they implemented a set of grammars to annotate complex questions in the medical domain, based on a named entity recognizer capable of recognizing references to people, places, organizations, diseases, and virus names, and extract from them their focus and topic.

– In "Integrated NooJ environment for Arabic linguistic disambiguation improvement using MWEs", Dhekra Najar, Slim Mesfar, and Henda Ben Ghezela present a system for Arabic that recognizes several types of morphosyntactic variations that can occur in a multi word expression (MWE). They have implemented this system in an Arabic language disambiguation system, and they evaluate the system by creating a set of tests and experiments.

– In "The digital text workshop cloud, new solutions for super calculation environments", Ilaria Veronesi, Rita Bucciarelli, Francesco Saverio Tortoriello, Andrea Rodrigo, Marianna Greco, Colomba La Ragione, and Javier Julian Enriquez aim to find links between quantum physics, computational linguistics, and quantum computing. Thanks to the tools they have developed to identify fixed structures in Charles Baudelaire's narrative text, they have developed a local grammar that highlights the importance of the verb in the sentence. They discuss then how their system could be used in conjunction with BuViTeMS's AW Digital Intelligence model to reformulate and translate the recognized sentences.

This volume should be of interest to all users of the NooJ software because it presents the latest development of its linguistic resources, as well as a large variety of applications, both in the digital humanities and in NLP software.

Linguists as well as computational linguists who work on Arabic, Belarusian, Croatian, English, Ancient Greek, Indonesian, Italian, Quechua, or Spanish will find advanced, up-to-the-minute linguistic studies for these languages.

We think that the reader will appreciate the importance of this volume, both for the intrinsic value of each linguistic formalization and the underlying methodology, as well as for the potential for developing NLP applications along with linguistic-based corpus processors in the social sciences.

Max Silberztein

Organization

Program Chair

Max Silberztein   Université de Bourgogne Franche-Comté, France

Organizing Committee

Max Silberztein	Université de Bourgogne Franche-Comté, France
Andrea Rodrigo	Facultad de Humanidades y Artes, UNR (IES No. 28), Argentina
Marcela Coria	Facultad de Humanidades y Artes, UNR, Argentina
Silvia Reyes	Facultad de Humanidades y Artes, UNR, Argentina
Bárbara Méndez	Facultad de Humanidades y Artes, UNR, Argentina
Carolina Tramallino	Facultad de Humanidades y Artes, UNR, Argentina
Silvina Palillo	Facultad de Humanidades y Artes, UNR, Argentina
Virginia Gonfiantini	Facultad de Humanidades y Artes, UNR, Argentina
Luciana Andrín	UTN, Argentina
María Yanina Nalli	UTN, Argentina
Silvana Pierabella	UNR, Argentina

Program Committee

Farida Aoughlis	Mouloud Mammeri University, Algeria
Xavier Blanco	Autonomous University of Barcelona, Spain
Stéfan Darmoni	Université de Rouen, France
Héla Fehri	University of Sfax, Tunisia
Zoe Gavriilidou	Democritus University of Thrace, Greece
Yuras Hetsevich	National Academy of Sciences, Belarus
Kristina Kocijan	University of Zagreb, Croatia
Walter Koza	Universidad Nacional de General Sarmiento and CONICET, Argentina
Philippe Lambert	Université de Lorraine, France
Danielle Leeman	Université de Nanterre, France
Laetitia Leonarduzzi	Université d'Aix-Marseille, France
Peter Machonis	Florida International University, USA
Ignazio Mauro Mirto	University of Palermo, Italy
Samir Mbarki	Ibn Tofail University, Morocco
Slim Mesfar	University of Manouba, Tunisia
Elisabeth Métais	Conservatoire National des Arts et Métiers, France
Mario Monteleone	University of Salerno, Italy
Johanna Monti	University of Naples "L'Orientale", Italy
Ralph Müller	University of Fribourg, Switzerland

Thierry Poibeau   Laboratoire Lattice, CNRS, France
Jan Radimský   University of South Bohemia, Czech Republic
Andrea Rodrigo   University of Rosario, Argentina
Marko Tadić   University of Zagreb, Croatia
Izabella Thomas   Univerité de Franche-Comté, France
François Trouilleux   Université Clermont Auvergne, France
Agnès Tutin   Université de Grenoble-Alpes, France

Contents

Natural Language Processing Applications

List of Contributors

Essia Bessaies Riadi Laboratory, University of Manouba Tunisia, Manouba, Tunisia

Rita Bucciarelli University of Siena, Siena, Italy

Xavier Blanco Universitat Autònoma de Barcelona, Cerdanyola del Vallès, Spain

Hajer Cheikhrouhou LLTA, University of Sfax, Sfax, Tunisia

Anna Dolgova Minsk State Linguistic University, Minsk, Belarus

Maximiliano Duran Université de Bourgogne Franche-Comté, CRIT, Besançon, France;
LIG, UGA, Grenoble, France

Javier Julian Enriquez Polytechnic University of Valencia, Valencia, Spain

Héla Fehri MIRACL Laboratory, University of Sfax, Sfax, Tunisia

Siarhey Gaidurau United Institute of Informatics Problems, Minsk, Belarus

Henda Ben Ghezela RIADI, University of Manouba, Manouba, Tunisia

Henda Ben Ghzela Riadi Laboratory, University of Manouba Tunisia, Manouba, Tunisia

Mariana González Centro de Estudios de Tecnología Educativa y Herramientas Informáticas de Procesamiento del Lenguaje, Instituto de Eduación Superior N°28 "Olga Cossettini", Rosario, Argentina

Marianna Greco Ministry of Education, Rome, Italy

Yuras Hetsevich United Institute of Informatics Problems, Minsk, Belarus

Yuras Hetsevich United Institute of Informatics Problems of the National Academy of Sciences of Belarus, Minsk, Belarus

Nizar Jarray University of Gabes, Zrig Eddakhlania, Tunisia

Kristina Kocijan Department of Information and Communication Sciences, Faculty of Humanities and Social Sciences, University of Zagreb, Zagreb, Croatia

Walter Koza Consejo Nacional de Investigaciones científicas y técnicas, Universidad Nacional de General Sarmiento, San Miguel, Argentina

Imed Lahyani LLTA, University of Sfax, Sfax, Tunisia

David Latyshevich United Institute of Informatics Problems of the National Academy of Sciences of Belarus, Minsk, Belarus

Slim Mesfar Riadi Laboratory, University of Manouba Tunisia, Manouba, Tunisia

Slim Mesfar RIADI, University of Manouba, Manouba, Tunisia

Mario Monteleone Università degli Studi di Salerno, Fisciano, SA, Italy

Dhekra Najar RIADI, University of Manouba, Manouba, Tunisia

Tsimafei Prakapenka United Institute of Informatics Problems, Minsk, Belarus

Rafael Pérez García Universidad Carlos III de Madrid, Getafe, Madrid, Spain

Colomba La Ragione University Pegaso of Naples, Naples, Italy

Silvia Reyes Centro de Estudios de Tecnología Educativa y Herramientas Informáticas de Procesamiento del Lenguaje, Facultad de Humanidades y Artes, Universidad Nacional de Rosario, Rosario, Argentina

Silvia Susana Reyes Centro de Estudios de Tecnología Educativa y Herramientas Informáticas de Procesamiento del Lenguaje, Facultad de Humanidades y Artes, Universidad Nacional de Rosario, Rosario, Argentina

Andrea Rodrigo Centro de Estudios de Tecnología Educativa y Herramientas Informáticas de Procesamiento del Lenguaje, Facultad de Humanidades y Artes, Universidad Nacional de Rosario, Rosario, Argentina

Viviana Román Pontificia Universidad Católica de Valparaíso, Valparaíso, Chile

Palina Sakava United Institute of Informatics Problems, Minsk, Belarus

Krešimir Šojat Department of Linguistics, Faculty of Humanities and Social Sciences, University of Zagreb, Zagreb, Croatia

Mikita Suprunchuk Minsk State Linguistic University, Minsk, Belarus

Mikita Suprunchuk United Institute of Informatics Problems of the National Academy of Sciences of Belarus, Minsk, Belarus

Constanza Suy Pontificia Universidad Católica de Valparaíso, Valparaíso, Chile

Francesco Saverio Tortoriello University of Salerno, Fisciano, Italy

Valery Varanovich Belarusian State University, Minsk, Belarus

Ilaria Veronesi University of Salerno, Fisciano, Italy

Tong Yang North China Electric Power University, Beijing, China

Nastassia Yarash United Institute of Informatics Problems, Minsk, Belarus

Yauheniya Zianouka United Institute of Informatics Problems, Minsk, Belarus

Yauheniya Zianouka United Institute of Informatics Problems of the National Academy of Sciences of Belarus, Minsk, Belarus

Morphological and Lexical Resources

The Architecture of SANTI-Morf's Guesser Module

Prihantoro[✉] [iD]

Universitas Diponegoro, Semarang, Indonesia
prihantoro@live.undip.ac.id

Abstract. SANTI-morf is a new morphological annotation system for Indonesian, implemented using Nooj [1, 2]. SANTI-morf is designed using multi-module pipeline architecture. The modules are the Annotator, the Improver, the Disambiguator, and the Guesser. The Guesser, as its name suggests, provides best guesses for words the Annotator fails to analyze. Due to the complexities of Indonesian morphology, multiple layers of rules are created to guess the morphological structures of unknown polymorphemic and monomorphemic words. These rules are incorporated into five morphological grammars, which are applied in a pipeline based on their priorities. In each grammar, there are two layers of rules. The first layer rules are prioritized, thus ending with a +UNAMB operator. The second layer rules only apply when the first layer rules fail to find any match. Thus, the rules are constructed without a +UNAMB operator. Reflecting on the complexity of this experiment, I therefore suggest an alternative to set priorities, whose method I simulate in this paper. I argue that using the proposed alternative, NooJ users can organize rules with multiple priorities in just one grammar file.

Keywords. NooJ · Indonesian · Morphology · Guesser · Priority

1 To Guess or Not to Guess

In certain cases, an annotation system may have exhausted all of its resources to annotate a corpus but still, to some extent, fails to annotate some tokens in the corpus. The reasons for this may vary, such as the paucity of the system's resources, the presence of proper nouns and newly coined words as also mentioned in [3], among many others. While these are common phenomena in unrestricted texts, for automatic linguistic annotation systems, they may pose considerable challenges.

There are several options to deal with these paucities. The first option is to leave the tokens unannotated, i.e. as they are. NooJ [1, 2] implements this by default (unless modified). The second option is to annotate them using some sort of 'unknown' tag, such as X, as in Morphind [4]. These two options have the same consequence in that all unknown units will be considered unanalyzed.

Implementing these two options does not improve the coverage score, accuracy, or other evaluative measures. For example, if a system fails to analyze 10 out of 100 words in a text, the coverage of the system is measured at 90%. It is impossible to improve the coverage of the system when we implement one of the alternatives.

M. González et al. (Eds.): NooJ 2022, CCIS 1758, pp. 3–13, 2022.
https://doi.org/10.1007/978-3-031-23317-3_1

The third option is to implement some sort of guessing mechanism, which allows the system to supply analysis for unknown tokens. Consequently, these guesses may be either correct or incorrect. Applying this option means that evaluative scores have the potential to improve if the system guesses correctly. For example, the system may have guessed 5 out of 10 words correctly, thus improving the coverage from 90% to 95%. In a case where all guesses are incorrect, the coverage remains at 90%. While the latter does not improve the coverage, this option should do no harm when applied. On this basis, I argue that the benefits of this alternative outweigh the risks.

Note that the discussion of a 'guesser' in this project is presented within the frame of corpus linguistics, particularly morphological analysis. The effectiveness of a guesser's morphological output for other purposes, such as Information Retrieval (as discussed in [5–7]), is not presented here. Next, while the guesser created in this project can also be used to target Indonesian words which can contain morphemes from languages not present in the system's resources, most examples presented in this paper are taken from English for ease of reading.

2   A Brief Look at SANTI-Morph's Architecture

This section briefly discusses the architecture of SANTI-morph [8], a morphological annotation system implemented using Nooj [1, 2, 9, 10] that targets Indonesian. Indonesian is a mildly agglutinative language [4], widely spoken in Indonesia [11, 12].

SANTI-morf is composed of four 'modules': the Annotator, the Guesser, the Improver, and the Disambiguator, applied respectively. In this case, the term *module* refers to a resource or group of resources dedicated to completing a particular task.

The Annotator is composed of a collection of resources to tokenize words into morphemes and label each morpheme with potential tag(s). This is the first module created for SANTI-morf. I tested to what extent the system can provide coverage for different Indonesian corpora. It turned out that 100% coverage cannot be consistently achieved. This means some words remain unknown even though all resources have been exhausted by the system.

The types of unknown words vary. Some are proper nouns like the names of places or institutions. Some others are newly coined words, misspelt words, acronyms, or foreign words. Other unknown words are composed of a combination of an Indonesian affix and a foreign root, such as *merestore* 'to restore', which is a combination of an Indonesian prefix *me-* and a foreign root *restore*.

These findings drive the creation of the Guesser module. Just like resources in the Annotator, those in the Guesser are used by the system to implement annotations. However, they specifically target words the Annotator fails to analyze. Using this module, the system manages to analyze all words, thus 100% coverage can always be achieved. A fuller description of the module will be presented in subsequent sections. I will now return to describing the Improver, another module in the SANTI-morf system.

The Improver contains resources which aim to evaluate the annotations applied by the Annotator and the Guesser. If the annotations applied by the previous two modules are deemed incorrect, new annotations (which are considered better) are added. This module, in principle, applies annotations, like the Annotator and the Guesser, but it only works when those two modules have completed their tasks.

The last module is the Disambiguator, which is dedicated to resolving ambiguities. It targets ambiguously annotated units and removes incorrect annotations. In a case where ambiguities cannot be resolved, those units will remain ambiguous. However, it will always try its best to eliminate ambiguities (Fig. 1).

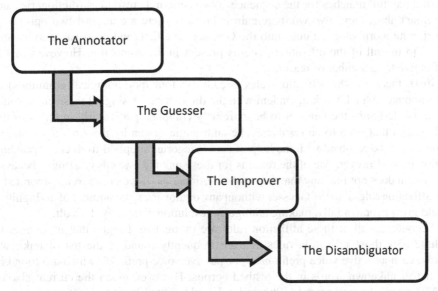

Fig. 1. SANTI-morf modules.

3 The Guesser

3.1 Morphological Cues

Identifying the characteristics of unknown words is crucial to the construction of the Guesser. This is because we can take cues from these unknown words and develop the Guesser's resources on the basis of these cues. Therefore, obtaining a list of unknown words from a corpus is a start.

To obtain a list of unknown words, I applied the Annotator to SANTI-morf's testbed corpus. From the observation of unknown words in the testbed, there are at least two important cues, on the basis of which, the Guesser's resources can be written: morphological cues, and capitalization.

Morphological cues such as affixes can be used to implement the morphological annotation of unknown words in this project. Let us consider two unknown Indonesian words: *memblacklist* 'to blacklist' and *merender* 'to render' as examples. These words begin with the prefixes *mem-* and *me-*, allomorphs of morpheme *meN-*. They are followed by foreign stems *blacklist* and *render*. Note that these foreign stems are analyzed as single roots in the SANTI-morf annotation scheme, regardless of whether they might be full word forms in the source language. Thus, even though *blacklist* can be analyzed as a compound, in this context, it is only analyzed as a root.

Following this scheme, *memblacklist* should be analyzed as <mem, meN, TAG> <blacklist, TAG> and *merender* should be analyzed as <me, meN, TAG> <render, TAG> (TAG in this paper is used to replace a full tag). However, the Annotator does not find any full matches for the sequences anywhere in its resources (dictionaries and grammar), thus, these two words remain unknown. There are at least two options to incorporate morphological cues into the Guesser. The first, and most straightforward, one is to use all of the affixation patterns present in the Annotator. However, this is ineffective for a number of reasons.

First, there are 484 affixation rules already (in four morphological grammars) in the Annotator, which work in tandem with the dictionaries. Using all these cues would cause the design of the Guesser to be extremely complex, particularly in terms of the ambiguities that need to be resolved. The ambiguities given by the Annotator can, to some extent, be resolved with the help of root categories supplied from corresponding dictionaries. However, one of the reasons for these unknown words existing is because the system does not find any matches in the dictionaries. If we chose to incorporate all 484 affixation rules into the Guesser without any dictionaries, the number of ambiguities would grow exponentially, making ambiguity resolution extremely difficult.

Second, not all of these affixation rules are productive. I argue that it is better to include only those affixation rules that are frequently found in the list of unknown words, such as active voice prefix *meN-* or passive voice prefix *di*, which are found in the list of unknown words in the testbed corpus. However, given the current size of SANTI-morf's testbed corpus (10k words), I could only manage to identify fewer than 10 rules. The size of the testbed corpus is quite small due to the difficulty of manual verification in SANTI-morf's evaluation [8].

To obtain a more reliable quantity of unknown words and to discover productive affixes present in unknown words, I created a 1-million-word corpus of Indonesian whose data are randomly extracted from the Indonesian subset in the Leipzig Corpora Collection. After running the Annotator, I discovered that the unknown words in this corpus consist of mostly monomorphemic words (74%). The remainder is polymorphemic words (26%).

For polymorphemic words, a number of affixes, and the roots to which they attach, are indeed ambiguous. In this case, only the most frequent affix categories are selected. For instance, *ke—an* circumfix can derive a verb or a noun. As *ke—an* as a nominalizer circumfix is more frequent, I chose to include only *ke—an* that derives a noun.

The root can also be ambiguous, typically between adjective, verb, or noun. In this case, I also chose the most frequent category found in unknown words, which is adjectives. In total, 34 frequent affixation cues (including allomorphic variations) were identified. These 34 rules serve as a reference to develop morphological grammars to be incorporated into the Guesser module.

3.2   Capitalization

From the list of monomorphemic words, 62% of the words are proper nouns, which begin with upper-case letters. Thus, in addition to morphological cues, another cue that

I found useful for guessing is capitalization. Person names such as James or George begin with a capital letter. Organisation names in acronyms are often written with full capitalization, such as UNHCR or FBI.

The dictionaries in the Annotator already included a number of proper name entries. However, a text may contain proper names that are absent from dictionary entries. As a result, when the system finds no match in the dictionaries, these proper names become unknown. A rule is then written to analyze unknown words with these capitalization cues as noun roots. Note that, at the moment, the SANTI-morf annotation scheme does not distinguish common noun and proper noun roots; thus, analyzing proper noun roots as just noun root <ROOT+NOU> is considered correct without further specifying a proper noun analytic label in the tag.

3.3   Final Guess

Finally, when all cues (morphology and capitalization) are exhausted, it is possible that some words may still remain unknown. To address this, I decided to create some sort of final guess rule, which guesses that these unknown words are noun roots. This method does not always produce correct results. For example, if a text contains a Javanese (one of the languages spoken in Indonesia, particularly on Java island) monomorphemic word *enom* 'young', which is an adjective root without any morphological or capitalization cues, the word will always be guessed as a noun root instead of a foreign root.

However, I have examined the application of the rule to different corpora whose content I created randomly from the Indonesian subset in the Leipzig Corpora Collection. Guessing that remaining unknown monomorphemic words are noun roots is accurate in 86% of instances on average. Conversely, using another POS gives a very low success rate. For example, when the final guess category is switched to adjective root, I only obtained only a 5% success rate on average. This is simply because most of the unknown words in each corpus that I experimented with are noun roots. Thus, it is reasonable to choose noun root as the final guess.

3.4   Ambiguity Problem

The first step to create the Guesser module is to devise guessing rules and incorporate them into morphological grammar files. Let us now focus on rules in which one or more morphological cues may be present. Consider the following rule (only formal tags are presented, functional tags are hidden) in a morphological grammar file. We can see here that the root is not dictionary-specified. The root output element in the rule ($X) refers to whatever letters follow *meng*.

```
MAIN = meng/<meng,PFX> $(X <L>* $)/<$X,ROOT>;
```

In this case, the cue is the *meng* prefix. If the rule is applied to the word *menggenerate* 'to generate', the word will be analyzed as a combination of an active verb prefix *meng-* and a root from a non-Indonesian word, *generate*. Whatever sequence of letters follows *meng-* is used as the root token output ($X), and will be tagged as ROOT. This in general is what a rule looks like in SANTI-morf's guesser module.

To allow the Guesser to guess more varieties of words, the incorporation of other rules is required. However, one problem to consider is to minimize ambiguity. Consider the following. If a new rule consists of 1) a sequence of letters identical to a sequence of letters in an existing rule, and 2) in the same position (e.g. both are prefixes), ambiguities are likely to be present. This happens for affixes that are allomorphs of the same morpheme. Consider the following rule in which a new morphological cue (*men*) is added.

```
MAIN=(meng/<meng,PFX>|men/<men,PFX>)$(X <L>*
$)/<$X,ROOT>;
```

With the addition of the above rule, it is possible to analyze *mentreat* 'to treat' as a combination of two morphemes: *men-* (active verb prefix) and *treat* (another non-Indonesian root). However, this accumulation of rules causes the earlier word *menggenerate* to undergo an unwanted analysis. In addition to being analyzed as *meng-* and *generate,* the system introduces an analysis that splits *menggenerate* into *men-* and *generate.* This is because the rule can indeed recognize words that begin with *men.* The rule does not know that tokenizing *menggenerate* into *men* and *generate* is incorrect.

Likewise, incorporating other morphological cues in different positions can also result in more ambiguities. For instance, we can incorporate *-kan,* a quite productive suffix in Indonesian.

```
MAIN=(meng/<meng,PFX>|men/<men,PFX>)$(X <L>*
$)/<$X,ROOT+FULL+VER> (kan/<SFX>|<E>);
```

This allows words such as *menggeneratekan* 'to generate (sth)' to be correctly analyzed into a three-morpheme word *meng-generate-kan.* However, due to the presence of *meng-* in the rule, as stated earlier, the incorrect analysis of *meng-generate-kan* is also generated. As an epsilon (here <E>), in union with *kan,* is present, the rule can also incorrectly analyze *menggeneratekan* as a two-morpheme word. It may also misunderstand *generatekan* as a single root instead of a combination of a root and a suffix.

3.5 Solution

To solve this ambiguity, rules in this grammar are organized based on the following principles. The first one is: *more morphological cues, higher priority.* This means that rules with more cues must have higher priority than rules with fewer cues. For example, rules *me—kan* and *me-* both target polymorphemic words. However, the former is composed of two morphological cues, *me-* and *kan,* while the latter is composed of only one cue, *me-.* In this case, the former rule must be prioritized. Thus, if the system finds an unknown word with *me—kan,* such as *menggeneratekan,* this word will not prompt two analyses <meng> <generatekan> and <meng> <generate> <kan>, just the latter.

This is because rule *me-* is not applied as the system has already found a match with *me—kan,* the rule with higher priority.

But what if two rules have the same number of cues? In this case, the second principle, *more letters, higher priority,* applies. For example, we have two rules *meng-* and *men-*. These two rules have one cue each. In this case, the rule *meng-* (4 letters) is prioritized over *men-* (3 letters) so that *men-* will not be applied, if and only if, *meng-* finds a match. If *meng-* does not find a match, then *men-* is applied. In this way, no ambiguity is introduced. Note that this does not apply for cues whose letter compositions are not very similar, e.g. *ber-* and *mem-*, and rules in different morphological positions (prefix and suffix). Also, this does not apply for cues with the same number of letters. For instance, *meng-* and *meny-* rules can be applied with the same priorities.

3.6 Architecture

The basic architecture of the SANTI-morf Guesser module can be described as follows. First, the module prioritizes the annotation of polymorphemic words. Once completed, all remaining words are considered monomorphemic. Second, the module will try to observe capitalization cues. Words which begin with a capital letter, fully written in uppercase, are annotated as noun roots. Finally, the remaining words are annotated as noun roots. This basic architecture is implemented as follows.

The Guesser consists of 38 rules, distributed into six different grammar files, and organized into six different priorities. All files end in G (guesser) followed by a number, thus, G1, G2 … G6. A lower number means a higher priority. As shown in the following illustration, the Guesser starts from H2 to L4. This is because the slots H9 to H3 are reserved for grammar and dictionary files that account for the Annotator (Fig. 2).

Preferences

| General | Lexical Analysis | Syntactic Analysis |

Lexical Resources for: id   Priorit

Priority	Resource
H5	EN-v5-YumiA2.nom
H4	EN-v5-YumiA3.nom
H3	EN-v5-YumiA4.nom
H2	EN-v5-YumiG1.nom
H1	EN-v5-YumiG2.nom
L1	EN-v5-YumiG3.nom
L2	EN-v5-YumiG4.nom
L3	EN-v5-YumiG5.nom
L4	EN-v5-YumiG6.nom

Fig. 2. Priorities of morphological grammars for the Guesser (ending in a G + Number).

Within each file, there are two categories of rules, prioritized and standard. Prioritized rules are marked by a +UNAMB operator, while standard rules do not include this, as shown in the following rules (abbreviated from YumiG1.nom, the morphological grammar for guessing, in the highest hierarchy).

```
Main = :Prioritized| :Standard;
Prioritised = :meng_meny_kan ;
meng_meny_kan
=(meng/<meng,PFX+UNAMB>|men/<meny,PFX+UNAMB>)$(X <L>*
$)/<$X,ROOT+UNAMB> (kan/<kan,SFX+UNAMB>);
Standard = :men_mem_kan;
men_mem_kan =(men/<meng,PFX>|mem/<meny,PFX>)$(X <L>*
$)/<$X,ROOT> (kan/<kan,SFX>);
```

We can see that rules with *meng* and *meny* are prioritized, while rules with *men* and *mem* are not. In addition, *kan* is not in union with epsilon. This means that these rules target only three-morpheme words. In fact, all rules in the morphological grammar (YumiG1.nom) are dedicated to analyzing unknown words with two morphological cues (plus one root). They are typically unknown words with three morphemes (prefix-root-suffix), but can also be unknown words with two morphemes on condition that the two cues represent a circumfix (opening part of a circumfix – root – closing part of a circumfix). The morphological grammars Yumi G1 to Yumi G3 are all dedicated to analyzing unknown words with three morphemes.

This prevents the system producing ambiguities, as discussed earlier. For a file with a higher hierarchy, once the system finds a match from one of the prioritized rules, standard rules are not applied. Conversely, if the system does not find a match from the prioritized rules, the system keeps looking. Once it finds a match from any of the standard rules, it will stop. In the case where an unknown word is composed of one morphological cue (for instance, unknown words with *meng, meny, mem* and *men,* but not *kan*), the system does not find a match anywhere in the rules in these morphological grammars (YumiG1-YumiG3).

However, the system continues checking in the next lower hierarchy morphological grammars, in this case YumiG4 and YumiG5. In these two morphological grammars, I incorporated rules that account for unknown words with one morphological cue. The following rules are abbreviated from the rules in YumiG4.

```
Main = :Prioritized| :Standard;
Prioritized = :meng_meny;
meng_meny
=(meng/<meng,PFX+UNAMB>|men/<meny,PFX+UNAMB>)$(X <L>*
$)/<$X,ROOT+UNAMB>;
Standard = :men_mem;
men_mem =(meng/<meng,PFX>|men/<meny,PFX>)$(X <L>*
$)/<$X,ROOT>;
```

The above rules account for the analysis of unknown words with one morphological cue. They have also been organized to prevent ambiguities. For instance, if an unknown word begins with *men*, the system only matches one of the standard rules as it fails to find a match in the prioritized rules. Conversely, when the word begins with *meng*, the system stops searching once it finds a match in one of the prioritized rules, thus, the standard rules do not apply.

Words that cannot be guessed using YumiG1 to YumiG5 are guessed using the following rules (see below) in YumiG6. These words are considered monomorphemic, thus they are always guessed as a root, particularly a noun root. This includes words with or without capitalization cues.

```
Main = :type1 | :type2 ;
#proper case
type1 = (<U><W>*)* <E>/ROOT+NOUN;
#mixed case
type2 = (<U>|<E>) <W>* (<U>*) (<W>*|<E>|<W>* <U>|<W>*)*
<E>/ROOT+NOUN;
```

4   The New +UNAMB Operator: A Proposal for Simplification

As described in an earlier section, the organization of rules and grammars in the Guesser follows two principles. First, words with more affixation units are prioritized (e.g. words with prefix + suffix combinations are prioritized over words with just a prefix). Second, if words have the same number of affixation units (e.g. prefixes), the units with a greater number of letters are prioritized (e.g. *meng-* is prioritized over *men-*).

I have tried my best to simplify the design of the Guesser module in SANTI-morf. I managed to reduce the number of morphological grammar files to just six, thanks to the +UNAMB operator. The operator allows two sets of rules with different priorities to be placed in a single morphological grammar file instead of two separate files with a different priority for each. Without this operator, there would be 15 morphological grammar files as a file would only be assigned rules with the same priority.

In this section, I suggest a new priority operator so that the number of files, if realized, can be reduced to just one. The implementation of this operator would also simplify the design of other SANTI-morf modules.

The +UNAMB operator is one of the methods for ambiguity resolution in NooJ. In principle, this operator assigns the highest priority to certain rules in a grammar file. The crucial point is that there can only be two sets of rules: prioritized and non-prioritized. This is an issue, for instance, for *meN-* allomorphs, which have three different sets of rules with three different priorities.

I propose an improvement to this operator so that there can be more than two levels of priority. In NooJ, this is nothing new as we can assign different priorities to grammars or dictionaries via Preferences by assigning codes such as H9 or H8 to each file. This method can be replicated. When multi-level priorities are required, the same priority codes used in Preferences are appended to the +UNAMB operator. The examples below serve to illustrate my point.

```
MENG = meng/<meng,PFX+UNAMB_H3> $(X <L>* $)/<$X,ROOT>;
MEN = men/<men,PFX+UNAMB_H2> $(X <L>* $)/<$X,ROOT>;
ME = me/<me,PFX+UNAMB_H1> $(X <L>* $)/<$X,ROOT>;
```

The above examples show three rules, with three different priority codes appended to the +UNAMB operator: H3 (high 3), H2 (high 2), and H1 (high 1). These rules are present in one grammar file. Let us simulate the situation by applying the grammar to the word *mereset*. This word is a combination of the active verb prefix *me-* and a verbal loan root *reset*. It is less likely to be recognized by the dictionaries and grammars in the Annotator, thus, it must be analyzed using the rules in the Guesser.

NooJ will first prioritize MENG (the rule with the +UNAMB_H3 operator). As no match is found, NooJ will automatically apply MEN, the rule with a lower priority, H2. The rule does not have any match so Nooj will apply ME, the rule with the lowest priority in the grammar, H1. As a match is found, *mereset* is annotated using the output in this rule.

Conversely, *menggenerate* 'to generate' (a combination of *meng-* and a foreign root *generate*) will be analyzed using the MENG rule, as it will find a complete match in the H3 rule. NooJ will not apply MEN and ME rules, H2 and H1, as a full match is already achieved by MENG, a rule with higher priority.

The benefit of using this improved operator is that all the rules can be contained in just one grammar file, but still adhere to the two principles I established earlier. Therefore, it is not necessary to incorporate rules into multiple grammar files as is currently implemented.

5 Conclusion

In this paper, I have described the position of the Guesser module within the SANTI-morf system. I have also described how I built the Guesser, which covers the selection of rules, identification of cues, incorporation of cues into rules, resolution of ambiguities and organization of the Guesser's files. I have also proposed an improvement to the + UNAMB operator. The simulation shows that the priority system is more compact, as users can organize all rules into just one grammar file even when each rule has a distinct priority. While, at present, this is just a hypothetical proposition, without any technical implementation details, the simulation of how the operators are applied can be used as a point of reference by NooJ developers to improve the NooJ prioritization system.

References

1. Silberztein, M.: NooJ Manual (2003). www.nooj4nlp.net
2. Silberztein, M.: Formalizing Natural Languages Nooj Approach. Wiley, London (2016)

3. Šmerk, P., Sojka, P., Horák, A.: Towards Czech morphological guesser. In: Proceedings of Recent Advances in Slavonic Natural Language Processing, Brno, pp. 1–4 (2009)
4. Larasati, S.D., Kuboň, V., Zeman, D.: Indonesian morphology tool (MorphInd): towards an indonesian corpus. In: Mahlow, C., Piotrowski, M. (eds.) SFCM 2011. CCIS, vol. 100, pp. 119–129. Springer, Heidelberg (2011). https://doi.org/10.1007/978-3-642-23138-4_8
5. Segalovich, I.: A fast morphological algorithm with unknown word guessing induced by a dictionary for a web search engine. In: MLMTA, Las Vegasmorph, pp. 273–280 (2003)
6. Harman, D.: How effective is suffixing. J. Am. Soc. Inf. Sci. **42**(1), 7–15 (1991)
7. Hull, D.-A.: Stemming algorithms: a case study for detailed evaluation. J. Am. Soc. Inf. Sci. **47**(1), 70–84 (1996)
8. Prihantoro: SANTI-morf: a new morphological annotation system for Indonesian (a PhD thesis: forthcoming). Lancaster University Press, Lancaster (2021)
9. Prihantoro: The morphological annotation of reduplication-circumfix intersection in Indonesian. In: Formalising Natural Languages: Applications to Natural Language Processing and Digital Humanities (2021)
10. NooJ 2020. Communications in Computer and Information Science. CCIS, Zagreb, pp. 37–48 (2021)
11. Prihantoro: Tweaking NooJ's resources to export morpheme-level or intra-word annotations. In: Bigey, M., Richeton, A., Silberztein, M., Thomas, I. (eds.) NooJ 2021, pp. 3–14. Springer, Cham (2021). https://doi.org/10.1007/978-3-030-92861-2_1
12. Mueller, F.: Indonesian morphology. In: Morphologies of Asia and Africa, pp. 1207–1230 Eisenbraums, Winnona (2007)

Formation and Evolution of Intensive Adverbs Ending in *-mente* Derived from the Adjectival Class <Causatives de Feeling: Fear> in Spanish and French

Rafael Pérez García[1] and Xavier Blanco[2(✉)]

[1] Universidad Carlos III de Madrid, 28903 Getafe, Madrid, Spain
Rafael.garcia.perez@uc3m.es
[2] Universitat Autònoma de Barcelona, 08193 Cerdanyola del Vallès, Spain
Xavier.Blanco@uab.cat

Abstract. This paper examines the history of some adverbs derived from adjectives belonging to the syntactic-semantic class <causatives of feeling: fear> in French and Spanish. While most of the lexical units in this class have acquired an intensive meaning in both languages, they have done so progressively. As usually happens in language history, the current paradigm of intensifiers, that is, the one we can find in modern Spanish and French, is the result of a grammaticalization process which began with one or two adverbs in particular and extended to many other semantically linked ones. However, the number of units involved, the dates of their conversion into intensifiers and their degree of grammaticalization depend on the idiosyncrasy of each language, although we cannot rule out the possibility that one these languages influenced the other, especially, as in the case here, when we are dealing with two closely related languages like French and Spanish.

Keywords: Intensifiers · Grammaticalization · History of the French language · History of the Spanish language · Adverbs ending in *-mente*

1 Introduction

This article, which is part of a research project devoted to studying intensifier collocations in mediaeval French and Spanish [2][1], focuses on the formation and evolution of a very specific group of intensifiers: those adverbs derived from adjectives belonging to the semantic class called <causatives of feeling> [1], and more specifically the subclass <causatives of feeling: fear>. The adjectives belonging to the class <causatives of feeling> are evaluative adjectives[2], many of which are derived ones (from nouns or from verbs), which share the fact that they have an actant subject considered the origin or cause of the feeling contained in the meaning of the lexeme itself. In this sense, from the semantic standpoint, they can be grouped into more specific subclasses. The

---

[1] RDI COLINDANTE (PID2019-104741GB-100), Ministry of Science and Innovation (Spain).
[2] For this concept in adverbs ending in *-mente* with interpretation of degree, see [3].

© Springer Nature Switzerland AG 2022
M. González et al. (Eds.): NooJ 2022, CCIS 1758, pp. 14–25, 2022.
https://doi.org/10.1007/978-3-031-23317-3_2

feeling of surprise, for example, is present in a variety of adjectives in Spanish like *asombroso, pasmoso, sorprendente*, etc.; the feeling anger in derivations like *irritante, enojoso, exasperante*, etc.; and the feeling of fear (*temor* in Spanish), which we are specifically focusing on here, can be found quite evidently in adjectives like *temeroso, terrible, tremendo, terrorífico*, etc.

In [6] demonstrated that not all intensifiers ending in -*mente* have undergone a simultaneous grammaticalization process, but that after the paradigm was established, it was progressively enriched with variable lexical-semantic additions and losses throughout history. It is also interesting to note in this case that even though the adjectival class <causatives of feeling: fear> can be considered fairly semantically homogeneous, not all adverbs ending in -*mente* stemming from it have given rise to units assigned an intensive meaning[3]. On the other hand, the morphological ascription of an adverb ending in -*mente* to this subclass does not guarantee that it is automatically grammaticalized, and in the cases in which this process does occur, the result is not necessarily identical, given that just like the majority of historical changes, grammaticalization is a matter of degree. We should not forget that the meaning of words is dynamic rather than static, and subject to constant adjustments, breakdowns and readjustments [5]. This means that while some units become prototypical because they have undergone this process fully, others are in intermediate stages that are closer to or further from the expected final stage. The factors involved are diverse, hence the need to undertake a detailed study of each of the units and their relations.

This study is presented from a contrastive perspective. For the evolution of these adverbs in Spanish, the main sources will be the *Corpus diacrónico del español* (CORDE) [13] and the *Corpus del Nuevo diccionario histórico del español* (CDH) [12][4]. For French, they will be the *Frantext Français Médiéval* [18] and the BFM [11], in an attempt to determine to what extent the two languages are similar or different. We should bear in mind that even though they both share a Romance language underpinning, they have also been associated with different sociocultural and political situations. The lexicons and part of the corpuses will be implemented through the NooJ [9] linguistic engineering platform.

---

[3] In Spanish, the adjectival bases of the subclass < causatives of feeling: fear > which give rise to the adverbial derivations with an intensive meaning were originally marked by a higher degree of intensity in the description of the feeling. Thus, adjectival bases like *temeroso, medroso* or *temible* (meant as causation of a medium-intensity feeling 'that instills fear') have not given rise to derivations with an intensive interpretation, as opposed to the bases *espantoso, horrible, horroroso, terrible, terrorífico, tremendo* or *pavoroso*, which implicitly entail the idea of horror or terror ('intense fear').

[4] This second corpus is particularly interesting due to the distinction it makes between the date the work was composed and the date of the manuscript in which the linguistic testimony appears. For several examples from the current era, we also draw from the CREA [15] and the CORPES XXI [14].

2 Intensive Adjectives Derived from the Class <Causatives of Feeling: Fear>

2.1 Terriblemente/Terriblement

The main adverb in both French and Spanish derives from the adjective coming from the Latin etymon TERRIBILIS, *terriblemente*, *terriblement*, equivalent cultivated forms. They are not the oldest from the standpoint of their morphological formation—in fact, they can both only be traced back to the fourteenth century—but they can be considered leaders from the standpoint of their grammaticalization, as they show a more steadfast tendency to become intensifiers. Hence they are worth taking as models here.

While these forms initially had a purely manner meaning, *e lo ál por las tentaçiones, males e tribulaçiones que aquélla o su cabsa, sin embargo del fuir, cruel e terriblemente en mí e en todo lo mío perpetró* (1424, Enrique de Villena, *Tratado de consolación*, ed. Pedro M. Cátedra); *Et pour tant Ceres, voiant la presompcion et cruauté de Euzithon, le fist terriblement morir en tant que par povreté il vendi sa propre fille* (*Archiloge Sophie*, 1400, p. 187), they soon were "delexicalized." The origin of this delexicalization can be found in their combination with gradable verbs: the fear that inspires a given action is often associated with the intensity of that action, hence verbs that express sound are frequent, *ung gros corbeau vint volleter sus sa teste en criant terriblement* (*L'Histoire de Jason*, 1460, p. 147), as are verbs involving physical contact *& non tienen lenguas & mueven las mexillas de ençima & muerden terriblemente & tienen las hunnas que son muy fuertes* (1350, *Translation of the "Historia de Jerusalem abreviada" by Jacobo de Vitriaco*, ed. María Teresa Herrera; María Nieves Sánchez). This later gave rise to grammaticalization based on a new process of metaphorical reinterpretation.

However, even though both forms coincided in their evolution, the data also show that French was slightly ahead of Spanish in completing the process. Indeed, in French it is striking that the first testimonies of *terriblement* already had a clearly intensive meaning, even though they were not totally disassociated from the manner meaning. It is also curious that in the earliest testimonies, *terriblement* is applied to adjectives instead of verbs: *cellui Gieffroy est chevalier de hault et puissant affaire, et si est terriblement crueulx* (*Mélusine*, 1392, p. 207)[5], *Puis des.II. laides faces dire [...] Tant sont laides terriblement* (*Le Livre de la Mutacion de Fortune* t.1, 1400, p. 125).

We find that these adjectives have negative connotations in the later examples (late fourteenth to early fifteenth century). In the second half of the fifteenth century, we continue to find similar examples: *terriblement mauvais, terriblement infortuné*... It is not until later, when the grammaticalization was more advanced, that we find examples of *terriblement* applied to adjectives with positive connotations ('alegre, feliz'). By that

---

[5] The DMF [17] contains this example but classifies it under the non-grammaticalized meaning of the adverb: 'De manière à inspirer la terreur, de manière effrayante'. Even though it clearly preserves part of this meaning, the intensive meaning also seems clear. The next example of LITTRÉ [21] (s.v. *terriblement*), which does not appear in FRANTEXT [18], also dates from the first half of the fourteenth century: *si le regarderent à merveilles, car il estoit terriblement grant* [*Perceforest*, t. IV, f° 53].

time in these cases, the manner meaning of the adverb was deactivated[6]: *Quant le roy d'Espaigne ouyt ceste promesse il fut terriblement joyeulx, et dit tout humblement au roy qu'il le mercioit.* (*Le roman de Jehan de Paris*, 1494, p. 2); *Lesquelz faisoit terriblement beau voir* (*Le voyage de Naples*, 1495, p. 180).

With regard to Spanish, we can say that the intensive meaning began to separate from the interpretation of mode or manner in the late Middle Ages *Llamentaron terriblemente y desygual: dieron vozes y gimieron: porque tan crudamente/rey que tanto los amaua/y era amado: era muerto* (1499 Gonzalo García de Santamaría, *Traducción de la Corónica de Aragón de fray Gauberto Fabricio de Vagad*, ed. José Carlos Pino Jiménez), although it would only definitively become fully independent in the Renaissance, which yielded numerous examples. Precisely, it is in Renaissance texts where the first testimonies of its position before verbal participles appear, which we should consider a first step in its subsequent conversion into an intensive quantifier of adjectives and adverbs. In this sense, we can assert that its grammaticalization process developed somewhat later than other intensifiers ending in -*mente*, which have been widely used and quite widespread in the language since the Middle Ages (see [6][7]).

Slightly later, in the Baroque, this intensive meaning can be considered to be sufficiently widespread in use: *Sintiólo terriblemente el licenciado Cebadilla (que así se llamaba)...* (1632 Alonso de Castillo Solórzano, *La niña de los embustes*, ed. Teresa de Manzanares).

The combination with pure, non-participle adjectives also took place in the seventeenth century with adjectives with negative connotations, with the adverb coming either before or after them: *Yo estaba enfadado y mohino terriblemente de ver que no podía alcanzar lo que tanto deseaba y tan fácil era...* (c. 1612 Miguel de Castro, *Vida de Miguel de Castro*, ed. José María de Cossío). The final stage in its grammaticalization—and in this sense, proof of its full conversion into an intensifier—unquestionably came with the shift from a selection of adjectives with negative connotations to a selection of adjectives considered neutral or even positive, just like today ([8], s.v. *terriblemente*). This is a considerably later phenomenon (nineteenth century), although it did not become widespread until the twentieth century *Entregóse a la cacería con pasión. Pero aquella mariposa era terriblemente sagaz, y siempre se colocaba fuera del alcance de la red, aunque no huía definitivamente de su vista* (1916, Leopoldo Lugones, *Cuentos fantásticos*, ed. Pedro Luis Barcia). In fact, negative connotations deriving from the context can still be found in the nineteenth century[8].

---

[6] We even find this with the verb *plaire*: "Et les Canariens en estoient toutz esbahis et leur plaisoit terriblement" (Le Canarien, 1490, p. 305). We also have cases in which *terriblement* combines with lexical units with neutral connotations. They are also clearly intensive uses, as the lexical meaning of < causative of feeling > does not fit: *Je suis terriblement pensif Que je ne voy ici personne* (*Sottie à cinq personnages..*, 1488, p. 158); *Ou peult il estre ? Je ne le vy depuis Qu'il s'est levé terriblement matin* (*Le Mystère de saint Martin*, 1496, p. 187).

[7] This study also highlights the hinge role performed by participles, a category halfway between verbs and adjectives.

[8] Naturally, today its meaning as an adverb of manner still continues when it accompanies nongradable verbs ([4], s.v. *terriblemente*).

2.2 Horriblemente/Horriblement

In the subsequent development of the paradigm, we should consider the possibility of French influencing Spanish, as the chronological gap between *horriblement* and *horriblemente* is fairly large. The oldest examples of the French *horriblement* are found in the AND [10] (s.v. *horriblement*), with one example from the twelfth century and two from the thirteenth, although only in the former (from *Le Romaunz de temptacioun de secle* by Guischart de Beauliu) do we perhaps see an intensive nuance (applied to 'vengarse') accompanying the dominant manner meaning *(s.xii; MS: s.xiii) Dunc s'en vengrad Deus tant oriblement* GUISCH 787.

The first example from FRANTEXT [18], however, dates from 1130. Even though *horriblement* can only be interpreted as an adverb of manner in approximately 25% of these examples, when combined with verbs like *répondre, fondre* ('fall, collapse'), *mourir, tuer* ('kill') and others, from the earliest testimonies we can find an intensive nuance (the thunder or wind that inspire horror are particularly powerful): *Et tonner trés horriblement, Venter, gresler, et fort plouvoir* (*Le Jugement dou Roy de Navarre contre le jugement dou Roy de Behaingne*, 1349, p. 147).

Both meanings also coexist in the adverb plus verb combinations like *gaster* ('devastate'), *pécher* ('sin') and *se souiller* ('get dirty or stained'). The combination of 'pecar horriblemente' (sin horribly) is relatively frequent, with three occurrences. Finally, we should note that the DMF [17] provides an example with *doubter horriblement*, now marked solely as intensive, although it would be possible to detect a nuance of fear[9]. The RH [22], in turn, dates the intensive meaning of *horriblement* (which it defines as 'extrêmement') from 1559, although it provides no examples. It also mentions an augmentative meaning 'très grand' of *horrible* which was found in Rabelais but must have disappeared by the seventeenth century.

In Spanish, the earliest examples of *horriblemente* came considerably later, specifically in the fifteenth century. It combined with verbs which could allow a possible intensive interpretation beneath the primary manner meaning because they are gradable. In the sixteenth century, we find it modifying pure, non-participial adjectives, although it essentially retained its initial meaning of manner, in line with the participial selection found throughout that entire century. There are only two cases. The first one comes from a translation of *Orlando Furioso* by Jerónimo de Urrea; the second is local: *Vino una nube espesa y tenebrosa/Abierta á ratos de espantoso fuego,/Que aumentó la tormenta peligrosa,/Y dejó el mundo horriblemente ciego* (1588, Cristóbal de Virués, *Historia del Monserrate*, ed. Cayetano Rosell).

Despite this relatively early selection of two non-participial adjectives, which, as we have seen, come before the word they modify, the intensive value took longer to become common in use. Just as in the aforementioned cases, the combination of the adverb with gradable verbs, which has been found since the fifteenth century, laid the groundwork for its grammaticalization. Only in the eighteenth century can we consider *horriblemente* to have separated from its manner meaning to instead intensify adjectives

---

[9] P. ext. [Avec une valeur d'intensif] 'Extrêmement': Et en cest meisme livre avoit il dit devant comme la gloire de grandeur et de latitude de empire ou de royalme est comparee a la joie ou leesce que l'en a d'une verriere fieble et clere, de laquele l'en est toujours en doubte horriblement qu'elle ne soit froissié soudainement. (ORESME, Pol. Arist. M., c.1372–1374, 292).

and participles with negative connotations ...*para que aquella noche acompañase a la señora condesa, que yacía horriblemente atribulada con la novedad de un tremendo y extraño ruido* (1743 Diego de Torres Villarroel, "Vida, ascendencia, nacimiento, crianza y aventuras, I-IV", ed. Castalia). However, many of the examples conserved are still somewhat ambiguous.

After the nineteenth century, especially in the second half, this connotation definitively spread through use, but the selection was still restricted to adjectives and adverbs with negative connotations, as it is even today ([8], s.v. *horriblemente*).

2.3 Espantosamente/Épouvantablement

The equivalents of EXPAVENTARE (*espantosamente* and *épouvantablement*), which are old in both languages (thirteenth and twelfth centuries, respectively), can be considered to have been grammaticalized at a similar historical time: the seventeenth century. The Spanish *espantosamente* was first combined with verbs and primarily meant manner, albeit with a twofold meaning, both causative and non-causative, the latter to a lesser extent, which corresponded to the twofold meaning of its adjectival base *espantoso*[10]. However, an intensive contextual interpretation began to take shape when it accompanied certain actions in which the fear supposedly caused was associated with the intensity of the actions. However, we cannot trace an intensive meaning *per se* in a habitual selection of verbal units until the seventeenth century. Even though we find an early example of a combination with participles in that same century, the adverb, with its new meaning, did not choose this type of verbal form and by extension pure non-participial adjectives with negative connotations until the nineteenth century: *Clemencia, observó llena de vergüenza Isabel, tú tendrás la culpa de que el señor vaya a encontrarme espantosamente torpe... ¿por qué eres así?* (1869, Ignacio Manuel Altamirano, *Clemencia*, ed. Salvador Reyes Nevares).

Generally speaking, it has been used less frequently in the selection of neutral or positive adjectives, and when it has been, it comes with a certain rhetorical effect[11]. We can assert that in reality, it still maintains a fairly close tie with its etymological meaning, which means that its grammaticalization has not reached the same degree as its synonym *terriblemente*[12]: *Normalmente, dentro del cinismo habitual de su discurso, se adivina una habilidad retórica para el convencimiento espantosamente inteligente* (2001. Fabio Murrieta: "Fidel Castro en la cumbre de Panamá". Revista Hispano Cubana).

---

[10] The non-causative meaning of the adjective was also in the minority, as in this example: "El espantoso ha miedo et spantase de lo que deue auer miedo et espantase de lo que non ha razon por que deue auer miedo" (1326, Juan Manuel, *Libro del caballero y del escudero*, ed. José Manuel Blecua). Hence, a phrase like *despertarse espantosamente* is interpreted as non-causative 'con espanto, espantado' (with fright, frightful) in this passage: "Del sueño son quando gorgean en el sueño e padecen ruimiento en los dientes e maxcan ansí como si tuviese algund cibo en la boca e tienen sueños espantosos e despiértanse espantosamente e con quexa e con ira" (1495, translation of the Lilio de medicina de Gordonio, ed. John Cull).

[11] This book title is significant: "Brujas y brujerías: Propuestas para pasarlo espantosamente bien.".

[12] In [8], only adjectives and adverbs with negative meanings in a familiar register are mentioned.

With regard to the adverb *épouvantablement* (*espoentablement*), the AND [10] offers one testimony from the twelfth century and another from the thirteenth: (s.xii1; MS: s.xiim) *espowentablement* (Latin: *terribiliter*) *essalças mei* Camb Ps 247.CXXXVIII.15; (1213; MS: 1213) *nostre sire omnipotent Qui tant espoentablement Lor quers esfreit e trobla* Dial Greg 102rb[13]. Psalms are certainly not easy to interpret, but setting aside the fear of God (*espowentablement* translates as *terribiliter* and this form was used in Christian Latin with a meaning similar to 'venerable, respectable'[14]), an added intensive meaning does not seem inappropriate in the aforementioned examples: *essalças* (from *essalcier*) means 'heed a prayer' and *magnifiez* (from *magnifier*) means 'exalt, glorify'.

With regard to the second example from the AND [10] mentioned above, the manner meaning seems to predominate due to isotopy: *épouvanter*[15], *effrayer*, *troubler*. However, the adverb is either pleonastic or introduces intensity.

The TL [23] shows, s.v. *espöentablement*, two examples in which the adverb has a manner meaning (combined with *se plaindre* 'complain' [human subject] and *lever la tête* ['raise one's head' [animal subject]). In one of the examples, *épouvantablement* is applied to *crier*, but the presence of *haut* shows that its interpretation should preferably be a manner one: *leur enseignes crient haut et espoventablement* (eb. II 5115).

The GDC [20] (s.v. *espoentablement*) presents different examples with <sound emission> verbs. Sometimes, the intensity is detached from the causative of feeling: *une voix qui dist moult halt et moult empoentablement*. Other times, the adverb encompasses both meanings: *Ilz les assaillirent en criant espouentablement*.

FURETIÈRE [19] dates the intensive meaning of *épouvantablement* from 1690: "d'une manière excessive," a date reported by the RH [22]. The TLFi [24], s.v. *épouvantable*, offers examples with an intensive meaning from the nineteenth century. In the latter, the adverb is applied to an adjective with a positive connotation: *Je m'ennuie épouvantablement ici! Voilà deux jours que je suis seule* (Crémieux, Orphée,1858, II, 3etabl., 1, p. 56); *Mais elle est épouvantablement ravissante!* (Rostand, Cyrano,1898, I, 2, p. 25).

2.4 Other Adverbs

The remaining adverbs deriving from adjectives in the subclass <causatives of feeling: fear> date from later; while they also end up joining the paradigm of intensifiers, they lag behind most likely because of the force with which their synonyms had already entered into the language. However, the fate of these new elements has been quite uneven.

The Spanish adverbs *horrorosamente* and *tremendamente* have spread quite widely as intensifiers. Their origin dates back to the seventeenth century. During that century and the ensuing one, the former appeared combined with verbs with a clear meaning of manner. Only after the nineteenth century did they work as intensifiers in combination

---

[13] We find a similar use in another psalm: *Je regehirai à tei, kar espowentablement ies magnifiez; merveilluses sunt les tues ovres, e la meie aneme conuistra mult.* Liber Psalmorum 216:13) [7] (p. 216).

[14] Cf. RH [22] s.v. *terrible*.

[15] We should note that *épouvanter* comes from vulgar Latin *expaventare,* from the Latin *expavere*'fear', with the prefix *ex-* that adds intensive value (cf. TLFi [24] s.v. *épouvanter*).

with participles or non-participial adjectives with negative connotations—in addition to gradable verbs—although at first without shedding their original meaning ...*por ser fraudulentos y fraudulentas con un género de dolo o engaño de los más malignos, avaros, crueles y horrorosamente abominables, y contrarios a la Constitución* (1820–1821, Juan Romero Alpuente, *Intervenciones en las Cortes Ordinarias*, ed. Alberto Gil Novales).

In the twentieth century, the intensive meaning permanently breaks away from the primary meaning in the adverb combined with both verbs and adjectives. However, it still shows a clear preference for choosing adjectives or adverbs with negative connotations. Just as happened in the two cases examined above, the selection of neutral or positive adjectives only became possible in the last few decades[16], but it is rare and implies significant rhetorical effects; in fact, this adverb has not managed to completely detach itself from its etymological meaning.

The second one, *tremendamente*, only appears in a single example in the seventeenth century, with the expected meaning of manner; however, there are no traces of it in the eighteenth century, so it truly spread in the nineteenth century, when it took on a clear intensive meaning in combination with participles and non-participial adjectives with negative connotations: *Por lo pronto, y desde el 20 de abril en adelante, fue y es, en nuestro sentir, no ya inútil, sino tremendamente nocivo el exigir responsabilidades y el desatarse unos contra otros en violentas recriminaciones* (1897, Juan Valera, "Notas diplomáticas").

The grammaticalization process accelerated at a good pace and was completed by the mid-twentieth century. In this sense, it should come as no surprise that since then and even today, the adverb can readily choose neutral or positive adjectives with a clearly intensive meaning. Thus, against all predictions—if we consider how relatively recent its appearance is—it has reached a high degree of grammaticalization which makes it resemble its model, *terriblemente*: *Que aclare por qué conservamos la inercia y que exija estar tremendamente activos ¡esta es la verdadera ética en estos momentos!* (1940, José Herrera Petere, Niebla de cuernos. (Entreacto en Europa), ed. Jesús Gálvez/José Esteban).

Compared to the previous examples, the Spanish *terroríficamente* coincides with the French *effroyablement* and *affreusement* in its lower frequency of use. There are few examples of *terroríficamente* in the corpus, which indicates that it initially experienced some difficulty carving a niche for itself among the set of intensifiers, probably because the paradigm was already somewhat saturated at the time it appeared. Just as with its synonyms, it was first used as an adverb of manner. After the mid-twentieth century, it appears before adjectives and an intensive meaning can be glimpsed, albeit still associated with its initial meaning. Throughout the twenty-first century, the intensity meaning has become independent, and despite its scarce use, it is apparently beginning to attain a high degree of grammaticalization, at least in the colloquial and oral language *Las criaturas no paran de bailar. Todo va terroríficamente bien (2018, Reina Ginolanda,* "Ponche de ácido lisérgico". Dilemas Yonkys).

The adverb *effroyablement* can be found in combination with verbs of sound (*tonner, rugir*) throughout the sixteenth century, and we can also find it in purely manner contexts. In the seventeenth century, we find some examples in which both meanings (manner and

---

[16] [8] (s.v. *horrorosamente*) attributes these usages to a marginal or even dialectal nature.

intensity) may coexist, although intensity applied to a minorative seems to dominate in this example: *Quelle-est la proportion de ce cerveau si effroyablement petit à une de ses parties constituantes ?* (Bonnet, Charles, 1769, *La Palingénésie philosophique ou Idées sur l'état passé et l'état futur des êtres vivans*: t. 1, partie 1, p. 172, Frantext N486).

In Molière's *Précieuses ridicules*, we find this context, no doubt paradoxical yet clearly intensive, given that *effroyablement* is applied to an adjective with positive connotations: Mascarille: *Vous ne me dites rien de mes plumes ! comment les trouvez-vous?*; Cathos: *Effroyablement belles.* (R364 I Molière, *Les Précieuses ridicules*, 1660, p. 96).

In FRANTEXT [18], we find no other clearly intensive contexts of *effroyablement* until the nineteenth century[17]: *Il se dirige vers la porte en faisant des zigzags. Don César, le regardant marcher à part. Il est effroyablement ivre !* (Victor Hugo, *Ruy Blas* (1838), act 4, scene 3, p. 425, Frantext N245).

With regard to the form *affreusement*, until the seventeenth century we do not find the following context in which the intensive meaning seems to dominate, especially because *affreusement* (*affreusement hypocondriaque*) is used in parallel with *fort* (*fort melancholique*): *il avoit hautement juré qu'à l'occasion de son bannissement de la cour il estoit devenu fort melancholique et affreusement hypocondriaque se voyant esloigné des delices de paris* (Q529 I Garasse François - *La Doctrine curieuse des beaux-esprits de ce temps* (1623) Book 1 Section 8, p. 54).

The intensive use of this adverb was entrenched by the eighteenth century, e.g.: *il m'ennuie affreusement, vous avez extrêmement tort d'en être jaloux.* (N953 Crébillon, Claude-Prosper Jolyot de - *Ah quel conte !* (1751) Book 3 Section 5 Chapter 26, p. 326.

TRÉVOUX [25] criticizes the intensive use of *affreusement* but implicitly considers the intensive use of *horriblement* acceptable. The RH [22] reports an intensive meaning of *affreusement* (in 1701) which it labels incorrect, but it offers no examples and does not state the source (this is a common practice in this dictionary, which prioritizes the legibility of its articles over the traceability of the information provided).

Finally, given the importance of the colloquial register in definitively anchoring many of these units in the linguistic system, the ascription of some of them to literary language may have contributed to their lower degree of grammaticalization. One example is the Spanish *pavorosamente*, a mediaeval derivation, though a considerably later one, as we find it for the first time in the fifteenth century. It began by selecting verbs and was interpreted unambiguously as an adverb of manner until the seventeenth century. Just like *espantosamente*, it had a dual causative and non-causative meaning, which corresponded to the dual meaning of its base *pavoroso*[18]. Only in the seventeenth century does it combine with adjectives—now only in its current causative meaning—but still as an adverb of manner. The grammaticalization process began in the nineteenth century: the

---

[17] The TLFi [24], in fact, contains this last quote as the first example of an intensive meaning in its entry for *effroyablement* (P. exagér., fam. De manière excessive). The RH [22] states that the classical authors used *effroyablement* as a simple intensive, while today its negative connotation ('désagrément', that is 'dislike, annoyance') prevails.

[18] The non-causative meaning came early, since it can be traced in texts from the thirteenth century, as revealed in the following excerpt: "Bienaventurado el omne que siempre está pavoroso d'esto, mas el que de yerta voluntat fuere contra esto, en mal caidrá" (in 1280, Alfonso X, General Estoria, ed. Pedro Sánchez-Prieto Borja).

original meaning can be glimpsed alongside a quantification of degree (9) according to the evolution 'de manera pavorosa' ('in a dreadful way') 'en tal grado que provoca pavor' ('to such an extent that causes dread'): *Consulté el cielo, y lo vi pavorosamente feo; consulté la mar, y la encontré muy sañuda* (1873 Benito Pérez Galdós, *Trafalgar*, ed. Crítica).

Only after the twentieth century do we find a combination with neutral or positive adjectives, where purely the intensive meaning prevails, although, just as with *espantosamente*, examples of this do not abound and they have a rhetorical effect, especially when the adverb retains fairly literary connotations[19]. This leads us to posit a limited grammaticalization process in this case as well: *El número de obras que desarrollan el tema del naufragio es pavorosamente ingente, y aunque éstas resulten de calidad muy dispar* (2004, Esperanza Guillén Marcos: Naufragios. Imágenes románticas de la desesperación. Ed. Siruela).

In the case of the French adverbs *horrifiquement* and *effrayamment*, we also find a much more limited and almost residual use. The former is rare; it is found in Rabelais[20]: "Quel diable, demanda Juppiter, est là bas qui hurle si horrifiquement?" E013 I RABELAIS François - Le Quart Livre (1552) (p. 893).

The latter is another literary form which is not found until the nineteenth century: *ses yeux s'agrandirent effrayamment, ses lèvres frémirent...* M539 I Goncourt Edmond de et Jules de - Charles Demailly (1860) (p. 404).

3 Conclusion

In this article, we have traced the history of the syntactic semantic class <causatives of feeling: fear> in French and Spanish and have seen that the majority of its lexical units have progressively taken on an intensive meaning in both languages. As tends to happen in the history of languages, the paradigm of intensifiers which we discover today is the outcome of a grammaticalization process that began with one or two adverbs in particular—specifically, the Spanish *terriblemente* and the French *terriblement* led the process although we find that the French *horriblement* was slightly ahead of Spanish *horriblemente*—and then spread as time went on to many other semantically linked adverbs. However, the number of units involved, the dates on which they turned into intensifiers and their degree of grammaticalization depend on the idiosyncrasies of each language. As we have seen, if the common thread of the paradigm is found independently in both languages and can be associated with merely linguistic causes (in this case, delexicalization of these adverbs through their combination with gradable verbs), the chronological difference in the incorporation of some units with the same Latin etymon (especially in the case of *horriblemente/horriblement*) may also reveal a possible influence of one

---

[19] Proof of this is its virtual non-existence in oral corpuses. In fact, DECH [16] (s.v. *pavor*) reports that the initial base noun is today a literary archaicism.

[20] Causative adjectives of feeling are found in Rabelais' titles, such as: *Les horribles et espoventables faictz et prouesses du très renommé Pantagruel*. The TLFi [24] offers an example of the use of this adverb with a modal meaning in the twentieth century: *Ils se seraient aperçus (...) que les bastilles horrifiquement nommées Londres et Paris n'étaient capables d'arrêter au passage ni blé, ni bœufs* (A. France, J. d'Arc, t. 1, 1908, p. 327).

language on the other as the paradigm was being constructed. The most notable semantic changes during the Middle Ages correspond to the adverbs *terriblemente/terriblement* and *horriblemente/horriblement*. The other adverbs come later; the acquisition of their intensive value may be explained precisely by the force that their older synonyms had gained.

References

1. Blanco, X.: Un inventario de clases semánticas para los adjetivos predicativos de estado. Verba **33**, 235–260 (2006)
2. Blanco, X., García Pérez, R.: Las estructuras comparativas intensivas aplicadas al adjetivo *negro* en español medieval en comparación con el francés. Romanica Olomucensia **33**(1), 21–39 (2021)
3. Bosque, I., Masullo, P.: On verbal quantification in Spanish. In: Proceedings of the 3rd Workshop on the Syntax of Central Romance Languages, pp. 1–47. Universitat de Girona, Girona (1996)
4. Fuentes, C.: Diccionario de conectores y operadores del español. Arco/Libros, Madrid (2009)
5. García Pérez, R.: Les dimensions multiples du sens lexical. Cah. Lexicol. **104**, 69–97 (2014)
6. García Pérez, R.: Fuertemente atados: adverbios intensificadores en -*mente* y colocaciones en castellano medieval. ELUA **36**, 273–292 (2022)
7. Michel, F.: Libri Psalmorum. Versio Antica Gallica. E typographeo academico, Oxonii (1860)
8. Santos Río, L.: Diccionario de partículas. Luso-Española de Ediciones, Salamanca (2003)
9. Silberztein, M.: Formalizing Natural Languages: The NooJ Approach. Wiley-ISTE, London (2016)

Dictionaries and Text Databases

10. AND = Anglo-Norman Dictionary, 2nd edn. Modern Humanities Research Association/Anglo-Norman Text Society, London/Oxford (2022). http://www.anglo-norman.net. Accessed 22 June 2022
11. BFM = Base de Français Médiéval. ENS de Lyon, Lyon (2019). http://txm.bfm-corpus.org. Accessed 22 June 2022
12. CDH = Real Academia Española: Corpus del Diccionario histórico de la lengua española (CDH) (2013). https://apps.rae.es/CNDHE. Accessed June 2022
13. CORDE = Real Academia Española: Banco de datos (CORDE). Diachronic Spanish corpus. http://www.rae.es. Accessed June 2022
14. CORPES XXI = Real Academia Española: Banco de datos (CORPES XXI). Corpus of twenty-first century Spanish (CORPES). http://www.rae.es. Accessed June 2022
15. CREA = Real Academia Española: Banco de datos (CREA). Reference corpus on current Spanish. http://www.rae.es. Accessed June 2022
16. DECH = Corominas, J., Pascual, J.A.: Diccionario crítico etimológico castellano e hispánico. Madrid, Gredos (1980–1991)
17. DMF = Dictionaire du Moyen Français (1330–1500). Laboratoire ATILF, Université de Lorraine. http://www.atilf.fr/dmf. Accessed 22 June 2022
18. FRANTEXT = Base textuelle Frantext. ATILF-CNRS & Université de Lorraine (1998–2019). http://www.frantext.fr. Accessed 23 June 2022
19. FURETIÈRE = Furetière, A.: Dictionnaire universel contenant généralement tous les mots françois, tant vieux que modernes, et les termes de toutes les sciences et des arts. Le Robert, Paris (1978 [1690])

20. GDC = Godefroy, F.: Complément du dictionnaire de l'ancienne langue française et de tous ses dialectes du IXe au XVe siècle. F. Vieweg Libraire-Éditeur, Paris (1895–1902)
21. LITTRÉ = Littré, É.: Dictionnaire de la langue française, Hachette, Paris (1873–1874). http://www.littre.org. Accessed 22 June 2022
22. RH = Rey, A.: Dictionnaire historique de la langue française, Dictionnaires Le Robert, Paris (1992)
23. TL = Blumenthal, P., Stein, A. (eds.): Tobler-Lommatzsch Altfranzösisches Wörterbuch. Franz Steiner Verlag, Wiesbaden (2002). https://www.ling.uni-stuttgart.de/institut/ilr/tobler lommatzsch. Accessed 22 June 2022
24. TLFi = Le Trésor de la Langue Française Informatisé. ATILF-CNRS & Université de Lorraine (1971–1994). http://www.atilf.atilf.fr/tlf.htm. Accessed 22 June 2022
25. TRÉVOUX = Dictionnaire universel françois et latin, 6th edn. Compagnie des libraires associés, Paris (1777)

Formalizing the Ancient Greek Participle Inflection with NooJ

Silvia Susana Reyes(✉)

Centro de Estudios de Tecnología Educativa y Herramientas Informáticas de Procesamiento del Lenguaje, Facultad de Humanidades y Artes, Universidad Nacional de Rosario, Rosario, Argentina
sisureyes@gmail.com

Abstract. The purpose of this paper is to present a preliminary formalization of the Ancient Greek participle using the (Modern) Greek NooJ Module [2]. To ensure its morphological processing, we first retrieved the secondary operators of the properties.def file of the (Modern) Greek NooJ Module from the doctoral thesis of Lena Papadopoulou. However, we added four definitions related to the Ancient Greek participle: V_Mood = PAR (participle), and the three other tenses—the PR (present) tense is included in the module—in which the participle was conjugated in Ancient Greek: FU (future), AO (aorist), and PF (perfect). The set of conjugational and declensional properties comprises: V_Mood = PAR; PAR_Case = nom | acc | gen | voc | dat; PAR_Gender = n | f | m; PAR_Number = s | p; PAR_Tense = PR | FU | AO | PF; PAR_Voice = act | mid | pas | mp. Our text corpus is made up of 150 animal fables written in prose by or associated with Aesop, a Greek fabulist and storyteller, who was born around 620 BCE. His fables contain a great variety of participles in their full forms, without final vowel elisions. We offer a brief account of the stages involved in the morphological processing and show we have been able to inflect, generate and recognize present active and middle-passive participles; future active, middle and passive participles; and aorist active, middle and passive participles.

Keywords: NLP · Ancient Greek participle · Morphology · Inflectional grammars · Greek NooJ module

1 Introduction

1.1 The Ancient Greek Participle

The purpose of this paper is to present a preliminary formalization of the Ancient Greek participle using the (Modern) Greek NooJ Module [2]. This work represents a small sample of the applied linguistics section of my future master's thesis concerning the automatic morphosyntactic processing of the Ancient Greek participle with NooJ.

The Ancient Greek participle was a heavily inflected category that has been usually defined as a verbal adjective, i.e. an adjective derived from a verb, since it includes the grammatical features of both a verb and an adjective. Although it was considered

M. González et al. (Eds.): NooJ 2022, CCIS 1758, pp. 26–38, 2022.
https://doi.org/10.1007/978-3-031-23317-3_3

a separate part of speech by the Greek grammarians, Anna Pompei [5] states that the participle "cannot be considered an autonomous word class," it "must be considered as a non-prototypical part of speech." It is in fact a complex unit combining a verb with an adjective. It can be defined as a non-finite verbal form that has tense/aspect and voice, which is also inflected for case, gender and number.

1.2 The Modern Greek Module

To ensure the morphological processing of the Ancient Greek participle –since the Ancient Greek NooJ Module [1] was not available for download–, we retrieved the secondary operators of the properties.def file of the (Modern) Greek NooJ Module from the doctoral thesis of Lena Papadopoulou [4]. However, we added four definitions related to the Ancient Greek participle: V_Mood = PAR (participle), and the three other tenses—the PR (present) tense is included in the module—in which the participle was conjugated in Ancient Greek: FU (future), AO (aorist), and PF (perfect).

The set of conjugational and declensional properties comprises the following: V_Mood = PAR; PAR_Case = nom l acc l gen l voc l dat (nominative, accusative, genitive, vocative, dative); PAR_Gender = m l f l n (masculine, feminine, neuter); PAR_Number = s l p (singular, plural); PAR_Tense = PR l FU l AO l PF; PAR_Voice = act l med l pas l mp (active, middle, passive, middle-passive).

Although Ancient Greek had three numbers (singular, dual, plural), dual has been omitted because it gradually disappeared and was not found in our corpus. On the contrary, we have added the perfect tense although perfect participles have not yet been processed.

1.3 The Text Corpus and the Participle Corpus

Our text corpus is made up of 150 animal fables written in prose by or associated with Aesop, a Greek fabulist and storyteller, who was born around 620 BCE. His fables offer a great number and variety of participles in their full forms, without final vowel elisions. Fables were randomly selected and are concerned with the following animals: ass, cicada, crab, crow, dog, dolphin, fox, lion, stork, swallow, swan, weasel, wolf (Fig. 1). The Ancient Greek texts follow E. Chambry's edition and were taken from [3].

We loaded and indexed a preliminary text corpus in NooJ [6] as a single text file of 150 complete animal fables. However, since we were interested in analyzing only one part of speech, we decided to have an abridged corpus that contained only participles, after carefully deleting all the other words or parts of speech from each fable. This abridged or participle corpus (Fig. 2) was ready for the annotation process or Text Annotation Structure after applying Linguistic Analysis.

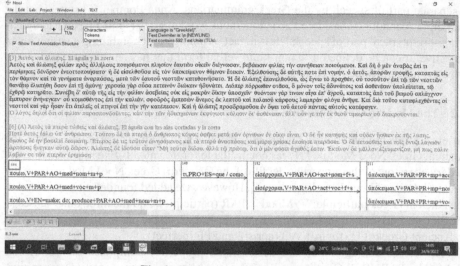

Fig. 1. Text corpus of Aesop's fables.

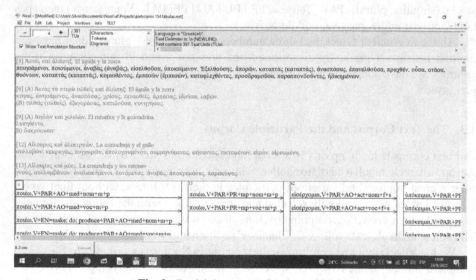

Fig. 2. Participle corpus of Aesop's fables.

2   Morphological Processing of the Ancient Greek Participle

2.1   Extraction of Participles

Participles were manually extracted from the text corpus and classified according to the two specific mood suffixes (-ντ- and -μεν-) that are involved in the inflection of most participles and that are used to inflect the thematic present, the sigmatic and thematic aorist, and the future stems. Participle mood suffixes combine verb roots or stems with adjectival or nominal endings indicating case, gender and number.

2.2 Selection of Participles

The participles to be processed belong to the first or thematic conjugation (with the *o*-grade thematic vowel in the present stem), that is, active -ω verbs (thematic vowel + active primary ending), and middle-passive or deponent -μαι verbs (thematic vowel + middle-passive primary ending). The first two stages of our work, participle extraction and selection, are summarized in Table 1.

Table 1. Tense//voice classification of participles according to mood suffixes including nominative/genitive endings, and examples with TAS.

Participle suffixes		
-ντ-(yα)-		-μεν-
Present Active (Thematic)	-ων, -οντος -ουσα, -ούσης -ον, -οντος	**Present Middle-Passive (Thematic)**	-μενος, η, ον -μένου, ης, ου
συγχωρῶν συγχωρέω,V+PAR+PR+act+nom+m+s		ἀναλισκόμενοι ἀναλίσκω,V+PAR+PR+mp+nom+m+p
Future Active	-σων, -σοντος -σουσα, -σούσης -σον, -σοντος	**Future Middle**	-σόμενος, η, ον -σομένου, ης, ου
κομίσων κομίζω,V+PAR+FU+act+nom+m+s		ἰασόμενον ἰάζω,V+PAR+PR+med+acc+m+s ἰάζω,V+PAR+PR+med+nom+n+s ἰάζω,V+PAR+PR+med+acc+n+s
Aorist Active (Sigmatic)	-σας, -σαντος -σασα, -σάσης -σαν, σαντος	**Aorist Middle (Sigmatic)**	-σάμενος, η, ον -σαμένου, ης, ου
κόψας κόπτω,V+PAR+AO+act+nom+m+s		ποιησάμενοι ποιέω,V+PAR+AO+med+nom+m+p
Aorist Active (Thematic)	-ών, -όντος -οῦσα, -ούσης -όν, -όντος	**Aorist Middle (Thematic)**	-όμενος, η, ον -ομένου, ης, ου
εἰσελθοῦσα εἰσέρχομαι,V+PAR+AO+act+nom+f+s		λαβόμενος λαμβάνω,V+PAR+AO+med+nom+m+s
Aorist Passive	-θείς, -θέντος -θεῖσα, -θείσης -θέν, -θέντος		
λυπηθέντα λυπέω,V+PAR+AO+pas+acc+m+s λυπέω,V+PAR+AO+pas+nom+n+s λυπέω,V+PAR+AO+pas+acc+n+s		

For reasons of space, the annotation of vocatives, whose morphological endings mostly coincide with the nominative in the active voice, have not been included.

We have inflected and generated future active, middle and passive participles, even though they are very rare in the corpus. We have not yet found any future passive participles, ending in -(θ)ησόμενος, η, ον, but some might appear as the corpus gets larger. We have also inflected and generated only three present middle-passive athematic participles of the verbs δύναμαι, κεῖμαι and πρόκειμαι, even though these verbs belong to the second athematic -μι conjugation, which does not have an *o*-grade thematic vowel in the present stem.

2.3 Lemmas Classification Criteria: Accented Vowels Before Verb Endings

Lemmas are represented in the first person singular of the indicative mood. They can have an accent on the second syllable from the end (βλέπω), or on the third syllable from the end (θεάομαι). They are grouped in dictionaries according to the last accented vowel or diphthong second vowel before the first person present indicative endings of -ω verbs. We distinguished two patterns or sequences, where V is the abbreviation for vowel and C for consonant: i) the last accented vowel (-V-) of verb roots/stems ending in a vowel (γηρά-ω); and the last accented vowel or diphthong's second vowel before the last consonant of verb roots/stems in sequences such as -VC-, -VCC-, (or even -VCCC-). In Tables 2, 3, 4, 5 and 6, one lemma per pattern is displayed, and participle nominative endings are provided for the different tenses inflected by different inflectional rule grammars.

Table 2. Lemmas of participle dictionaries compiled with present rule grammars.

Lemmas	Accented vowels and -V-/-VCC- sequences	PR participle nominative endings
θεάομαι	-ά-ο-μαι, -ῶ-μαι	-α-ό-μεν-ος
γηράω-ῶ	-ά-ω, -ῶ	-ά-ων,-ῶν
πυνθάνομαι	-άC-ο-μαι	-αν-ό-μεν-ος
ἄγω	-ἄC-ω	ἄγ-ων
κράζω	-άC-ω	-άζ-ων
λανθάνω	-άC-ω	-άν-ων
πάλλω	-άCC-ω	-άλλ-ων
ἀφικνέομαι	-έ-ο-μαι, -οῦμαι	-ε-ό-μεν-ος
δέχομαι	-έC-ο-μαι	-εχ-ό-μεν-ος
λέγω	-έC-ω	-έγ-ων
ἔχω	ἔC-ω	ἔχ-ων
φθέγγομαι	-έCC-ο-μαι	-εγγ-ό-μεν-ος
ἔρομαι	ἔC-ο-μαι	ἐρό-μεν-ος
μέλλω	-έCC-ω	-έλλ-ων
προσήκω	-ήC-ω	-ήκ-ων
θνήσκω	-ήCC-ω	-ήσκ-ων
ἥκω	ἥC-ω	ἥκ-ων
οἴομαι	-ἴ-ο-μαι	οἰόμεν-ος
γίνομαι	-ίC-ο-μαι	-ιν-ό-μεν-ος
κλίνω	-ίC-ω	-ί (αἱ/εἱ)-ν/β/γ/λ/π/ρ/-ων
γίγνομαι	-ίCC-ο-μαι	-ιγν-ό-μενος
ἀναλίσκω	-ίCC-ω	-ί-σκ/κτ/τν-ων
ἀλαζονεύομαι	-ύ-ο-μαι	-υ-ό-μεν-ος
βούλομαι	-ύC-ο-μαι	-υλ-ό-μεν-ος
φεύγω	-ύC-ω	-ύγ-ων
διώκων	-ώC-ω	-ώκ-ων
λιμώττω	-ώCC-ω	-ώττ-ων
δύναμαι	-ύCα-μαι	δυνά-μεν-ος
κεῖμαι	-ῖ-μαι	κείμεν-ος
πρόκειμαι	-όCει-μαι	προ-κεί-μεν-ος

2.4 Creation of Dictionaries and Grammars

Dictionaries (.dic files) and inflectional rule grammars (.nof files) were created in order to compile these dictionaries (.nod files). These compiled dictionaries were added to

Table 3. Lemmas of participle dictionaries compiled with aorist rule grammars.

Lemmas	Accented vowels and -V-/-VCC- sequences	AO participle nominative endings
θεάομαι	-ά-ο-μαι	-ασάμενος
γηράω	-ά-ω	-άσας, ασάμενος
τολμάω	-ά-ω	-ά/έ-ω, -ήσας
αἱμάττω	-άCC-ω	-άσσ/ττ-, -άξας
ἀνάπτω	-άCC-ω	-άψας, -αψάμενος
αἰσθάνομαι	-άC-ο-μαι	-αθόμενος
βάλλω	-άλλ-ω	-αλ-ών
βρυχάομαι	-ά-ο-μαι	-ησάμενος
βλέπω	-έC-ω	-έψας, -εψάμενος
βρέχω	-έC-ω	-έξας, -εξάμενος
φθέγγομαι	-έCγ-ο-μαι	-έγξάμενος
πέμπω	-έCπ-ω	-έ-μπ/ρπ-,- έψας
ἡγέομαι	-ή-ο-μαι	-ησάμενος
πτύπτω	-ύCC-ω	-ύπτ/σσ-, -ύξας
ἔρχομαι	ἔCC-ο-μαι	ἐλθ-ών
εἴδω	εἴδ-ω	ἰδ-ών
ἐξ-έρχομαι	ἐξ-έρχ-ο-μαι	ἐξελθ-ών
ἔπω	ἔπ-ω	εἰπ-ών
ἐπι-λανθάνομαι	ἐπι-λανθάC-ο-μαι	ἐπι-λαθ-όμενος
εὑρίσκω	εὑρ-ίσκ-ω	εὑρ-ών
κατ-είδω	κατ-είδ-ω	κατ-ιδ-ών
λαμβ/λανθ/τυγχ-άν-ω	-άC-ω	λαβ/λαθ/τυχ-ών

Table 4. Lemmas of -έω participles compiled with present and future grammars.

Lemmas	Accented vowel and -V- Sequence	PR and FU nominative participles
κινέω, -ῶ	-έω, -ῶ	κινέων-ῶν-, ή-σ-ων

Info > Preferences so that participles can be recognized after performing Linguistic Analysis. After the compiling process, lexical entries can also be inflected (-flx.dic files) in order to check the generated forms.

Lexical entries or lemmas are introduced in lowercase in the first person singular of the present indicative: θεάομαι, V + FLX = ΘΕΑΟΜΑΙ.

Table 5. Lemmas of participle dictionaries compiled with present/aorist rule grammars.

Lemmas	Accented vowels and -V-/-VCC-/ -VCCC- sequences	PR and AO participle nominative endings
κάμπτω	-άCCC-ω	-άμπτ-ων, -άμψας
ρίπτω	-ίCC-ω	-ίπτ-ων, -ίψας
κόπτω	-όCC-ω	-όπτ-ων, -όψας
βιόω	-ό-ω, -ῶ	-ιόων-ῶν, -ώσας
μαντεύομαι	-ύ-ο-μαι	-υ-ό-μενος, σά-μεν-ος
κύπτω	-ύCC-ω	-ύπτ-ων, -ύψας
λύω	-ύ-ω	-ύ-ων, -ύ-σας

Table 6. Lemmas of participle dictionaries compiled with present/future/aorist rule grammars.

Lemmas	Accented vowels and -V-/-VCC-/ sequences	PR, FU and AO participle nominative endings
βαστάζω	-άC-ω	βαστάζ-ων, -άσ-ων, -άσας
ἐργάζομαι	-άC-ο-μαι	ἐργαζό-σό-σά-μενος
ἐρίζω	-ίC-ω	ἐρίζων, -ίσων, -ίσας
λογίζομαι	-ίC-ο-μαι	λογιζό-σό-σά-μενος
πιέζω	-έC-ω	πιέζων, -έσων, -έσας
ἐσθίω	-ί-ω	ἐσθίων, -ίσων, -ίσας

The rule grammar to which the dictionary is linked in order to be compiled and with which lemmas are inflected is also named in the first person singular of the present indicative, but in uppercase: ΘΕΑΟΜΑΙ-PAR-PR.nof.

We have created 66 dictionaries made up of a different number of entries and have linked them to different inflectional paradigms or rule grammars comprising one, two, or three tenses (Table 7):

Table 7. Dictionaries, entries and associated rule grammars.

Dictionaries	Entries		Rule grammars
	*flx-.dic	*.dic	
30	19650	318	Present
22	27143	311	Aorist
1	23865	111	Present-future
7	21110	125	Present-aorist
6	31078	128	Present-future-aorist

Some excerpts of dictionaries, grammars and inflected participles are displayed in Fig. 3 and Fig. 4 below:

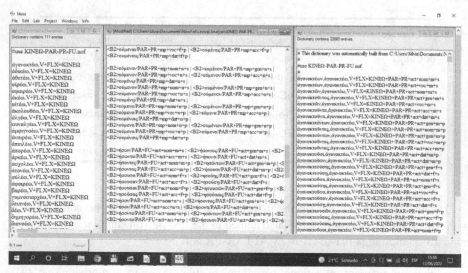

Fig. 3. Excerpts of the ε-contract dictionary (ἀγανακτέω, ἀδικέω, etc.) of the rule grammar associated with it (KINEΩ-PAR-PR-FU.nof) that inflects present (active and middle-passive) and future (active, middle and passive) participles, and of inflected forms.

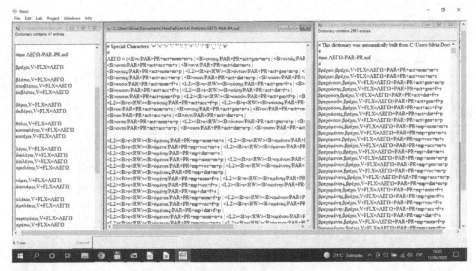

Fig. 4. Excerpts of the -έCω pattern dictionary (λέγω, βρέχω, etc.) whose consonant stems are preceded by an accented vowel έ, of the rule grammar associated with it (ΛΕΓΩ-PAR-PR.nof) that inflects present participles, and of inflected forms.

2.5 Linguistic Analysis and TAS

After performing Linguistic Analysis and getting the Text Annotated Structure (TAS), we entered strings of characters such as συγχωρῶν, ἀναλισκόμενοι, κόψας, ποιησάμενοι, εἰσελθοῦσα, λαβόμενος, and λυπηθέντα, which were already shown in Table 1, to check their inflection. We also entered NooJ regular expressions (<V+PAR>, <V+PAR+PR>, <V+PAR+AO>, <V+PAR+FU>) in the Locate window to check that participles were successfully recognized and inflected, as it can be seen in Fig. 5, Fig. 6, Fig. 7 and Fig. 8:

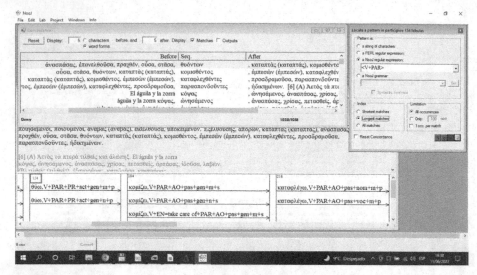

Fig. 5. <V+PAR> search with Locate.

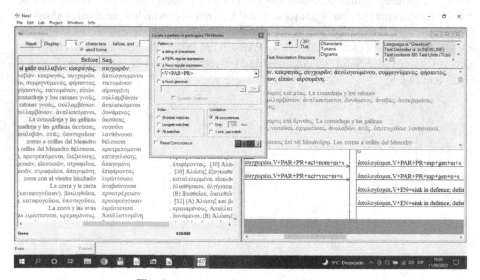

Fig. 6. <V+PAR+PR> search with Locate.

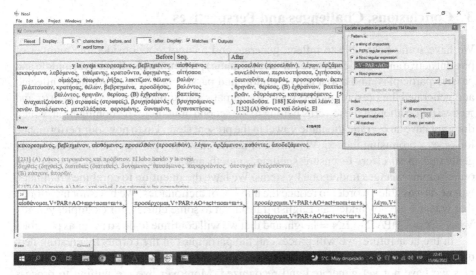

Fig. 7. <V+PAR+AO> search with Locate.

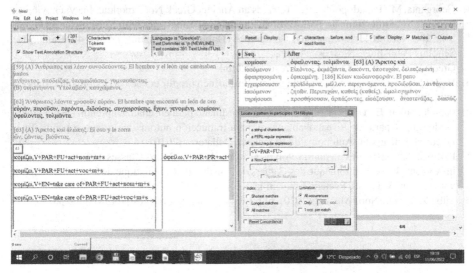

Fig. 8. <V+PAR+FU> search with Locate.

3 Conclusions, Challenges and Perspectives

We have so far been able to inflect, generate and recognize a considerable number of present active and middle-passive (mostly thematic) participles; future active, middle and passive participles; and aorist active, middle and passive participles. We have inflected and generated the present middle-passive athematic participles of δύναμαι, κεῖμαι and πρόκειμαι, although these verbs belong to the second athematic -μι conjugation, which does not have an *o*-grade thematic vowel in the present stem. Up to now, our performance looks very promising indeed. We will continue to check the participles we have already generated in an effort to ensure spelling, smooth and rough breathings, accents, and orthographic changes undergone by stems. We have the intention to combine grammars, whenever possible, in order to reduce the number of dictionaries. We have not mentioned that we have already added an English translation to some entries, for example, γελάω, V + FLX = ΓΗΡΑΩ + EN = laugh, and that we will continue to do so as far as possible.

In the near future, we will process all the participles in the corpus by creating new dictionaries and new rule inflectional paradigms for the thematic conjugation participles we have not yet generated and recognized. Moreover, we are willing to process all the verbs of the athematic conjugation. However, our greatest challenge lies in the formalization of the perfect active and middle-passive participles.

In the long run, our intention is to use the graphical editor to create inflectional grammars.

References

1. Georganta, M., Papadopoulou, E.: Towards an Ancient Greek NooJ module. In: Vučković, K., Bekavac, B., Silberztein, M. (eds.) Formalizing Natural Languages with NooJ: Selected Papers from the NooJ 2011 International Conference (Dubrovnik, Croatia), pp. 41–49. Cambridge Scholars Publishing, Newcastle (2012)
2. Greek Module. http://nooj4nlp.org/resources.html
3. Hodoi Electronikai, Du texte à l'hypertexte. http://mercure.fltr.ucl.ac.be/Hodoi/concordances/intro.htm#Esope
4. Papadopoulou, E.: Diccionario monolingüe coordinado para enseñanza/aprendizaje del griego moderno por parte de hispanohablantes y para traducción automática griego-español, Tesis Doctoral. Universitat Autónoma de Barcelona, Bellaterra (2010)
5. Pompei, A.: Participles as non-prototypical word class. In: Word Classes and Related Topics in Ancient Greek. Bibliothèque des Cahiers de l'Institut de Linguistique de Louvain (BCILL), vol. 117, pp. 361–388. Peeters, Louvain-la-Neuve (2006)
6. Silberztein, M.: NooJ Manual (2020). http://www.nooj4nlp.org/files/NooJManual.pdf

Automatic Analysis of Appreciative Morphology: The Case of Paronomasia in Colombian Spanish

Walter Koza[1]([⊠]), Viviana Román[2], and Constanza Suy[2]

[1] Consejo Nacional de Investigaciones científicas y técnicas, Universidad Nacional de General Sarmiento, San Miguel, Argentina
wkoza@campus.ungs.edu.ar
[2] Pontificia Universidad Católica de Valparaíso, Valparaíso, Chile
{viviana.roman,constanza.suy}@pucv.cl

Abstract. Paronomasia is defined as the substitution of one lexical item for another, based on partial homophony. While this phenomenon has been the subject of several studies focused on stylistic aspects [1, 2] - and, to a lesser extent, those of grammar [3] - computational linguistics approaches are practically nonexistent. Previous barriers include difficulties in automatically assigning correct labels (both semantic and morphological) due to ambiguity in these expressions. To this end, this paper analyzes a group of Colombian Spanish nouns and their corresponding paronomastic variants from the Generative Lexicon Theory [4, 5] (GLT) with a view toward computational modelling and automatic recognition by means of NooJ [6]. The methodology consists of the following steps: (i) selection of a list of Colombian Spanish nouns included in Varela's work [7]; (ii) creation of semantic structures (SS) according to GLT; and (iii) elaboration of productive morphological and constrained syntactic grammars [8]. The resources are tested on a set of sentences, yielding promising results to further investigate the automatic analysis of paronomasia from this perspective.

Keywords: Paronomasia · Colombian Spanish · Generative Lexicon theory · Automatic analysis · NooJ

1 Introduction

Among the studies of linguistic creation resources, paronomasia - understood as the substitution of one lexical item for another, on the basis of partial homophony - has been the subject of several stylistic studies [1, 2]. Additionally, though to a lesser extent, grammatical approaches have also been observed [3]. However, to the best of our knowledge, no studies account for the phenomenon from the computational linguistics field. Indeed, there are difficulties in automatically assigning correct labels (both semantic and morphological) due to the ambiguity inherent to such expressions. Thus, for example, while

© Springer Nature Switzerland AG 2022
M. González et al. (Eds.): NooJ 2022, CCIS 1758, pp. 39–49, 2022.
https://doi.org/10.1007/978-3-031-23317-3_4

'*alcamonías*' (condiment seeds) is a *plurale tantum*, it had seen use[1] as a paronomastic form of '*alcahuete*' (brothel-keeper), which produced structures like those in (1):

(1)   Juan is an *alcamonías*. (→ *alcamonías*: masculine, singular)
       Juan and Pedro are *alcamonías*. (→ *alcamonías*: masculine, plural)
       Maria is an *alcamonía*. (→ *alcamonías*: feminine, singular)
       María and Susana are *alcamonías* (→ *alcamonías*: feminine, plural).

In this regard, this paper analyzes a group of Colombian Spanish nouns and their corresponding paronomastic variants from the perspective of Generative Lexicon Theory (GLT) [4, 5]. Specifically, we propose computational modelling and automatic recognition by means of a constraint grammar [8] through NooJ [6], a tool for linguistic analysis with utilities like electronic dictionaries and computer grammars. The methodology is as follows: (i) selection of a list of Colombian Spanish nouns from Varela's work [7]; (ii) creation of an electronic dictionary with associated semantic and morphosyntactic information; and (iii) elaboration of productive morphological and syntactic constraint grammars [8] for recognition. The resources are then tested on a set of sentences validated by native speakers of Colombian dialects. The results show that, in some cases, paronomasia implies a constraint of the semantic structure (SS) ('billete>Villegas') or generates a new one ('mano>Manuela'); in others, it remains unchanged ('mierda>miércoles'). This process of automatic analysis yields promising results for further investigation of the phenomenon from this perspective.

The article is organized as follows. Section 2 presents the theoretical framework that supports the proposal. Section 3 discusses methodology, consisting of the creation of semantic structures (SS) according to the principles of GLT [4] and the elaboration of morphological and syntactic grammars. In Sect. 4, the results obtained are described. And in Sect. 5, the conclusions derived from the present work are reported.

2 Theoretical Framework: The Phenomenon of Paronomasia, Generative Lexicon Theory and Constraint Grammar

This section first presents the theoretical framework that supports the research: first, the works that have addressed the phenomenon of paronomasia; second, a synthesis of GLT [4]; and third, a brief description of what a constraint grammar consists of [8].

2.1 Paronomasia: Description of the Phenomenon

Paronomasia is defined by Moreno [9] as a derivative linguistic operation – and, therefore, morphological - in which one lexical unit with phonic similarity to, takes the signifier of, another lexical unit recognized in the language, but without modification in the meaning. Thus, in (2), 'cana' ceases to have the meaning of 'white hair', to refer to 'prison'.

(2)   Juan is in *cana* ('*cana*' = '*jail*').

---

[1] Archaic, as of 2022.

The definitions, typologies and analyses of paronomasia that have been considered in this paper are basically framed in two lines: one descriptive [7, 9, 10]; and another formal and generativist [3]. Within the first group, Varela [9] defines paronomasia as the modification of a term so that it adopts the signifier of another term with which it only shares the initial phonetic structure. For this author, the alteration is not fortuitous, but intentional, and its phonetic nature results in the appearance of homonyms. In order to support this assertion, he carries out an exhaustive analysis, which allows that author to identify 903 of what they term "*homónimos parasitarios*" (parasitic homonyms) in Spanish.

In a grammatical approach, Bohrn's work [3] conceives of paronomasia as an association of two words of the language, based on their phonological similarity. Their contribution – framed around the assumptions of Distributed Morphology [11] – proposes that the schema of the process involves the phonological form of base # 1 toward base #2, which provides the meaning, and a paronomastic unit, or the association of the bases. This scheme includes certain grammatical categories, which can be in any of the bases: 'hambre>ambrosio'; 'mozo/a>mosaico'; 'corto/a>cortina'. The grammatical category of the resulting word is that of the unit that provided the meaning, not that of the word that lends its phonological form. Evidence in support of this argument is the concordance: where the two nouns involved have different genders, the gender of base #1 prevails.

(3)   *El mosaico* brought me cold coffee (The waiter brought me cold coffee).
       La mosaico brought me cold coffee. (The waitress brought me cold coffee.)

Notwithstanding, the literature raises a number of valid questions: (i) Is all phonetic similarity a case of paronomasia? (ii) What happens with the semantic information of the base? (iii) What happens with the morphosyntactic information of the base? And (iv) What drawbacks might exist for automatic parsing? Regarding the lattermost, difficulties have been described for automatic parsers that do not take paronomasia into account, see, e.g., the following taken from TreeTager, Conexor and FreeLing [12] (Fig. 1).

un	ART	un
melón	NC	melón
de	PREP	de
pesos	NC	peso

1	Juan	juan	subj>3	@NH N MSC SG Prop
2	se	se	obj>3	@NH PRON Pers Refl P3 ACC
3	hace	hacer	main>0	@MAIN V IND PRES SG P3
4	un	uno	det>5	@PREMOD DET MSC SG
5	Billegas	billegas	oc>3	@NH Heur N SG Prop
6				

Qué	qué		DE0CN0	0.104136
perro	perro		NCMS000	1
de	de		SPS00	0.999984
miércoles	[X:??/??/??.??.??.??]		W	1

Treetagger   **Connexor**   **Freeling**

Fig. 1. Examples of mislabeling for the cases of 'million>melon', 'billete>Billegas' and 'mierda>miércoles'.

Here it is evident that the phenomenon of paronomasia implies ambiguity, where wrong labels are assigned (Treetagger and Connexor); or, worse still, no assignment takes place (Freeling). In order to provide solutions to these complexities, this paper takes an approach from GLT [4] under constraint grammar [8], as discussed below.

2.2 The Generative Lexicon Theory

GLT [4, 5] establishes an organizational model for lexical entries in relation to the meanings they generate in combination with other units. The theory proposes the existence of four levels of representation that structure such information:

(i)   the *argument structure*, which specifies the number of arguments of a predicate, the semantic class and the way they are syntactically effected;
(ii)   the *eventive structure*, which indicates the type of event denoted by a predicate;
(iii) the *Qualia structure*, which includes information on the fundamental characteristics of the entity to which it refers, and how the eventive and argumentative structures are related. These are:

- the *Constitutive quale*, which encodes the relationship between an object and its parts;
- the *Formal quale*, which encodes that which distinguishes the object within a larger domain;
- the *Telic quale*, which encodes the purpose and function of the object, and
- the *Agentive quale*, which encodes the factors involved in the origin or production of the object.

and (iv) The *lexical constructionalization structure*, which explains how one word is related to another in the mental lexicon.

Then all lexical entries have the following structure (Fig. 2):

```
[lexical sign
EVENT STRUCTURE
ARGUMENT STRUCTURE
LEXICAL STRUCTURE
QUALIA STRUCTURE:
     [FORMAL ROLE
     AGENTIVE ROLE
     TELIC ROLE
     CONSTITUTIVE ROLE]
```

Fig. 2. SS of lexical entries in the GLT [4].

Since the identification of meaning is given from the combination with syntaxes, a constraint grammar [8] would provide a suitable tool for disambiguation.

2.3 Constraint Grammars

Constraint Grammar was proposed by Karlsson, Voutilainen, Heikkilä and Anttila [8] and considers that all relevant structure is mapped directly from morphology (considered in the electronic dictionary) and from simple mappings from morphology to syntax.

According to Galicia and Gelbukh [13], a constraint grammar can be defined as a formalism for writing rules of disambiguation. It divides the parsing problem into three modules: morphological disambiguation, assignment of clause boundaries within sentences, and assignment of superficial syntactic labels. The labels indicate the superficial syntactic function of each word and the basic dependency relations within the clause and sentence. In the present work, grammars of this type are developed in order to disambiguate whether a word refers to its *original* or *paronomastic meaning*.

3   Methodology

The methodology contemplates the following stages: (i) selection of Colombian Spanish nouns, together with their paronomastic pairs and elaboration of SS; (ii) elaboration of productive morphological grammars; and (iii) creation of constrained grammars.

3.1   Selection of Colombian Spanish Names

Varela's work [9] includes an appendix with a list of words together with their paronomastic pairs of the Spanish spoken in Latin America. For the present work, with the assistance of three native speakers of Colombian Spanish, the words currently used in that variety were selected and extracted as follows: cárcel>cana, mano>Manuela, risa>Risaralda, teta>tecla, virgen>Virginia, millón>melón, pipi>pirulo, rabo>rábano, billete>Villegas/Billegas, mierda>miércoles.

Once the units had been selected for analysis, we proceeded to the elaboration of the SS, both for the base and for their paronomastic pairs. For the latter, the interviewees answered about the use they give to these words. Figure 3 shows that in cases such as 'cárcel>cana', the base remains unchanged.

cárcel	cárcel>cana
EA: Arg0: x: +hum	EA: Arg0: x: +hum
EE: el estado (x, estar en)	EE: el estado (x, estar en)
EQ:	EQ:
QF: institución.lugar	QF: institución.lugar
QC: rejas, paredes	QC: rejas, paredes
QT: resguardar X	QT: resguardar,
QA: poder judicial	QA: poder judicial

Fig. 3. SS for 'cárcel' and 'cana'.

Notwithstanding, in the case for example of 'Villegas' (or 'Billegas') as a paronomasia of 'billete', the SS is reduced to the argument structure and the telic quale, so that interviewees consider sentences like (4.a) possible, but not sentences like (4.b):

(4)   a. Juan is a guy with a lot of Villegas.
        b. *Juan found a Villegas of one hundred pesos.

Therefore, the SS for 'billete>Villegas' would be as shown in Fig. 4:

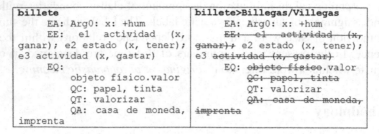

billete	billete>Billegas/Villegas
EA: Arg0: x: +hum	EA: Arg0: x: +hum
EE: e1 actividad (x, ganar); e2 estado (x, tener); e3 actividad (x, gastar)	~~EE: e1 actividad (x, ganar);~~ e2 estado (x, tener); e3 ~~actividad (x, gastar)~~
EQ: objeto físico.valor QC: papel, tinta QT: valorizar QA: casa de moneda, imprenta	EQ: ~~objeto físico~~.valor ~~QC: papel, tinta~~ QT: valorizar ~~QA: casa de moneda,~~ ~~imprenta~~

Fig. 4. SS for 'billete>Villegas'.

Based on these SS, computational resources were developed based on the creation of productive grammars and syntactic constraint grammars.

3.2   Computer Work

For the computational work, a Spanish dictionary developed in previous works [14] was used, and productive and constrained grammars were developed.

Productive Grammars
For the creation of a constrained grammar, the following rule was proposed:

- Paronomastic derivation rule: A word is a paronomasia of another word if and only if: (i) it belongs to a word in the lexicon; (ii) it is phonically similar to another word also belonging to the lexicon; and (iii) the phonic similarity is not the product of another derivational process.

In this way, cases such as 'nacer' and 'nacimiento', where the second word is the product of a nominalization, are discarded. Figure 5 gives the case of 'cárcel>cana' is presented:

Fig. 5. Productive grammar for the recognition of 'cárcel>cana'.

This grammar starts with the 'Base' variable, which consists of a set of at least one letter, followed by the first constraint, which consists of combining $Base with another set of letters, in this case 'árcel'[2]. Thus the combination 'cárcel' is formed, which must

---

[2] In this example, only the letter 'c' and not 'ca' was considered as a base, because the word from which it is derived has a tilde ('cárcel').

be listed in the electronic dictionary (<$Base#ana=:N>). Secondly, we declare the constraint that the same initial node is combined with a new set of words and thus, forms another word, which is also in the dictionary (<$Base#ana=:N>), thereby, producing 'cana', so it is assigned a new meaning, plus the indication that it is a paronomastic pair of 'cárcel' (<$Base#ana=:N+C1+fem+PAR=cárcel>). Third, an ad-hoc syntactic class was assigned. Figure 6 shows the output of the analysis of the sentence 'Juan está en cana'.

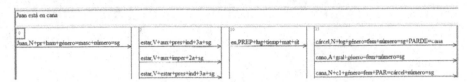

Fig. 6. Output of the analysis of the sentence 'Juan está en cana'.

As can be seen, the lexical analysis of 'cana' yields three results: in addition to the two noun tags, the adjective tag ('su cabeza cana') is added. This complexity, as mentioned above, can be approached from a constraint grammar.

Constraint Grammar
For the elaboration of the constraint grammar that would allow the disambiguation of possible meanings, in addition to the semantic aspect, the gender and number of each element of the pair had to be taken into account. This resulted in four classes, as detailed in Table 1.

Table 1. Classification of the cases of paronomasia analyzed.

Case	Basis		Paronomasia		Class
	Gender	Plural	Gender	Plural	
cárcel>cana	fem	-s	fem	-s	1
mano>Manuela	fem	-s	fem	-s	1
risa>risaralda	fem	-s	fem	-s	1
teta>tecla	fem	-s	fem	-s	1
virgen>virginia	fem	-es	fem	-s	1
millón>melón	masc	-es	masc	-es	2
pipi>pirulo	masc	-s	masc	-s	2
rabo>rábano	masc	-s	masc	-s	2
billete>Billegas/Villegas	masc	-s	común	0	3
mierda>miércoles	fem	-s	masc	0	4

Which yields the following syntactic grammar, as shown in Fig. 7:

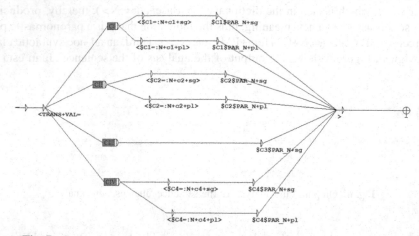

Fig. 7. Constraint grammar for the disambiguation of paronomastic derivatives.

The description of class 4 (CIV), corresponding to 'mierda>miércoles', will be exemplified below. In this case, the base 'mierda' is feminine and forms the plural by adding the suffix '-s', while 'miércoles', in the original sense, is masculine (5.a). When paronomasia occurs, there is a modification in the inflectional properties (5.b).

(5)   a. The film opens on miércoles.
       b. I don't believe that miércoles.

This allows, by means of a finite state grammar, to identify the cases where 'miércoles' corresponds to 'mierda', like the one shown in Fig. 8:

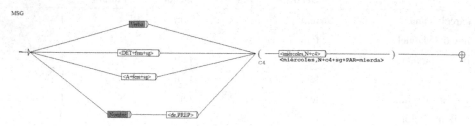

Fig. 8. Constraint grammar for the disambiguation of 'miércoles'.

This includes two embedded grammars: Verb and: Noun, which are displayed in Figs. 9 and 10, respectively.

Verbo

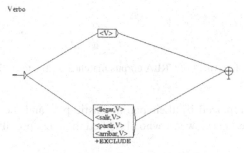

Fig. 9. Embedded grammar: Verb.

Nombre

Fig. 10. Embedded grammar: Noun.

Both propose a noun or a verb as a node; however, they exclude exceptions that are insufficient for disambiguation, such as: 'partir miércoles', 'tarde de miércoles', etcetera. Although this finite state grammar is not entirely exhaustive, since it would recognize agrammatical sequences of the type '*estar miércoles', it is adequate enough for the purposes of the present work. In Fig. 11, a fragment of the recognition and disambiguation is presented.

Before	Seq.	After
'¿Meñiques?, vete a	la miércoles/<TRANS+VAL=<miércoles,N+c4+sg+PAR=mierdas>mierda>	' Bueno, miñi, ya nos despedim
'¿Meñiques?, vete a	la miércoles/<TRANS+VAL=<miércoles,N+c4+sg+PAR=mierdas>mierdas>	. ' Bueno, miñi, ya nos despedim
ɔs a sepultar nuestra	propia miércoles/<TRANS+VAL=<miércoles,N+c4+sg+PAR=mierdas>mierda>	que estamos creando lo vamos
ɔs a sepultar nuestra	propia miércoles/<TRANS+VAL=<miércoles,N+c4+sg+PAR=mierdas>	que estamos creando lo vamos
bomba atómica nos	manda a la miércoles/<TRANS+VAL=<miércoles,N+c4+sg+PAR=mierdas>mierda>	, la gente se cabrea porque

Fig. 11. Recognition and disambiguation for 'mierda>miércoles'.

In the following section, the results obtained are presented.

4   Results Obtained

For the evaluation, we proceeded as follows. First, we searched the CREA corpus [15] for oral texts of Colombian Spanish and extracted the first 100 matches. Figure 12 shows a fragment of 'billete'. For the case 'mano>Manuela', as it was not found in the corpus, the interviewees were asked to propose two examples each, obtaining 6 sentences.

```
Nº   CONCORDANCIA                                                                                                          AÑO
1    imaginable, sin tener en ese momento que tocar un billete a girar un cheque para pagar. Eso, eso no le  **  1992
2    eroz enmantecada, resulta casi imposible sacar el billete para pagar los 100 pesos de un pedazo de piña  **  1988
3    s más fáciles, tocar de todo para  "rebuscarse el billete". En otras palabras, seguir la fórmula de Jul  **  1988
4    7.000 pesos y 1.029 aproximaciones. El valor del billete es de 30 pesos. Pero la echan toda. En el Baz  **  1987
5    Así como no se dice billet, taburet, toret, sino billete, taburete, torete, no debe decirse disquet, s  **  1996
```

Fig. 12. Fragment of CREA corpus matches for the term 'billete'.

They were then replaced by their paronomastic pair and the resulting constructs were validated by the interviewees, who classified them as 'possible' or 'not possible' (Table 2).

Table 2. Classification of the cases of paronomasia analyzed.

Left context	Unit	Right context	Evaluation
I had to change the	VILLEGAS	to return [traveling]	Not possible
I like the	villegas	because I like to work	Possible

The overall result obtained was as shown in Table 3:

Table 3. Overall results obtained.

Total	Recognized	Wrong	Precision	Recall	F-measure
562	362	2	99.4	64.05	77.9

The partial results are distributed as shown in Table 4.

Table 4. Overall results obtained.

Case	Total	Recognized	Wrong	Precision	Recall	F-measure
billete>Villegas	8	7	1	87.5	87.5	87.5
cárcel>cana	100	97	0	100	97	98.4
mano>Manuela	6	6	0	100	100	100
risa>Risaralda	100	90	0	100	90	94.7
teta>tecla	100	12	0	100	12	21.4
virgen>Virginia	10	6	1	90.9	60	74.1
millón>melón	36	29	0	100	80.5	89.2
pipi>pirulo	2	0	0	–	–	–
rabo>rábano	100	13	0	100	13	24.3
mierda>miércoles	100	100	0	100	100	100

In relation to the information in this table, automatic recognition is more efficient when the base and the paronomastic pair differ both in semantic features ('billete>Villegas'; 'mano>Manuela') or there is a reassignment of gender and number ('mierda>miércoles').

5 Conclusions

This research constitutes a first approach to the study of Spanish paronomasia from computational linguistics. The analysis allows us to observe that this morphological process does not merely consist of the replacement of a word by a similar sounding one, but also involves issues at the lexical-syntax interface. Automatic analysis showed promise, with disambiguation reaching an F-measure of 77.9%. On the other hand, although sentences alone might not seem sufficient for disambiguation, the authors attribute this to performance issues, which are beyond the scope of the present research.

Future work will be organized around the following pillars: (i) to build a corpus for the study of Colombian paronomasia; (ii) to continue with the analysis of new units; and (iii) to compare this methodology with the paronomasia of Rio de la Plata Spanish.

References

1. López, M.: La paronomasia como recurso conceptual, expresivo y humorístico en la lengua española actual. Ph.D. thesis. Universidad de Granada, Granada (2005)
2. Musté, F.: Análisis lingüístico de un corpus de eslóganes y frases publicitarias de marcas comerciales. Ph.D. thesis. Universidad Politécnica de Valencia, Valencia (2015)
3. Bohrn, A.: ¿Qué me contursi? Mi mujica se fue con un vizcacha. Paronomasia en el español del Río de la Plata. In: Kornfeld, L., Kuguel, I. (eds.) El español rioplatense desde una perspectiva generativa. Editorial FFyL-UNCuyo & SAL, Mendoza (2013)
4. Pustejovsky, J.: The Generative Lexicon. MIT Press, Cambirdge (1995)
5. Pustejovsky, J., Batiukova, O.: The Lexicon. Cambridge University Press, Cambridge (2019)
6. Silberztein, M.: Formalizing Natural Languages. The NooJ Approach. ISTE, London (2016)
7. Varela, D.: Un sistema peculiar de creación de palabras en español: descripción y análisis de la homonimia parasitaria. Ph.D. thesis. Universidad Autónoma de Madrid, Madrid (2016)
8. Karlsson, F., Voutilainen, A., Heikkilä, J., Anttila, A.: Constraint Grammar: A Language-Independent System for Parsing Unrestricted text. Mouton de Gruyter. Berlín/New York (1995)
9. Moreno, L.: Expresión de la afectividad en el español de Chile: Estudio lingüístico de cuatro fenómenos relevantes. Ph.D. thesis. Universidad Complutense de Madrid, Université Blaise Pascal, Madrid (2015)
10. Castañeda, L.: Caracterización lexicológica y lexicográfica del parlache para la elaboración de un diccionario. Ph.D. thesis. Universidad de Lleida, Lleida
11. Halle, M., Marantz, A.: Morphology distributed and the pieces of inflection. In: Hale, K., Keyser, J. (eds.) The View from Building 20. The MIT Press, Cambridge (1993)
12. http://www.elv.cl/nazar/nlp/. Accessed 10 June 2022
13. Galicia, H., Gelbuk, A.: Investigaciones en el análisis sintáctico en español. Instituto Politécnico Naciona, México D.F. (2007)
14. Koza, W., Suy, C.: Automatic detection and generation of argument structures within the medical domain. In: Bigey, M., Richeton, A., Silberztein, M., Thomas, I. (eds.) NooJ 2021. CCIS, vol. 1520, pp. 198–207. Springer, Cham (2021). https://doi.org/10.1007/978-3-030-92861-2_17
15. https://www.rae.es/banco-de-datos/crea. Accessed 11 Apr 2022

Prosodic Segmentation of Belarusian Texts in NooJ

Yauheniya Zianouka(✉), Yuras Hetsevich, Mikita Suprunchuk, and David Latyshevich

United Institute of Informatics Problems of the National Academy of Sciences of Belarus,
Minsk, Belarus
ssrlab221@gmail.com

Abstract. The article describes the syntactic grammar for automatic text segmentation into syntagms in Belarusian by means of NooJ. It is based on the principle of defining sequences of linguistic elements associated with certain semantic relationships and aimed at searching structural and semantic components of utterances and delimiting them into accentual units. Its implementation is essential for improving the synthetic speech generated by Belarusian text-to-speech systems using prepared syntactic grammars in NooJ.

Keywords: Syntactic grammar · Intonation · Syntagm · Prosodic delimitation · Segmentation · Text-to-speech system

1 Introduction

To date, there are no general rules or mechanisms for automatic prosodic delimitation and an unambiguous definition of syntagms in a written text or speech flow. The study of prosodic speech organization is conducted on the basis of auditory and experimental analyses, with the help of which the parameters of super-segmental means are distinguished. They are the limits of the speech flow segmentation, types of intonation constructions (IC), tonal, dynamic and quantitative signals of the IC center, changes in the speed and intensity of sound. All these components are difficult to transfer as a unified component at the computer level and reproduce identically to natural speech.

This problem is quite common for text-to-speech (which converts arbitrary text into speech) and recognition (which automatically converts a speech signal into written text) systems. Despite the achievements in the field of synthesized speech, the problem of qualitative speech synthesis is only partially developed [1, 2]. Firstly, over time, new technologies are emerging to better solve certain issues of speech synthesis. Secondly, a number of algorithms, as well as many linguistic resources necessary for speech synthesis, are language-dependent and have not yet been developed for all languages, including Belarusian. Therefore, the research in the field of speech synthesis, in particular Belarusian text-to-speech (TTS), is relevant to this day.

This work is a continuation of previous research dedicated to automatic speech delimitation. At previous stages of the research, punctuation was used as the major means of separating analyzed text into syntagms [3, 4]. Now we have applied a technique

M. González et al. (Eds.): NooJ 2022, CCIS 1758, pp. 50–62, 2022.
https://doi.org/10.1007/978-3-031-23317-3_5

for automated phrase segmentation not only at the punctuational level but also at the semantic. The keystone is the number of syntagms in a sentence that can significantly exceed the number of punctuation marks in the text [5]. Morphological and syntactic principle is the main core of the research. The approach is confined to the ability of a particular speech part to match with words of other lexical and grammatical classes and occupy a certain syntactic position. The concept is grounded in a superficial syntactic analysis of a text with an emphasis on grammatical characteristics of speech parts that combine accentual units.

2 Relevance of the Study: Lack of Automatic Prosodic Segmentation in TTS

The perception of oral speech is characterized by the fact of how the listener recognizes the meaning of what he has heard. With any chosen approach to assessing the quality of synthesized speech, the main accepted verification parameters are intelligibility of speech, naturalness of speech, evaluation of individual modules of the system, evaluation of recognition, understanding of meaning, expressiveness, emotionality.

The noted parameters of high-quality speech are indicated not only by the developers of language computer technologies, the problem of localizing intonation boundaries in the voiced text is one of the main tasks of the prosodic processor, which is a mandatory block in any automatic speech synthesis system. Syntagmatic articulation of the speech stream identifies minimal semantic units and displays the structural and semantic components of utterances.

The lack of depth syntactic analysis complicates automatic syntagm allocation. It leads to the search for alternative approaches to the development of machine algorithms, methods and techniques for determining the sequence of language elements associated with certain semantic relationships. The delimitation of speech primarily depends on the structure of the sentence, the word order, homogeneous terms, the nature of the word combinations and other language parameters. These complications should be considered and marked in separate syntagms during the development of such systems.

For us, this direction is quite topical. Text-to-text speech synthesis includes a set of questions to ensure the possibility of high-quality processing of arbitrary text into artificial speech [6]. This technology has a wide potential, as proven by numerous TTS for different languages. For the Belarusian language, the most famous is the system called *"Multyfon-4"*, on the basis of which the staff of the Speech Synthesis and Recognition Laboratory of the United Institute of Informatics Problems (UIIP) [7] of the National Academy of Sciences of Belarus has created an Internet version of the Belarusian-language synthesizer, which is publicly available and free to use (Fig. 1). It converts electronic text into a speech signal in Belarusian, Russian and English with Belarusian accent [8].

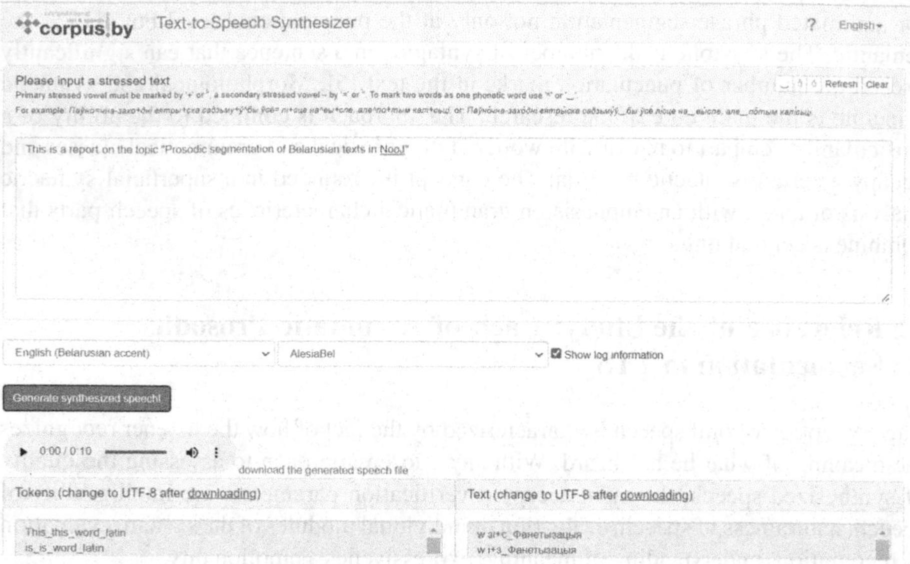

Fig. 1. The interface of Belarusian text-to-speech synthesizer.

Today, new functions are still being incorporated into this synthesizer and already developed ones are being improved. It processes Belarusian texts quite qualitatively, but not perfectly. This is due to a prosodic processor where intonation is almost absent. Belarusian TTS still lacks more or less clear (adequate) intonation – that is, the unity of interrelated components of speech, such as melody, intensity, duration, tempo and timbre, which are inherent in any living utterance. All this reflects a low level of qualified artificial voice and prevents the creation of high-tech national products. In connection with the above, programmers and linguists are faced with the question to consider the phonetic and prosodic characteristics of speech in conjunction with computer technologies where the need for good prosodic processing is the main point to analyze.

3   Text Sources: Corpus of Literary and Medical Texts

In the framework of the research, we composed a text corpus which contains 200 sentences of medical and 200 sentences of literary domains (Fig. 2). The total number is 400 syntactic-accentual units. Stylistic and genre diversity of the selected material is associated with the desire to cover all possible communicative and syntactic types of sentences inherent in the modern Belarusian standard language. Styles differ in the set of linguistic means and their use under the content, tasks and situations of the utterance. So, if a literary text (stylistically enclosed) is focused on evoking an emotional response, influencing the psycho-emotional sphere of the reader/listener, then medical texts are characterized by a strict, almost expressionless nature of scientific and journalistic content using special vocabulary, terminology, abbreviations, a few syntactic constructions. A variety of syntactic constructions of both styles allows considering a variety of word models interaction in the combination of "the main word-dependent components".

Within previous research, the staff of Speech synthesis and recognition laboratory created a text corpus of a medical domain. It was compiled on the basis of medical news published in following medical Internet portals: *Health Committee of Minsk City Executive Committee, Minsk City Gynecological Hospital, 1st Central Regional Clinical Polyclinic of the Central district of Minsk, 4th City Clinical Hospital named after M.J. Sajčanka.* Our laboratory works on Russian-Belarusian-English translations of these sites. On the rights of authors of bilingual translations, we took the news and formed the corpus. Literary texts are taken from works of Belarusian writers, including the publication *"Belarusian literary heritage: an anthology. In 2 books".*

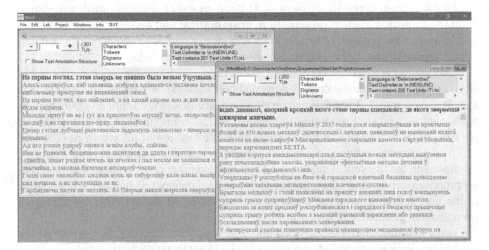

Fig. 2. Text corpus of literary and medical domains.

Initial corpus processing showed the next peculiarities for different styles (journalistic and literary). Literary texts are full of auxiliary parts of speech, have free word order, expressive phrases, and lots of punctuation marks. On the contrary, medical texts are characterized by long sentences, numerous constructions of adjectives and nouns, only nouns, nouns, adjectives and nouns. Auxiliary parts of speech, as a rule, are represented by particles and conjunctions. Punctuation is not so widespread, the most frequent is comma. These regularities were considered during the compilation of the list of rules.

4   Extraction of Syntagms

For the moment, there are no general rules for the syntagm extraction of Belarusian speech. But the results of the statistical analysis based on experimental data give grounds for developing a general algorithm for its delimitation. The system that is planned to find the intonation boundaries of syntagms is based on a superficial syntactic analysis with an emphasis on grammatical characteristics of speech parts. The primary task of this work is to develop rules and an algorithm of formal syntactic grammars that will divide a sentence into syntagms. To develop an algorithm, it is necessary to take into account all punctuation marks, phraseological units and directly a list of formal rules for dividing a sentence into lexical syntagms.

While delimiting text into syntagms, the next points should be considered: the sentence structure, word order, the presence of homogeneous members, the nature of word combinations and other linguistic parameters. Also, each language has specific rules for syntactic relations and their application. Most of the sentences can be read purely syntactically based on the surface syntactic structure, which in the Belarusian written text is fully displayed by punctuation marks. But sometimes the syntactic information is not enough for the correct delimitation, especially for the ambiguity of the context. This is because of the stylistic and genre diversity.

As it was noted in previous papers [4, 5], three groups of syntagms are distinguished within this research, such as **punctuation, grammatical and lexical.**

A punctuation syntagm (PS) refers to a sentence or part of a sentence that is limited to punctuation marks. Belarusian punctuation includes next marks: ".", ",", ";", ":", "-", "…", "!", "?", "?!", "!!!", "???", "(";")". A *Grammatical Syntagm (GS)* marks stable word combinations (phraseological units and collocations). A *Lexical Syntagm (LS)* is a short sentence of 2–3 words or a part of a sentence that is not limited to punctuation marks and is expressed according to personal lexical signs (through certain words or phrases) or rules. The task of this study is correct extraction of all syntagms (PS, GS, LS) by developing, testing and improving syntactic grammars based on NooJ [9].

Based on the theoretical analysis and applied computer processing of text material, we propose a step-by-step algorithm for determining syntagms and intonation boundaries in the text. It comprises three major blocks according to the definition of syntagms (punctuation, grammatical, lexical).

In the first stage, the text is divided into sentences. Punctuation marks, which define the end of a sentence (a period, a question mark, an exclamation mark, a question mark with an exclamation mark, three exclamation marks) are used for this. The next step is partitioning the sentence into syntagms, namely the sequential extraction of syntagms (punctuational, grammatical and lexical). After determining each type of syntagm, the syntagm boundary is arranged with the input of the corresponding marker. PS are distinguished according to punctuation marks that characterize syntactic relations within a sentence (comma, semicolon, dash, colon, brackets, quotation marks). Numbers, abbreviations and proper names are allocated in a separate syntagm precisely because the problem of their decoding has not been solved in the Belarusian TTS. This is done separately by the system user. The search for stable word combinations is carried out on the basis of Belarusian digitized dictionary of phraseological units by I. Liepiešaŭ. They form a separate syntagm (GS). Next, the search for conjunctions and placing the marker of the syntagm boundary before conjunction according to their category by functional meaning: connective (combinative, enumerative-distributive, comparative, gradational) and subordinate (explanatory, temporary, conditional, causal, target, introductory, final, comparative, of place, mode of action, measures, of degrees). The last point is applying the list of formal rules for dividing the text into lexical syntagms in accordance with the computer legend. The result is an output of all sentences delimited by intonation boundaries with their formal markers.

Figure 3 shows the algorithm for determining syntagms and intonation boundaries in sentences.

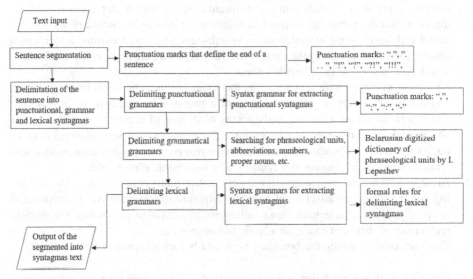

Fig. 3. The algorithm for extracting syntagms and intonation boundaries.

Separating lexical syntagms is the most difficult problem, which are interconnected at the semantic and syntactic levels. This group of lexemes can be determined on the basis of creating general syntactic grammars for a computer expert system, which will search for similar syntactic constructions in a database or a corpus. Each grammar must be presented with a personal syntactic rule to isolate their intonation boundaries in a specific sentence.

In the research, following syntactic rules were used for the arrangement of syntagm boundaries. They are based on the semantic and formal union of two (or more) full-meaning words connected by subordinate relations of the Belarusian standard language. According to the number of principal parts of speech that can serve as the main component, there are 6 types of phrases. They are extracted according to the main word/component and some subordinate members of the sentence:

1. An attributive syntagm that includes a noun and several dependent or interdependent components; a noun and a group of words that convey the same related concepts; a noun and a compound name; a noun and a syntactically indivisible phrase. In these combinations, the main component is the noun.
2. Attributive syntagm with prepositional arrangement separates combinations of prepositions, adjectives with nouns; combinations of prepositions, nouns or a verb group.

3. Predicative syntagm, where the verb or adverbial part is the grammatical and semantic core of the sentence which enters subordinate relations with numerous subordinate
   members of the sentence: a verb with adverbs; a verb with nouns in different cases;
   a verb and preposition with nouns in different cases; a verb with participles, subordinate numerals, pronouns, dependent infinitive, a consistent auxiliary verb *to be*;
   also a verb and several semi-dependent or sub-dependent components; a verb and a
   group of words that convey the same related concepts; a verb and a compound name;
   a verb and syntactically indivisible phrase.
4. An object syntagm with a pronoun as the main component, including a pronoun
   and a noun in different cases; a pronoun, a preposition and a noun in different
   cases; a pronoun, an adjective in the forms of degree of comparison with adverbs
   and particles; a pronoun with an infinitive; a pronoun and several dependent or
   interdependent components; a pronoun and a group of words that convey identical
   related concepts; a pronoun and syntactically indivisible phrase, etc.
5. Adverbial Syntagm, where an adverb acts as the main component in the following combinations: an adverb and qualitative/quantitative/qualitative-circumstantial
   adverb; qualitative/quantitative/qualitative-circumstantial adverb with a preposition
   and a noun in different cases; an adverb and pronouns.
6. Conjunctional syntagm: the boundary is placed before all types of conjunctions.

Using theoretical knowledge in the delimitation of Belarusian texts the authors have
developed a list of formal rules for determining lexical syntagms based on the corpus of
literary and medical domains (see Fig. 4).

$$I+N+I+N \rightarrow I/V//PUNKT/$$
$$I+N+I+J+N+V \rightarrow I/C//PUNKT/$$
$$I+N+D+J+J+N \rightarrow I/C/V//PUNKT//L/PART2$$
$$I+N+N \rightarrow I/C/V//PUNKT/L/J$$
$$I+N+N+I+N \rightarrow C/V//PUNKT/L/MV$$
$$I+N+N+J+N \rightarrow I/C/V//PUNKT//L/PART2/R$$
$$I+N+N+N/NPG \rightarrow NPN/I/V//PUNKT/C$$
$$I+N+N \rightarrow I/C/V//PUNKT/L/PART2$$

Fig. 4. The fragment of a list of formal rules for determining lexical syntagms.

Each line describes a combination of speech parts that are included in one syntactic
rule. The computer system must consistently analyze each rule until it finds the item
that matches the combinations of certain words in the sentence and automatically sets
the boundaries of syntagms. The main principle is to consider the right and the left
contexts that separate syntagms. Uppercase of Latin letters marks a part of speech and
its case, the "+" signs a combination, the right arrow "→" indicates the parts of speech
that separates previous and subsequent syntagms (starts a new syntagm), forward slash
"/" suggests possible variants of those parts of speech that begin the next syntagm.
The "/PUNKT/" symbol describes any of the punctuation marks that possibly separates
punctuational syntagms. It is important to note that syntactic grammars are designed for

the computer processing of syntactic-accent units at the machine level. For the moment, the list consists of 300 formal rules. However, their number may increase during the analysis of a larger volume of material and testing the system for defining new types of syntagms.

For a clearer understanding, consider two sentences of the literary and medical domains.

An example of medical sentence:

Haradskaja   kliničnaja   balnica   chutkaj   dapamohi horada Minska zjaŭliajecca viadučaj ustanovaj u krainie pa akazanni kruhlasutačnaj spiecyjalizavanaj ekstranaj dapamohi roznym katehoryjam nasielnictva: [Haradskaja kliničnaja balnica (JN+JN+N→JR+NR+NG+NG)] [chutkaj dapamohi horada Minska (J+N+N+N→I/C/V//PUNKT/L/PART2)] [zjaŭliajecca viadučaj ustanovaj u krainie (V+J+N+I+N→I)] [krainie pa akazanni kruhlasutačnaj spiecyjalizavanaj ekstranaj dapamohi (I+N+JG+JG+NG+NG→I/J/C/V//PUNKT/L/PART2/J)] [roznym katehoryjam nasielnictva (J+N+N→V/R/I//PUNKT)].

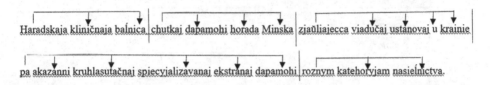

An example of a literary sentence:

Hosć davierliva prytuliŭ halavu da jaho halavy, niby najliepšy siabra albo navat brat, abniaŭ.: [Hosć davierliva prytuliŭ halavu (N+R+V+N→I/R/P/INF)] [da jaho halavy (I+P+N→I/C/V//PUNKT/)] [niby najliepšy siabra (R+J+N→C//I//PUNKT/)] [albo navat brat (C+R+N→C/I//PUNKT)] [abniaŭ (/PUNKT/→V→/PUNKT/)].

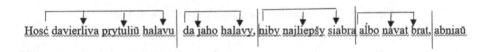

5 Syntactic Grammar for Extracting Syntagms in NooJ

The work carried out on prosodic segmentation makes it possible to automate the created and systematized resources based on NooJ [10]. The developed algorithm and formal rules for determining syntagms form the basis for creating a syntactic grammar for computer processing of grammatical structure of syntagm. Based on the segmentation methods proposed above, we improved syntactic grammar (Fig. 5), which represents the initial stage of prosodic text processing for Belarusian-language speech synthesis systems. It consists of 8 graphs which search syntagms according to parts of speech. They are adjective, prepositional, pronoun, noun, verb, adverbial, conjunctional, particle groups. They are considered as the first component in the sequence of parts of speech that form a new syntagm.

The principle of grammar is as follows: the system consistently analyzes the formal grammatical indicators of words/phrases in a sentence. If it finds a coincidence of morphological and syntactic characteristics of speech parts according to the formal rules of each subgraph, it encloses them in a syntagm. It also notes the graph to which the syntagm corresponds. The characters *SYNT, (,),* in the subgraph reflect the beginning and the end of the syntagm, which the system automatically highlights in the sentence. The right and left contexts are indicated before and after these symbols. Then combinations of speech parts should coincide with a separate formal rule given in the list of formal rules. After finding the correct subgraph corresponding to a certain rule from the list, the system analyzes the right context: formal markers indicating the boundary between syntagms (main/auxiliary parts of speech or punctuation marks). This marker is an indicator of the next syntagm. Thus, a boundary is drawn between the combination of words of one subgraph and certain markers that begin a new syntagm. In accordance with this principle, syntactic grammar works.

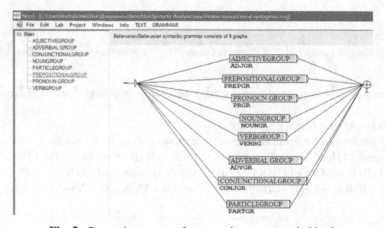

Fig. 5. Syntactic grammar for extracting syntagms in NooJ.

For instance, the adverbial graph consists of nine subgraphs (Fig. 6). The main principle of this grammar is the combination of adverbs as the first component of a syntagm and their subordinate components.

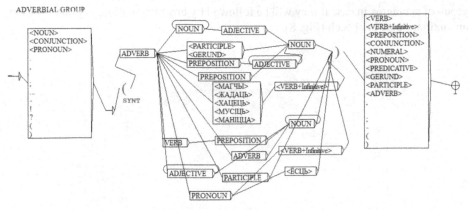

Fig. 6. The graph for extracting adverbial syntagms.

It's very important to consider the right and the left context (words/expressions) which surround this syntagm for delimiting its boundaries. According to this subgraph, the left context can be a noun, a conjunction, a pronoun or some punctuation marks represented in this figure. The right context can be represented by any main part of speech, some auxiliary parts of speech or punctuation marks.

Figure 7 demonstrates the search of verbal syntagms where a verb is the main component.

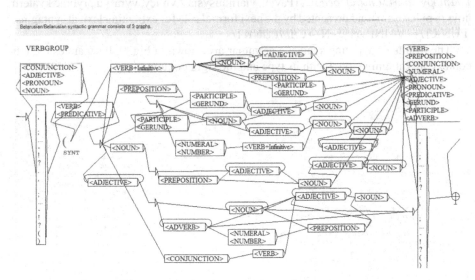

Fig. 7. The graph for extracting verbal syntagms.

For a clearer understanding of grammar, let's analyze the first line of the graph: a verb in combination with an infinitive, noun, adjective and noun forms the first verb group of syntagms in case if they will be followed by any punctuation, notional word or an auxiliary part of speech (Fig. 8).

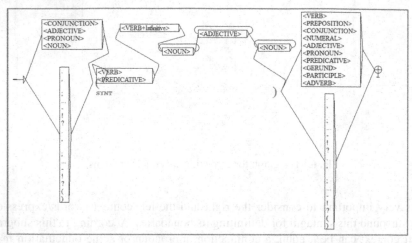

Fig. 8. The graph for extracting verbal syntagms according to the rule /PUNKT/→ V+INF+N+J+N→ C/I///PUNKT/

It is realized in the sentence *"Павел, вярнуўшыся з вуліцы, вырашыў прыбраць кватэру новым пыласосам"*. (Paviel, viarnuǔšysia z vulicy, vyrašyǔ prybrać kvateru novym pylasosam) and presented by the next formal rule for extracting lexical syntagms: /PUNKT/→ V+INF+N+J+N→ C/I///PUNKT/

The results of applying syntactic grammar are shown in Fig. 9. It separates the left context, a syntagm marked with its type and the right context.

Before	Seq.	After
Бароўскі) Галена ўссунула яе Зосі	праз галаву./PREPGR	абцягнула. (Г. В. Далідовіч) Ён
(Г. В. Далідовіч) Ён нібы	з неахвотаю прыклаў/PREPGR	да яе спіны далоні. (Я
В. Далідовіч) Ён нібы з	неахвотаю прыклаў да/NOUNGRнеахвотаю прыклаў	яе спіны далоні. (Я. Сіпакоў
яе спіны далоні. (Я. Сіпакоў)	Яна прыпаднялася на/NOUNGRЯна прыпаднялася	дыбачкі, ён адчуў гэты рух
спіны далоні. (Я. Сіпакоў) Яна	прыпаднялася на дыбачкі./VERBG	ён адчуў гэты рух, прыгнуўся
далоні. (Я. Сіпакоў) Яна прыпаднялася	на дыбачкі,/PREPGR	ён адчуў гэты рух, прыгнуўся
Сіпакоў) Яна прыпаднялася на дыбачкі	, ён адчуў гэты рух./PRGR	прыгнуўся, і яны пашалаваліся. (Я
ён адчуў гэты рух, прыгнуўся,	і яны пашалаваліся./CONJGRCONgr	(Я. Зарэцкі) Слова ўпірастае трывае
Зарэцкі) Слова ўпірастае трывае, I	са здымкаў усё/PREPGR	ажывае - Толькі пах, Толькі смак
смак не той. (Р. Барадулін)	А ён збаяўся ўжо/CONJGRCONgr	гэтага яе намеру, бо не
зусім разумеў яго і не	быў у думках пад/VERBG	-рыхтаваны. (Г. В. Далідовіч) А
разумеў яго і не быў	у думках пад/PREPGR	-рыхтаваны. (Г. В. Далідовіч) А
нашто ты, татачка, майго міленькага	выгнаў з палаца,/VERBG	што аж за морам апынуўся
ты, татачка, майго міленькага выгнаў	з палаца,/PREPGR	што аж за морам апынуўся
выгнаў з палаца, што аж	за морам апынуўся/PREPGR	? (Я. Купала) У пацука кароткае
з палаца, што аж за	морам апынуўся?/NOUNGRморам апынуўся	(Я. Купала) У пацука кароткае
апынуўся? (Я. Купала) У пацука	кароткае жыццё і/NOUNGRкароткае жыццё	хуткая змена пакаленняў. (К. Крапіва
У пацука кароткае жыццё і	хуткая змена пакаленняў./NOUNGRхуткая змена пакаленняў	(К. Крапіва) Ды яшчэ пра
пакаленняў. (К. Крапіва) Ды яшчэ	пра слаўную дзедаву стрэльбу і/PREPGR	пра сваё досыць цікавае знаёмства
(К. Крапіва) Ды яшчэ пра	слаўную дзедаву стрэльбу і/NOUNGRслаўную дзедаву стрэльбу	пра сваё досыць цікавае знаёмства
Крапіва) Ды яшчэ пра слаўную	дзедаву стрэльбу і/NOUNGR дзедаву стрэльбу	пра сваё досыць цікавае знаёмства

Reset Display: 5 ⊂ characters before, and 5 after. Display: ☑ Matches ☑ Outputs
                 ⊙ word forms

Fig. 9. Applying syntactic grammar in the corpus of medical and literary domains.

The grammar has some flaws and demands follow-up revision. The main hypothesis of the grammar is sequential processing of each subgraph from the most complex to the simplest. The same is necessary for graphs. Unfortunately, for today this problem is not resolved. The system analyzes the corpus randomly, the same sentences are checked according to different formal rules. Also, there is a problem with homonyms, numbers and abbreviations which are not taken into account in the grammar.

The next step of the research is detailed grammar testing on the whole corpus for searching new word combinations into syntagms, adding them into graphs and correcting mistakes.

6 Conclusion

The article presents the syntactic grammar for automatic extraction of syntagms and highlighting the intonation boundaries between syntagms at the syntax level in NooJ. The main core is the morphological and syntactic principle that lies in the ability of a particular speech part to match with other words or word forms and occupy certain positions in the sentence. The concept is grounded in a superficial syntactic analysis of different texts (based on the corpus of literary and medical domains) with the emphasis on grammatical characteristics of speech parts that combine accentual units. The purpose of preparing the corpus of different domains is to search and define syntactic constructions in the Belarusian language, not separated by punctuation marks and conjunctions. Their detailed analysis (mostly manual processing of every sentence) provides the source for compiling a list of formal syntactic rules that will later be used by an expert system as the means of searching for identical structures in the input text and determining intonation boundaries within every sentence in NooJ. Identified prosodic aspects estimate the value of intonation peculiarities of Belarusian. Obtained results will be used for further research in automatic processing of prosodic structure of Belarusian, in particular for computer systems with voice accompaniment.

References

1. Lobanov, B., Levkovskaya, T.: Multi-stream word recognition based on a large set of decision rules and acoustic features. In: Proceedings of the 5th International Title Suppressed Due to Excessive Length 9th Workshop Speech and Computer SPECOM 2000. Revised Selected Papers, St.-Petersburg, pp. 75–78 (2000)
2. Lobanov, B., Tsirulnik, L., Zhadinets, D., Karnevskaya, E.: Language- and speakerspecific implementation of intonation contours in multilingual TTS synthesis. In: Speech Prosody: Proceedings of the 3rd International Conference, Dresden, Germany, 2–5 May, Revised Selected Papers, vol. 2, pp. 553–556 (2006)
3. Okrut, T., Hetsevich, Y., Lobanov, B., Yakubovich, Y.: Resources for identification of cues with author's text insertions in Belarusian and Russian electronic texts. In: Monti, J., Silberztein, M., Monteleone, M., di Buono, M.P. (eds.) Formalising Natural Languages with NooJ 2014. Revised Selected Papers, pp. 129–139. Cambridge Scholars Publishing, Newcastle (2015)
4. Hetsevich, Y., Okrut, T., Lobanov, B.: Grammars for sentence into phrase segmentation: punctuation level. In: Okrut, T., Hetsevich, Y., Silberztein, M., Stanislavenka, Hanna (eds.) NooJ 2015. CCIS, vol. 607, pp. 74–82. Springer, Cham (2016). https://doi.org/10.1007/978-3-319-42471-2_7

5. Zianouka, Y., Hetsevich, Y., Latyshevich, D., Dzenisiuk, Z.: Automatic generation of intonation marks and prosodic segmentation for Belarusian NooJ module. In: Bigey, M., Richeton, A., Silberztein, M., Thomas, I. (eds.) NooJ 2021. CCIS, vol. 1520, pp. 231–242. Springer, Cham (2021). https://doi.org/10.1007/978-3-030-92861-2_20
6. Lobanov, B.: Computer Synthesis and Cloning of Speech. Bielaruskaja Navuka, Minsk (2008)
7. Speech Synthesis and Recognition Laboratory. https://ssrlab.by/en/. Accessed 29 July 2022
8. Text-to-speech synthesizer. https://corpus.by/. Accessed 01 Aug 2022
9. NooJ: A Linguistic Development Environment. http://www.nooj4nlp.org/. Accessed 18 Feb 2021
10. Silberztein, M.: Formalizing Natural Languages: The NooJ Approach. Wiley, Hoboken (2016)

Syntactic and Semantic Resources

Zellig S. Harris' Transfer Grammar and Its Application with NooJ

Mario Monteleone$^{(\boxtimes)}$

Università degli Studi di Salerno, 84084 Fisciano, SA, Italy
mmonteleone@unisa.it

Abstract. In 1954, with his article entitled *Transfer Grammar* (published in "The International Journal of American Linguistics", Vol. 20, No. 4, pp. 259–270, University of Chicago Press), Zellig S. Harris was the first linguist to approach the nascent Automatic Translation (AT) from the point of view of structuralist and formal linguistics. This article, written in the pivotal period for the first AT attempts in the US, outlines a translation method that wants to:

– Formally measure the difference between languages, in terms of grammatical structures;
– Define the point of minimum difference (or maximum similarity) between any type of language pair;
– Define the difference between the languages as the number and content of grammatical instructions needed to generate the utterances of one language from the utterances of the other.

At the time, the purposes of Harris's article were therefore extremely innovative, since they considered translation as a process in which meaning transfers could only be achieved based on morphosyntactic analyses and evaluations. Moreover, it is worth stressing that at the time the first AT experiments performed word-for-word translations, without taking into account (not even statistically) the contexts in which the words co-occurred. As is known, this method proved to be unsuccessful, as regards the quality, time and costs of the translations made automatically. In 1966, this led ALPAC [1] to end AT research in the US, and cut off the flow of funding to it.

Keywords: NooJ · NooJ automatic translation · Lexicon-Grammar · Transfer Grammar · Structural linguistics · Distributional linguistics

1 Introduction

Today, AT is basically achieved by means of Computational Statistics (CS). One of the most recent methods exploited by AT is Neural Machine Learning (NML), based on Neural Transition Networks (NTM), but which fails to guarantee constant satisfactory results, as demonstrated by tools like Google Translate. As for the approach elaborated

© Springer Nature Switzerland AG 2022
M. González et al. (Eds.): NooJ 2022, CCIS 1758, pp. 65–75, 2022.
https://doi.org/10.1007/978-3-031-23317-3_6

by Zellig S. Harris, it is worth stressing that up to today, it has remained almost unrealized. During the 90s, there have been several important experiments regarding AT based on the formalization of language morphosyntax. However, all these experiments, including the one in the Logos system, have been abandoned for a long time. Currently, as we intend to demonstrate here, the only software tool and automatic procedures capable of implementing Harris's AT method is NooJ [2, 3]. In fact, we will see how NooJ FSA/FSTs, if used for AT, can apply and develop the aforementioned methodological steps indicated by Harris. Furthermore, we will again demonstrate how, always in its AT grammars, NooJ can use Lexicon-Grammar [4] methodological tools, which formalize morphosyntax using always the same parameters for all natural languages, hence allowing a more straightforward automatic translation between language pairs. Therefore, the ultimate aim of this study will be to demonstrate, with practical examples, how NooJ AT grammars are the most suitable application tools of Harris' Transfer Grammar.

2   On-Line Translation Portals and Tools

According to [5, 6], the most known and used on-line translation portals and tools are (in alphabetical order):

- Amazon Translate
- Bing Microsoft Translator
- Collins Dictionary Translator
- DeepL Translator
- Google Translate
- ImTranslator
- PROMT Online Translator
- Reverso
- SpanishDict
- SYSTRAN Translate
- Translate.com
- Translatedict

Despite the efforts of many analysts (very often prone to commercial interests), it is not possible to sort the list based on the reliability of the translations. As is well known, the evaluations of the translations offered by these portals and tools are at best subjective, and in addition conditioned by the target language competences of the person requesting a translation. What we can say with greater certainty is that Google Translate is the most used system, and it is for this reason that our initial analysis will focus on it.

2.1   A Brief Outline of Google Translate Errors

Being a rule-less system, not based on linguistic engineering, most of Google Translate errors are due to incorrect handling of morphosyntactic constructions, of which we will give a rapid sketch here. For instance, the English and French translations shown in Figs. 1 and 2 contain errors caused by the incorrect processing of a double negation in Italian, which in this specific sentence produce an affirmation and not a negation:

Fig. 1. Google Translate error in Italian-French double negation translation.

Fig. 2. Google Translate error in Italian-English double negation translation.

Apart from the lowercase for *je* in French, the translations offered in French and English have the opposite meaning of the source sentence. The correct translations are: *(FR) Jamais je n'ai pas le temps de lire* and *(ENG) Never I do not have time to read*, the backtranslation of which produce the same reversed errors[1] (Figs. 3 and 4):

---

[1] As for this study, listing other types of Google Translate errors would require a large number of pages. For summarizing purposes only, we indicate here some of them, i.e. erroneous translations of: idioms and frozen sentences; well-known prose and poetry passages already translated into many languages; both simple and terminological compound words. Besides, it is very important to underline that similar errors occur with languages that are not low-use, but with a high number of speakers in the world, such as English, French and Italian.

Francese
Italiano
Jamais je n'ai pas le temps de lire
Non ho mai tempo per leggere
Forse cercavi: Jamais je n'ai pas le temps de ...
Apri in Google Traduttore • Feedback

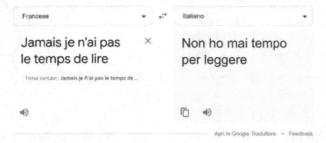

Fig. 3. Google Translate backtranslation error from French to Italian.

Francese
Inglese
Jamais je n'ai pas le temps de lire
I never have time to read
Apri in Google Traduttore • Feedback

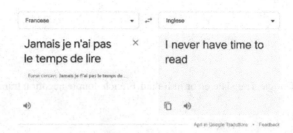

Fig. 4. Google Translate backtranslation error from French to English.

Another Google Translate error due to the absence of formalized morphosyntactic rules affects the management of dependence and co-reference relationships within free noun groups, as shown in Fig. 5:

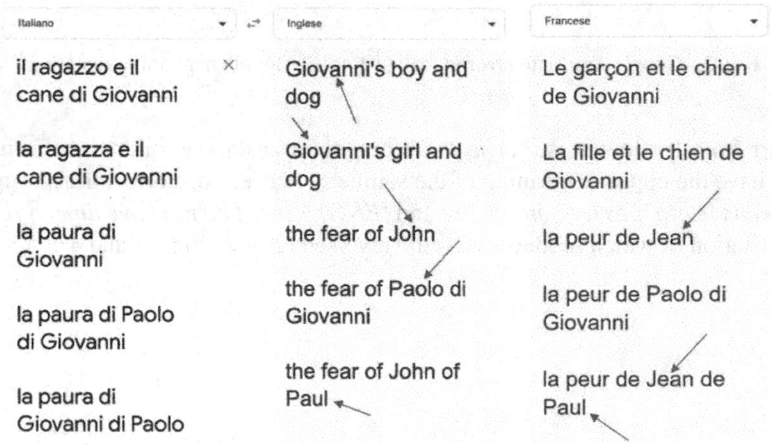

Italiano
Inglese
Francese
il ragazzo e il cane di Giovanni
Giovanni's boy and dog
Le garçon et le chien de Giovanni
la ragazza e il cane di Giovanni
Giovanni's girl and dog
La fille et le chien de Giovanni
la paura di Giovanni
the fear of John
la peur de Jean
la paura di Paolo di Giovanni
the fear of Paolo di Giovanni
la peur de Paolo di Giovanni
la paura di Giovanni di Paolo
the fear of John of Paul
la peur de Jean de Paul

Fig. 5. Google Translate errors in dependence and co-reference relationships translations.

In this case, the Italian noun groups are ambiguous, as the word *paura* (fright) may have an internal reference (Giovani frightens someone), or an external one (Giovanni is afraid of someone/something). Here, only the French translations always respect the initial Italian ambiguity. At the same time, we note the use of the Saxon genitive in English, which incorrectly "solves" the ambiguity inside the noun group, assuming that both *the boy* and *the dog* "belong" to Giovanni. Finally, we note the erratic translations of proper names, both in English and French.

A quite odd and difficult to explain error affects the translations of the following noun groups, as shown in Fig. 6. Modifying from singular to plural, the head of the noun group produces a remarkable change of meaning and translation:

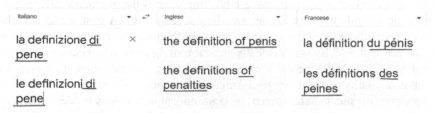

Fig. 6. Google Translate errors in singular/plural noun-groups translations.

As already stated, this various typology of errors is due to Statistical Machine Translation (SMT) not using Rule-Based Natural Language Processing but computational statistical procedures, which lacks consistent tools to handle specific lexical and morphosyntactic features, such as those in the previous figures/examples. The recent adoption of Neural Machine Translation (NMT) based on Artificial Neural Network [7] (Google Neural Machine Translation started in 2016 [8]) has slightly improved translation results, but only because in some phases, as pre-editing and post-editing, it requires massive control by humans.[2]

3 Zellig S. Harris' Transfer Grammar

Harris first described his approach to AT in the article *Transfer Grammar,* published in October 1954 by the University of Chicago Press in the *International Journal of American Linguistics*, (Vol. 20, No. 4, p. 259–270).[3] In the 1950s machine translation already was a very important area of research, also due to the Cold War and its resulting scientific espionage between the United States and the USSR, especially with regard to nuclear weapons research. Therefore, research funding for AT came primarily from the

---

[2] *Per se*, NMT limits mainly depend on the fact that Neuroscience research has not yet been able to establish how Natural Neural Networks work. There is therefore no model to replicate, and the distance between the functioning of Artificial and Natural Neural Networks is still very evident and remarkable, as for language and translation production. Therefore, it ensures that NMT works well with simple texts, formed by short sentences and free of semantic violations, as regards the rules of co-occurrence and selection restriction established by Lexicon-Grammar [9].

[3] Currently, this article is included in the reprint of *Papers in Structural and Transformational Linguistics* [10].

Pentagon, but also companies such as IBM were interested in AT.[4] On the Web today, it is very easy to find interesting information on the history of AT [11, 13, 14], so we will not dwell on it any further. The only aspect worth stressing is that the initial AT was achieved word by word.[5] In that same period, on the contrary Harris wanted to define a formal theoretical-practical framework to translate automatically from one language to another not word by word, but by the identification of the structural (therefore syntactic) similarities and differences between languages.

Harris [15] considers languages as sets of instructions that we can formalize and compare to each other. Specifically, he wants to measure the diversity between languages, as for grammatical structure, establishing what is the minimum difference (or the maximum similarity) between any two-language systems. A similar method could lead to a proceduralized system of translation, in the form of routine instructions for machine translations.[6] By systematically superimposing these sets, Harris states that it is possible to identify the specific sectors in which there is a maximum of difference or maximum similarity between two given languages. In this sense, he intends to define the differences as the number and content of grammatical instructions needed to generate the utterances of one language out of the utterances of the other.[7] However, there will be cases in which the list of changes that transform one language back to the other one may not be simply their reverse, but will form a different list.[8]

In brief, according to Harris, to have an effective machine translation, we need to:

• Formally measure the difference between languages, in terms of morphogrammatical (hence, semantic) structures;
• Define the point of minimum difference (or maximum similarity) between any type of language pair;
• Define the difference between the languages, which is the number and content of morphogrammatical instructions needed to produce the utterances of one language starting from the utterances of the other.

---

[4] IBM was the first major company to build a computer, called The Brain, specifically intended for machine translation. In 1954, IBM and Georgetown University teamed to produce the first English-to-Russian language computer translation program [12].

[5] AT was hence decontextualized, and it worked only for sentences/phrases with strictly compositional semantics. Due to the many errors produced, every translation had to be double-checked by human translators. This led AT to have higher costs than fully human ones, also in terms of time required.

[6] This method might also be relevant for the learning or teaching of foreign languages, proving possible to acquire a language by learning only the differences between the new language and the old.

[7] However, according to Harris, investigating the structural differences between languages does not suffice to define distance among their structures. *For instance, it will not be possible to state that the difference between English and German is some specified function of the English-Danish and the Danish-German differences.* [16, p. 157].

[8] To a certain extent, albeit unintentionally, here Harris seems to predict all the problems which today backtranslation creates in almost all machine-translation tools and systems.

Therefore, to structure a similar measurement procedure, it is necessary to formalize the morphosyntax of each language, using for all languages the same formalization NLP method, as for instance Maurice Gross' Lexicon-Grammar [14], which we know is the natural language formalization method to which NooJ mainly refers.

4   NooJ and Harris' Transfer Grammar

Conceptually and practically, NooJ [2, 3] grammars for machine translation are strongly similar to those theorized in Harris' Transfer Grammar, since they require the insertion of structural transfer rules that take into account each language specific morphosyntactic properties. Besides, in NooJ, machine-translation grammars are structured explicitly to perform transformations. Therefore, it is indeed possible to affirm that NooJ translations are transformations/transductions "measuring" the differences existing between two (or even more) languages. As previously stated, when translating from one language (L1) to another (L2), it may often be necessary to apply morphosyntactic and semantic rules to L2 that differ from those of L1. For instance, the Italian intransitive verb *piacere* (to like) may be translated into French with both the intransitive verb *plaire* and with the transitive verb *aimer*. In the first case, we will have translations like:

It. *Paolo piace a Maria* =: Fr. *Paul plaît à Marie* (Paul likes Mary)

In fact, from this translation, we can see that both *piacere* and *plaire* form nuclear sentences which have the syntactic structure typical of an intransitive verb with two arguments, in which N0 has the semantic role of the Patient, while N1 has the one of Agent. The set of translation instructions can be formalized as follows, for both languages:

- N0 (Noun, Human Proper Name, Patient, grammatical subject)
- V (Operator, intransitive verb)
- PREP (preposition)
- N1 (Noun, Human Proper Name, Agent, indirect object, semantic subject).

On the contrary, if we translate the Italian intransitive verb *piacere* with the French transitive verb *aimer*, as for N0 and N1 we must preview a distributional mirroring, which produces the following:

It. *Paolo piace a Maria* =: Fr. *Marie aime Paul*

Therefore, the set of translation instructions needed are as follows:

Italian Structure:

- N0 (Noun, Human Proper Name, Patient, grammatical subject)
- V (Operator, intransitive verb)
- PREP (preposition)
- N1 (Noun, Human Proper Name, Agent, indirect object, semantic subject).

French Structure:

- N0 (Noun, Human Proper Name, Agent, grammatical and semantic subject)

- V (Operator, transitive verb)
- N1 (Noun, Human Proper Name, Patient, direct object).

NooJ grammars allow two types of translation: the first is achieved by means of instructions inside grammars; the second by means of the NooJ command GRAMMAR -> TRANSFORMATION[9], which uses electronic dictionaries instructions as those shown in Fig. 7:

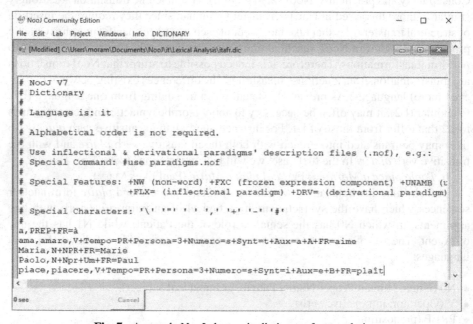

Fig. 7. A sample NooJ electronic dictionary for translation.

These instructions can use variables to transduce and translate sentences. As shown in Fig. 8, NooJ grammars[10] translations can be multilingual. In these cases, we inserted also the English translation for the Italian sentence, using *to like*, which has the same syntactic behavior as *plaire*. The concordance in red of Fig. 9 shows how outputs occur inside a given text.

NooJ grammars can also produce transformed-sentence translations, as shown in Fig. 10, in which the Italian declarative sentence is translated into French and English extrapositions. As for English it is worth stressing the use of the accusative pronoun *whom*, due to the specific syntactic profile of the verb *to like*:

---

[9] Here, due to the pre-established number of pages at our disposal, we will focus only on the first and less complex method, i.e. the one that uses instructions inside NooJ grammars.

[10] Each of the figures that follow include at the bottom a debug window used in NooJ to verify if the instructions inserted inside the specific grammars are correct. If there are no errors, the language elements being debugged will appear in green.

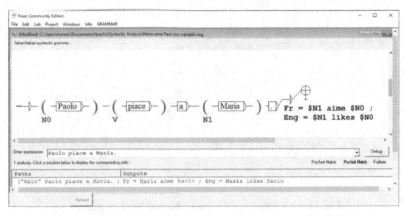

Fig. 8. A sample NooJ grammar using variables for multilingual translation. (Color figure online)

Fig. 9. Sample translation outputs inside texts.

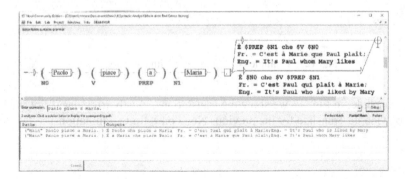

Fig. 10. A sample NooJ grammar for multilingual and transformed-sentences translations.

With specific instructions, in translation NooJ grammars it is also possible to address the choosing of an L2 specific verb. For instance, in Fig. 11, the verb variable is written in order to select from the electronic dictionary only the French translation B.

In NooJ grammars, states can only account for categories, hence producing a quite high number of translations. In Fig. 12, as for the two variables N0 and N1, we show the use of the tag *N+NPR*, which inside electronic dictionaries accounts for forenames.

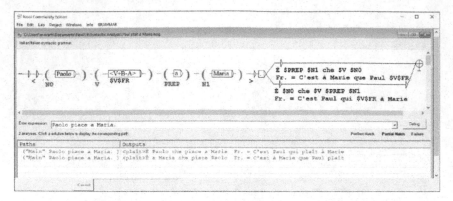

Fig. 11. A sample translation-addressed NooJ grammar.

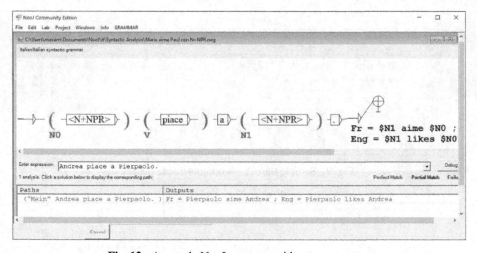

Fig. 12. A sample NooJ grammar with category states.

To conclude, in Fig. 13 we show the translations, mostly irregular if not incorrect, given by Google Translate for the previous NooJ ones for extrapolations:

Italiano		Inglese		Francese	
È Paolo che piace a Maria	×	It is Paul that Maria likes		C'est Paul que Maria aime	
È a Maria che Paolo Piace		It is Maria that Paolo likes		C'est Maria que Paolo aime	

Fig. 13. Google Translate solutions for Italian, English and French extrapolations.

5 Conclusions and Future Work

As previously shown, since they concretely put into practice Harris theoretical and formal approach, NooJ grammars can achieve efficient and effective machine translation, also demonstrating that no correct translation procedures is achievable without formalized morphosyntactic rules about contexts, co-occurrence and selection restriction. Therefore, to achieve these same results, any and all automatic translation tool must necessarily use:

- Bilingual/multilingual tagged electronic dictionaries;
- Bilingual lexical instructions (some of which are to be inserted inside NooJ electronic dictionaries, by means of specific tags);
- Syntactic instructions (also by means of NooJ variables) accounting for all the different behaviors of the predicates occurring in the sentences to be translated (as seen with the pair It. *Piacere* vs. Fr. *Aimer/plaire*, vs. Eng. *to like*).

The enhancement of such tools, i.e. the building of more grammars to broaden morphosyntactic coverage, in addition to being a goal for the future work, will make the NooJ machine-translation process even more accurate. This will especially be evident inserting inside NooJ grammars all those instructions accounting for homogeneous sets of distributional/transformational rules, that is, for all pairs of verbs having the same syntactic and translation features as *piacere/aimer/plaire/to love*. Eventually, using the NooJ grammar command GRAMMAR - > TRANSFORMATION, we will be able to produce correct translations for a very large number of declarative and/or transformed sentences, a goal that at the current state of the art it is impossible to achieve for statistical automatic translation tools, including those using artificial neural networks.

References

1. https://nap.nationalacademies.org/resource/alpac_lm/ARC000005.pdf. Accessed 25 Sept 2022
2. Silberztein, M.: The NooJ Manual (2006). http://www.nooj-association.org. Accessed 17 Sept 2022
3. Silberztein, M.: Formalizing Natural Languages: The NooJ Approach. ISTE Ltd and Wiley, London (2016)
4. https://en.wikipedia.org/wiki/Lexicon-grammar. Accessed 23 Sept 2022
5. https://www.makeuseof.com/tag/best-online-translators/. Accessed 17 Sept 2022
6. https://weglot.com/blog/machine-translation-software/. Accessed 17 Sept 2022
7. https://en.wikipedia.org/wiki/Artificial_neural_network. Accessed 17 Sept 2022
8. https://en.wikipedia.org/wiki/Google_Neural_Machine_Translation. Accessed 17 Sept 2022
9. Gross, M.: Grammaire Transformationnelle du Français: Tome 1 - Syntaxe du Verbe. Cantilène, Paris (1968)
10. https://link.springer.com/book/10.1007/978-94-017-6059-1. Accessed 17 Sept 2022
11. https://en.wikipedia.org/wiki/History_of_machine_translation. Accessed 17 Sept 2022
12. https://en.wikipedia.org/wiki/Georgetown%E2%80%93IBM_experiment. Accessed 17 Sept 2022
13. https://www.freecodecamp.org/news/a-history-of-machine-translation-from-the-cold-war-to-deep-learning-f1d335ce8b5/. Accessed 17 Sept 2022
14. https://en.wikipedia.org/wiki/ALPAC. Accessed 17 Sept 2022
15. Harris, Z.S.: Transfer grammar. Int. J. Am. Linguist. **20**(4), 259–270 (1954)

Formalization of Transformations of Complex Sentences in Quechua

Maximiliano Duran[1,2]($\boxtimes$)

[1] Université de Bourgogne Franche-Comté, CRIT, Besançon, France
duran_maximiliano@yahoo.fr
[2] LIG, UGA, Grenoble, France

Abstract. In the case of some languages, such as English, when a complex sentence consists of a main clause and a subordinate clause, these two clauses are joined together by either a subordinate 'completive' conjunction (that, so that), a circumstantial conjunction (when, before that, while) or a relative pronoun (who, that), e.g. "Because Mom said so, I talked to María". The subordination in Quechua is induced by a morpho-syntactic marker, applied to the dependent verb of the sentence (e.g. *chayta mamai niptin, Mariata rimarqani/* it's because my mother said that, I talked to María), where the suffix *-ptin* marks the causative circumstance 'because'.

The case of participial relative clauses was partially studied by W.F.H. Adelaar, In this paper, I complement his work by proposing new methods to formalize the clause-subordination based on the verbal suffixes {*-pti, -spa, -stin*}.

I have constructed specific grammars to obtain paraphrases of the sentences containing an adverbial subordinate clause. A few instances of transformations are also presented to illustrate how Quechua sentences containing a dependent clause can be translated into French.

Keywords: Quechua · Complex sentences · Clausal subordination · Adverbial subordination

1 Introduction

A complex sentence in Quechua is formed by adding one or more subordinate clauses to the main clause. e.g. *tutaya-ru-pti-n quyllur-kuna-ta rikun-chik/*As soon as it becomes dark, we may see the stars, here *quyllur-kuna-ta rikun-chik* is the independent clause.

Among the different classes of subordination in Quechua, there are internally headed relative clauses (IHRC) studied by R. Hastings [7], headless relative clauses (HRC) presented by Peter Cole et al. [3], and participial relative clauses partially studied by W.F.H. Adelaar, [1]. In this paper, I complement the last study by proposing some methods to formalize the clause-subordination strategies of the language.

The main formal distinction between subordinate clauses (adverbial case) and non-subordinated ones in Quechua is that the content term in a subordinate clause is morphologically derived by the relative suffixes {*-spa, -pti, -stin*} or the verbal repetition n...n.

© Springer Nature Switzerland AG 2022
M. González et al. (Eds.): NooJ 2022, CCIS 1758, pp. 76–88, 2022.
https://doi.org/10.1007/978-3-031-23317-3_7

Adverbial subordinate clauses have the function of adverbial modifiers, that is, they are subordinated to the main clause to which they contribute information. The verbal suffixes {*-pti, -spa, -stin*} allow to construct such adverbial dependent sentences (e.g. *tapuptii chayta willawarqa*/he told me that, because I asked him; *Kay qellqata tukuspai yanukuita qallarisaq*/I will start cooking after I finish writing; *asikustin sipasqa llamkaq richkan*/the girl goes to work laughing).

This work is aimed at formalizing the subordination induced by the {*-spa, -pti(-qti), -stin*} subordination suffixes.

These suffixes can agglutinate with the derivational verbal suffixes. To detail these combinations, following Duran [4, 5], I have constructed the Boolean matrix of the syntactic combinations of {*-pti, -spa, -stin*) with the set of the interposition suffixes IPS {*-chka, -yku, -paya...*}, see Duran [6] and Table 1.

Table 1. Grammatical combinations of IPS and subordination suffixes

	CHAKU	CHI	CHKA	YKACHA	YKACHI	YKAMU	YKAPU	YKARI	YKU	YSI	KACHA	KAMU	KAPU	KU	LLAV	MPU	MU	NAYA	PA	PAYA	0	0	RI	RPARI	RQU	RU	TAMU	SPA	STIN	PTI	YMANA
CHAKU	0	1	1	0	1	1	1	1	1	1	1	0	0	0	1	0	0	0	0	0	0	0	0	0	1	1	1	1	1	1	0
CHI	0	1	1	0	1	1	1	1	1	1	0	1	0	1	1	0	1	0	0	0	1	0	0	1	0	0	1	1	1	1	0
CHKA	0	0	0	0	1	1	1	0	0	1	0	0	0	0	0	0	0	0	0	0	0	0	0	0	0	0	0	1	0	1	0
YKACHA	1	1	1	0	0	0	0	0	0	1	0	1	0	1	1	0	1	0	1	0	1	0	1	0	1	1	0	1	1	1	0
YKACHI	0	0	1	0	0	1	1	1	0	1	0	1	1	1	1	0	1	0	0	1	1	1	1	0	1	1	1	1	1	1	0
YKAMU	0	0	1	1	1	0	1	1	0	1	1	0	0	0	0	1	0	1	0	1	0	1	0	1	1	1	1	1	1	1	0
YKAPU	0	1	1	1	1	0	0	1	0	1	1	0	0	1	1	0	1	1	0	1	1	0	1	1	1	1	1	1	1	1	0
YKARI	0	1	1	0	0	0	0	0	1	1	0	1	0	1	0	0	1	1	0	0	1	1	0	1	1	0	1	1	1	1	0
YKU	0	1	1	0	0	0	0	0	0	1	0	0	1	1	1	0	1	0	0	1	1	0	1	0	1	1	0	1	1	1	0
YSI	0	1	1	0	0	0	0	1	1	0	0	0	0	1	1	1	0	0	1	1	0	1	0	0	0	0	1	1	1	1	0
KACHA	1	1	1	0	0	1	1	0	1	0	0	1	1	1	0	1	0	1	0	1	1	1	1	0	1	1	0	1	1	1	0
KAMU	0	0	1	1	1	1	1	1	0	1	0	0	1	1	0	0	1	0	1	0	1	0	1	1	1	1	1	1	1	1	0
KAPU	0	1	1	1	1	1	1	0	1	1	0	0	0	0	0	1	0	0	0	0	0	0	1	0	1	0	0	1	1	1	0
KU	0	1	1	0	0	1	1	0	1	0	0	1	0	0	0	0	0	0	0	1	0	0	0	1	1	0	1	1	1	1	0
LLAV	0	1	1	1	0	0	0	0	1	1	0	0	0	0	0	0	1	0	0	0	1	0	0	0	0	0	1	1	1	1	0
MPU	0	0	1	0	0	0	0	0	0	0	1	1	0	0	0	0	0	0	0	0	0	0	1	0	1	0	0	1	1	1	0
MU	0	0	1	0	0	0	0	0	0	0	0	0	0	1	0	0	0	0	0	0	0	0	1	0	0	0	1	1	1	1	0
NAYA	0	1	1	0	0	0	0	0	0	1	0	0	0	1	0	1	0	0	1	1	0	0	1	1	0	0	0	1	1	1	0
PA	1	1	1	1	1	1	1	1	1	1	1	0	0	0	1	0	1	0	0	1	0	1	0	1	1	1	1	1	1	1	0
PAYA	1	1	1	1	0	0	0	1	1	1	1	1	1	1	1	0	1	1	0	0	1	1	1	0	1	1	1	1	1	1	0
PU	0	0	1	0	1	1	1	0	0	0	0	0	0	0	0	0	0	0	0	0	0	0	0	0	0	0	0	1	1	1	0
RAYA	0	1	1	1	1	1	1	0	0	1	0	0	0	1	1	0	1	0	0	1	0	0	0	0	0	0	0	1	1	1	0
RI	0	1	1	1	1	1	1	1	1	0	1	1	1	1	0	1	1	0	1	0	1	1	0	0	1	0	0	1	1	1	0
RPARI	0	1	1	0	1	1	1	0	1	1	0	1	1	1	0	1	0	0	0	0	1	0	0	0	1	0	0	1	1	1	0
RQU	0	0	1	0	0	0	0	0	0	0	0	0	1	0	0	0	0	0	0	0	0	0	0	0	0	0	1	1	1	1	0
RU	0	0	1	0	0	0	0	0	0	0	0	0	0	0	0	0	0	0	0	0	0	0	0	0	0	0	0	0	1	1	0
TAMU	0	1	1	1	1	1	1	1	0	0	0	0	0	0	0	0	0	0	0	0	0	0	0	0	0	1	0	0	1	1	0
SPA	0	0	0	0	0	0	0	0	0	0	0	0	0	0	0	0	0	0	0	0	0	0	0	0	0	0	0	0	0	0	0
STIN	0	0	0	0	0	0	0	0	0	0	0	0	0	0	0	0	0	0	0	0	0	0	0	0	0	0	0	0	0	0	0

I select those agglutinations that preserve the subordination (bearing the value 1 in the table) like {*-chkapti, -ykuspa, -payachkapti, -payastin...*}, e.g. *miku**chkapti**i chayaramun*/he arrived at the moment I was eating; *miku**ykuspan** llamkaiman rin*/he went to work after he ate.

This new set of combined suffixes will be used to build new paradigms in order to get a much larger number of paraphrases.

2 Gerund Subordination Classes

In what follows, I symbolize a verbal clause by CV. I mainly consider the complex phrases of type CV1 CV0, where V0 stands for the main verb and V1 is the dependent verb. The subordination gerund suffixes {*-pti, -spa, -stin*}, considered as nominalizers by Rios [10], agglutinated to the verb V1, give rise to dependent adverbial clauses.

Each of them induces specific relationships among the subjects and the sequence of tenses for each of the verbs composing the complex sentence. The tense of the subordinated clause depends on that of the main verb. The main verb V0 has its own derivation and inflection behavior.

To formalize the corresponding syntactic grammar, I use the NooJ language platform created by Silberztein [12]. I begin by calling GER, GER1, GER2, and GER3 the different Quechua gerund forms generated by the above-mentioned gerund suffixes. Let's describe the semantics that each of them induces in the dependent verb.

GER: the subjects S1 and S0, corresponding to verbs V1 and V0, are the same and the sequence of their grammatical tenses are simultaneous. In our formalization, we name it SPA_S (s: simultaneous) and use the suffix -*spa*.

Asispa chayta willawarqa/he told me that, laughing (both events in the past).

Asispa, kunan chayta willawan/he tells me that now, laughing (both events at present).

GER1: the subjects S1 and S0 are the same. The tense of the dependent clause appears before that of the main clause, or at has least, started before it. We name it SPA_NS (NS: non-simultaneous). It uses the suffix -*spa* combined with the transformed present tense endings and gives: {-*spai*, -*spaiki*, -*span*, -*spanchik*, -*spaiku*, -*spaikichik*, -*spanku*}.

Kay qellqata tukuspai yanukuita qallarisaq/I will start cooking after finishing writing (*qellqay*/to write, precedes *yanukuy* /to cook)

Waytakunata pallaruspan mamanman aypunqa/after gathering the flowers he will offer them to his mother (the event *pallay*/to gather in gerund, *pallaspa*, precedes *aypuy*/to offer, *aypunqa*/will offer)

GER2: the subjects S1 and S0 are not the same. The tense of the dependent clause takes place before and might have ended when the main event takes place. It uses the suffix -*pti* combined with the same set of modified present endings as for GER1, agglutinated to -*pti*: {-*ptii*, -*ptiiki*, -*ptin*, -*ptinchik*, -*ptiiku*, - *ptiikichik*, -*ptinku*}.

Kay qellqata tukuptii yanukuita qallarinki/You'll start cooking after I finish writ-ing (the subjects, which are embedded in the inflected verbs, are different: I and You).

Waytakunata pallaruptiiki mamaiiman apasaq/after you have gathered the flowers, I will take them to my mother (the subjects, which are also embedded in the inflected verbs, are different: I and You. The verb *pallay*/to gather in gerund, *pallaruptiiki*/when you had gathered, precedes apay/to take to, *apasaq*/I will take to)

GER3: the subjects S1 and S0 are the same, also the tense of the dependent clause is the same as that of the main event. It uses the suffix -*stin* for all persons.

Asikustin sipasja llamkaq richkan/the girl goes happy to work (the subjects and the tenses of both clauses are the same).

Waytakunata pallastin takichkan/she sings while she gathers the flowers.

These properties allow us to propose a classification of the complex phrases composed of two subordinate clauses of the type CV1 CV0. In these clauses, the dependent clause bears one of the cited gerunds, for the details see Duran [5]. I group them in the following classes:

a.   CV1_GER CV0_I (same subject and same tense for V1 and V0)
       Asispa willawarqa/he told me laughing
b.   CV1_GER1 CV0_I (same subject, with different tenses for V1 and V0)
       qellqata tukuspai yanukuita qallarisaq/I will start cooking once I finished writing

c. CV1_GER2 CV0_I (different subjects for V1 and V0 and same tenses)

    qellqata tukuptii yanukuita qallarinki/You will start cooking after I finish writing

d. CV1_GER3 CV0_I (same subjects and same tense)

    Asikustin sipasqa llamkaq richkan/the girl goes happy to work

e. In the case both clauses contain a verb at gerund, we will have the following classes:

    CV1_GER CV0_GER2_I (same or different subjects for V1 and V0, same tense)

f. *rimaspa richkaptin wichiikun*/he felt while he was talking

    CV1_GER CV0_PROG (same or different subjects for V1 and V0 and the dependent verb V0 is in the progressive mood) *takispa suyachkani*/I am waiting talking.

2.1 Concordance Grammars

We may now formalize the grammars, allowing us to retrieve the corresponding concordances out of a given corpus, as follows.

The grammar of Fig. 1, corresponding to the class (a) applied to our 8-Story corpus, recognizes 34 complex phrases of the form V1 + GER V0, which are shown in Fig. 2.

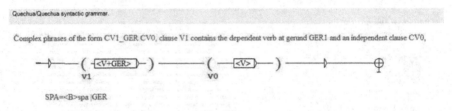

Quechua/Quechua syntactic grammar.

Complex phrases of the form CV1_GER CV0, clause V1 contains the dependent verb at gerund GER1 and an independent clause CV0,

SPA=<B>spa |GER

Fig. 1. Concordances of the form CV1_GER CV0_I found in the text.

Text	Before	Seq.	After
Ña Markaspataman	chayaspan	rimakachan	chaypi yachaqkunawan
imatapas gobernadormanta	chaskispa	rin	Kahaman lluqsina
siylu quyllurkunata	qawaspan	mana	atipaqchu imapas
Karu unaymanta	hamuspan	kay	rurananta tarispancha
Aw mamáy?	nispa	nin	mamaytañataq. Aw
didunkama traguta	tupuspan	quq	wantinumanqa. Kikinpaqñataq
qalluykipas chilakurunman -	nispa	ñaupa	timpu amigunqa
mankakunata pakaychik!	nispa	niq	wasiyuq mamakuna
pukllaypiwan kaptinqa,	nispa	nin	ñan purikuq
patiyunkunapipas, muyuriqninpi	tiyaspa	sayaspa	rimanakuchkaqta, kusisqa
qalluykipas chilakurunman -	nispa	ñaupa	timpu amigunqa
-ku mikuita	maskaspanku	mana	wañurunankupaq. Chaynam
trigo akllaypi	kaspan	mana	saqiikuptin wallpakuna

Query   34/34

Fig. 2. Concordances of the form CV1_GER CV0_I found in the text.

In Fig. 3 we show the concordance grammar of the class (b) CV1_GER1 CV0_I and the output of the corresponding query, on the same corpus.

Similarly, we have built other concordance grammars, taking into account the different gerund paradigms. For the *pti*-gerund for instance we have:

GER2 (the PTI_gerund):

```
PTI_PRM2 = ptiiki/GER2+2+s | ptiiku/GER2+1+pex|
   ptinku/GER2+3+p | ptii/GER2+1+s | ptin/GER2+3+s |
   ptinchik/GER2+1+pin| ptiikichik/GER2+2+p;
```

The corresponding formula for GER3 (the STIN gerund) is:

STIN =stin/GER3;

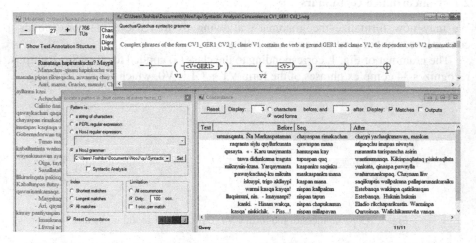

Fig. 3. Concordances found in the text "Huit contes" by the grammar CV1_GER1 CV2.

3 Basic Transformations (BT)

I present some grammars that formalize the transformations of a complex Quechua sentence, containing at least one subordinate clause. Following the ideas of Ben et al. [2], Languella [8], and Silberztein [11], I have built elementary NooJ grammars to build transformations of a canonical sentence[1].

3.1 Permutation [PERM]

[PERM] CV1 CV0 → CV0 CV1

---

[1] A canonical QU sentence is a simple sentence (no subordinates), assertive (declarative: no questioning, etc.), neutral on all levels (not negative, without highlighting procedures...), with the words in the simplest order, the most characteristic of their function. That order is: subject - object (complement (s))/attribute) – verb.

This is a basic permutation transformation [PERM], where the subordinate clause containing the verb at gerund may permute its position with the main clause, keeping an equivalent meaning is described in Fig. 4: *takispa suyasaq* → *suyasaq takispa.*

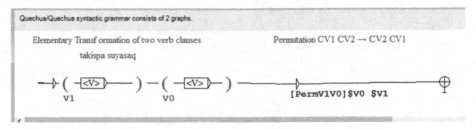

Fig. 4. Basic transformation: Permutation CV1 CV0 → CV0 CV1.

3.2 Interrogation [INT]

INT transforms an affirmative sentence into an interrogative one by agglutinating the suffix *chu,* either to the verb of the subordinated clause or to the main one as shown in Fig. 5, depending on the context of the complex sentence

$$[INT] \; CV1 \; CV0 \to CV1\_chu \; CV0?$$
$$\to CV1\_chu \; CV0?$$

The sentence

(1) *Takispa suyani*/I wait for someone while talking →
     Becomes
(2) *Takispachu suyani* ?/Do I wait for someone while talking?

3.3 Past2 [PASS_G]

[PASS_G] CV1_GER CV0 → CV1_GER CV0_Pass
     The sentence
     rimaspa rinchik/we march while talking → becomes *rimaspa riranchik*/we marched while talking
     Its corresponding grammar appears in Fig. 6.
     The elementary transformation Past2 consists in putting the verb V0 of clause 2 in the past tense, whereas the dependent clause remains unchanged (CV1_GER). The subjects remain the same.
     The next elementary transformation takes in consideration a variant of this transformation, in which the dependent clause contains the gerund GER1.

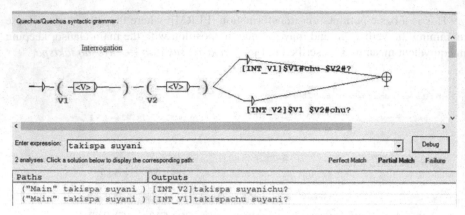

Fig. 5. The Interrogative elementary transformation.

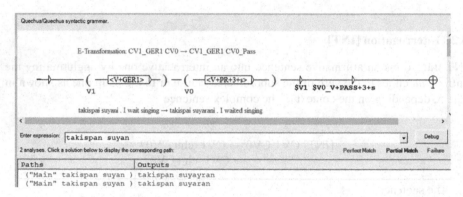

Fig. 6. Basic transformation Past2 CV1_GER CV0 > CV1_GER CV0_PASS.

3.4 Past1 [PASS_G1]

[PASS_G1] CV1_GER1 CV0 → CV1_GER1 CV0_Pass
  Here are three examples:

rimaspai rini/I march while talking → *rimaspai rirani*
rimaspaiki rinki/you march while talking → *rimaspaiki riranki*
rimaspan rin/he marches while walking → *rimaspan reran...*

  The elementary transformation [Past1] consists in putting in the past tense the verb V0 in clause 2, whereas the dependent clause is marked by the corresponding personal ending GER1[2]. The subjects remain the same.
  To get it, we apply the grammar of Fig. 7.

---

[2] Inflected GER1 endings: (*spa-i, spa-iki, spa-n, spa-nchik, spa-iku, spa-ikichik, spa-nku*).

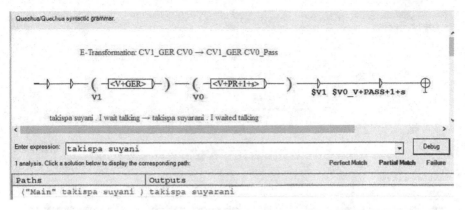

Fig. 7. Basic transformation Past1 CV1_GER CV0 → CV1_GER CV0_Pass.

3.5   Future [F]

For the Future elementary transformation, we have.

 [F] CV1 CV0 → CV1 CV0_F

Takispa suyani/I wait singing → *takispa suyasaq*/I will wait singing; I am going to wait singing.

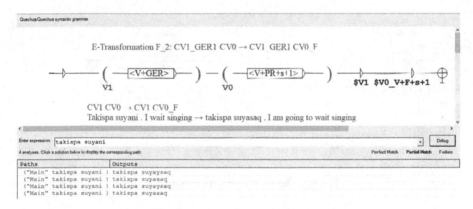

Fig. 8. Basic future transformation.

Applying the operation <Grammar> <Show debug> to the sentence *takispa suyani* in Fig. 8, we obtain 3139 transformations in the future[3]. We'll find the explanation in the morphology of the language: the combination of the IPS suffixes is very productive in QU, as these suffixes give rise to derivations of the verb V0, by combining 1, 2 or 3 suffixes, which can additionally be conjugated, for instance in the future tense shown in Fig. 9.

---

[3] Note: It contains however many duplicated outputs.

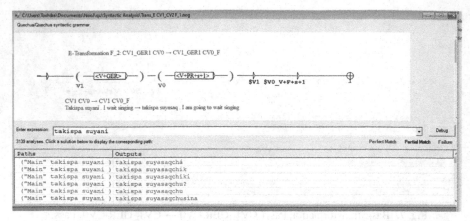

Fig. 9. Future transformation in different moods, aspects and circumstances.

3.6 Progressive [Prog_2]

```
[Prog_2] CV1 CV0 → CV1 CV0_Prog
```
    Takispa suyani/I wait singing → *takispa suyachkani*/I am waiting singing.

For the complex sentences, in which the clauses have the same subject and the same tense for V1 and V0, we propose the grammar of Fig. 10.

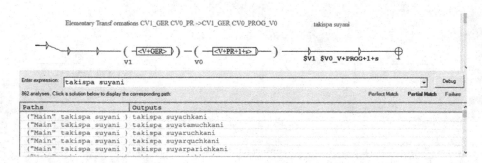

Fig. 10. The Progressive transformation.

Is it possible to analyze any binary clause subordinate complex sentence?

To answer this question, let's consider the phrase: *rimachkaspanchu pantarqan?*/Did he make a mistake while he was talking? The dependent clause *rimachkaspan-chu* can be glossed as follows:

    rima-chka-spa-n-chu

talk PROG GER 3 + s INT which actually suggests that it is the result of a sequence of three elementary transformations of the verb stem *rima_*(talk): [GER] *rima → rimaspa* (talking); then [PROG] *rimaspa-n → rimachkaspa-n* (while (he was) talking) and putting into the interrogative:

[INT] *rimachkaspa → rimachkaspachu* (while talking?).

Inspired by this analysis, and because of the agglutinative property of the QU, we propose an affirmative answer to the question, i. e. *any verbal dependent Quechua sentence can be obtained by the composition of elementary transformations.*

4   Paraphrasing Subordinate Clauses

To construct a paraphrasing NooJ grammar, I take into account the morpho-syntactic constraints for the main verb V0 as well as for the dependent verb V1. We find the following cases.

a.   **the dependent clause remains unchanged in gerund mood:**

takispa taytaikita suyanki/you wait your father singing;

takispa remains unchanged during the transformations and *suyanki* will derive into different moods or circumstances like *suyachkanki*/you are waiting, *suyachakun-ki*/ you are waiting quietly, …

V1+GER N+POS+s+2+ACC V0+PR+s+2→ V1+GER TR(N)+TR(V0) (TR: transformation)

The noun N and the main verb V0 may inflect using their respective inflectional suffixes (nominal and verbal). Taking into account the syntactic valid sequences, we obtain those which represent a paraphrase of the initial phrase, as can be seen in the following examples.

In (1), V0 is derived by the circumstantial suffix *-ri*, (2) shows the derivation by the progressive suffix *-chka*, (3) by the modal suffix *-chaku* and so on.

(1)   *takispa taytakita suyarinki*/you wait (for a little bit) for your father singing
(2)   *takispa taytachaikita suyachkanki*/you are waiting while singing for your beloved father
(3)   *takispa taytaikita suyachakunki*/you wait (having a little fun) your father singing

Or other derivations like *suyaykachanki* (ACAV), *suyapayanki* (FREQ)…

Figure 11. Shows the corresponding grammar.

b.   **the dependent clause is inflected and the main clause remains unchanged:**

V1+GER N+POS+s+2+ACC V0+PR+s+2 → V1+GER TR(N) + TR(V0) (TR: transformation)

takirispa taytaikita suyanki/you wait for your father while singing (smoothly)

takikuspa taytaikita suyanki/you are waiting for your father singing (for yourself)

takiykachaspa taytaikita suyanki/you wait for your while singing father (different songs)

c.   **both relative clauses may be derived additionally by the post-position suffixes ips.**

V1+GER N+POS+s+2+ACC V0+PR+s+2 → V1+GER TR(N)+TR(V0) (TR: transformation)

takirispa taytaikita suyachkanki/you are waiting for your while father (smoothly).—V1 is derived by the suffix *-ri* and V0 by the suffix *-chka*.

takirispayá taytaikita suyachkankipuni/you are stubbornly waiting for your father while singing really smoothly).

takiykachaspa taytaikita suyachkankiraq/you are still waiting for your father while singing different songs).

In order to automate the generation of paraphrases, we use the inflection paradigms corresponding to the gerund suffixes applied to V1 and the derivation grammars applied to the main verb V0 using IPS_drv suffixes and the mixed paradigms, like the following.
V_MIX1= (:SIP1_TI_V) (:SPP1_V) | (:SIP1_TI_C)(:SPP1_C) | (:SIP1_TIM_V) (:SPP1_V) | (:SIP1_TIM_C)(:SPP1_C); This mixed paradigm contains 1 SIP suffix (ending in a vowel or a consonant) and 1 SPP suffix (combined to endings finishing in a vowel or a consonant).

Considering the formulations found in the work of Duran [6], I propose NooJ grammars based on the syntactically compatible mixed paradigms, like those presented in Fig. 11. This grammar generates a large amount of paraphrases (3940 lines) for a complex sentence such as *takispa taytarayku suyanki paytachu takispa suyanki?*

takispachu payta suyanki?

takispa taytachata suyanki...

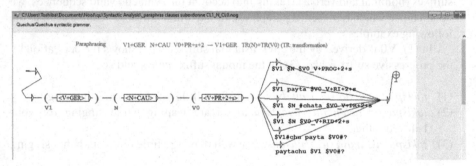

Fig. 11. Paraphraser performing inflections on N and derivations on V0

5 Transformation and Machine Translation

A certain kind of transformation grammars that we have presented, may be utilized to obtain a set of bilingual machine translation NooJ grammars like in Fig. 12. These help to build a database of aligned paraphrases with their corresponding French and Spanish translations.

I have used the resulting paraphrase grammar to create aligned pairs of Quechua-French and Quechua-Spanish lexicon, a useful resource for our planned MT applications.

I present a simple grammar that generates translated sentences of dependent clauses of the form CV1 + GER CV0 + F into French:

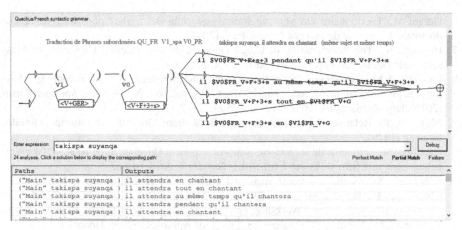

Fig. 12. Translation of -spa dependent clauses from QU into FR.

6 Conclusion

I have proposed several methods to formalize the automatic transformations of some particular classes of complex sentences, the clause-subordinate sentences.

I have presented the subordination suffixes {-*pti, -spa, -stin*}, formalized the construction of adverbial dependent clauses constructing paradigms of their grammatical combinations with the Interposed Suffixes (IPS) and Postposed Suffixes (PPS), and obtained an important number of transformed sentences out of a given one. Some of these transformations may serve to produce paraphrases.

I have also shown a set of specific transformation grammars allowing to automatically translate into French, complex Quechua sentences containing subordinate clauses.

I plan to extend these grammars to study other syntactic structures and enhance the current set of multilingual translation grammars to obtain a large database of aligned translated QU_FR and QU_SP complex sentences to be used in MT.

References

1. Adelaar, W.: Participial clauses in Tarma Quechua. Subordination in native South American languages. Edited by: Van Gijn, Rik; Haude, Katharina; Muysken, Pieter. University of Zurich Main Library, Zurich (2010)
2. Ben, A., Fehri, H., Ben, H.: Translating Arabic relative clauses into English using the Nooj platform. In: Monti, J., Silberztein, M., Monteleone, M., di Buono, M.P. (eds.) Formalizing Natural Languages with Nooj 2014, pp. 166–174. Cambridge (2015)
3. Cole, P., et al.: Headless relative clauses in Quechua. Int. J. Am. Linguist. **48**(2), 113–124 (1982)
4. Duran, M.: Formalizing Quechua verbs Inflexion. In: Proceedings of the NooJ 2013 International Conference, Saarbrücken (2013)
5. Duran, M.: The annotation of compound suffixation structures of Quechua verbs. In: Okrut, T., Hetsevich, Y., Silberztein, M., Stanislavenka, H. (eds.) NooJ 2015. Communications in Computer and Information Science, vol. 607, pp. 29–40. Springer, Cham (2016). https://doi.org/10.1007/978-3-319-42471-2_3

6. Duran, M.: Dictionnaire électronique français-quechua des verbes pour le TAL. Thèse doctorale. Université de Franche-Comté, Paris (2017)
7. Hastings, R.: The interpretation of Cuzco Quechua relative clauses. University of Massachusetts Occasional Papers in Linguistics, vol. 27 (2001)
8. Langella, A.M.: Paraphrases for the Italian communication predicates. In: Barone, L., Monteleone, M., Silberztein, M. (eds.) NooJ 2016. CCIS, vol. 667, pp. 196–207. Springer, Cham (2016). https://doi.org/10.1007/978-3-319-55002-2_17
9. Muysken, P.: Relative Clause Formation in Ecuadorian Quechua, manuscript, Otavalo, Ecuador (1976)
10. Rios, Annette. Esquema de anotaciones sintácticas para el Quechua Sureño (2014). www.cl.uzh.ch/dam/jcr:ffffffff-d043-9c87-ffff-ffffb112cc62/TR_2014_01.pdf
11. Silberztein, M.: Automatic transformational analysis and generation. ln: Gavriilidou, Z., Chatzipapa, E., Papadopoulou, L., Silberztein. M. (eds.) Proceedings of the NooJ 2010 International Conference and Workshop, pp. 221–231. University of Thrace, Komotini (2011)
12. Silberztein, M.: Language Formalization: The NooJ Approach. Wiley, Hoboken (2016)
13. Weber, D.: Relativization and Nominalized Clauses in Huallaga Quechua. University of California Publications in Linguistics, vol. 103. University of California Press, Berkeley (1983)

Automatic Extraction of Verbal Phrasemes in the Electrical Energy Field with NooJ

Tong Yang[✉]

North China Electric Power University, Beijing, China
tongyang@ncepu.edu.cn

Abstract. The abundant presence of prefabricated sequences attracts the attention of linguists. Phraseological units are often problematic for foreign learners both receptively and productively. In addition, they think that the number of phraseological units is greater in FOS (French for specific purposes) than in general French. In the field of electrical energy, the abundant presence of phrasemes [verb + nominal group or not + preposition + nominal group] pose many problems for non-native engineer-learners. The modeling is done based on the observation of our corpus and dictionaries in electricity. By using three grammars (rational grammar, algebraic grammar and contextual grammar.), NOOJ allows us to extract 1389 phrase sequences for teaching. Also, a disambiguation can be set up to reject useless phrasemes by using the + EXCLUDE operator. At the end, for the selection of phrases for teaching, three criteria (frequency, fixation and pragmatic criterion) seem relevant to us for the identification or classification of phrases from the professional field for foreign learners.

Keywords: NooJ · Automatic extraction · FOS · Phrasemes · Modeling · Disambiguation · Electrical energy field

1 Introduction

Our study fits the teaching method FOS, a methodology from the FLE (French as a foreign language). As a major energy country, France and China have long-term cooperation in energy (for example, Daya Bay Nuclear Power Plant, Ling'ao Nuclear Power Plant and Taishan Nuclear Power Plant). The "carbon peak, carbon neutral" strategic goal has made great contributions. In order to cultivate successor talents for Sino-French cooperation, since 2010, China Guangdong Nuclear, Sun Yat-sen University, the French Atomic Energy Commission, EDF (French Electricity), Areva Group, and the University of Grenoble have jointly launched full-time university education. It is the first step towards cooperation. Non-native engineer-learners will find it difficult to acquire knowledge, not only because of the novelty represented by the French business environment, but also because of their language level, which is sometimes inadequate to the situation. These

---

This article is supported by the Fundamental Research Funds for the Central Universities (JB2021059).

© Springer Nature Switzerland AG 2022
M. González et al. (Eds.): NooJ 2022, CCIS 1758, pp. 89–99, 2022.
https://doi.org/10.1007/978-3-031-23317-3_8

difficulties of integration in the French company mainly concern allophone learners of level A2 of the CEFR (Common European Framework of Reference for Languages), because the latter is the minimum level for foreigners to be able to obtain a visa to study in France. Above all, it should be remembered that these French-speaking engineers find themselves in a professional environment where – as in many professions – the language is important to master in order to do the job well: the learner must quickly understand the professional instructions and must also briefly understand with his co-workers. As a result, due to the expansion of professional and student mobility [6], French-language training courses oriented towards the electrical energy domain are increasingly in demand.

2   Phraseology Criteria

Linguists and didacticians have observed the need for the use of phraseology among foreign learners. The first observation established (among others [7, 17]) consists of the abundant presence of phraseological units. Regarding this idea of recurrence, [16] remarks that native speakers commonly use *prêt à parler*, but they do not realize it. Take the example of [7]: native speakers forget the usual meaning of the verb to *poser* in the collocation to *poser une question*, while non-native speakers tend to apply the verb to ask in a concrete way: to put the question on the table. Despite the considerable interest raised by research in the field of phraseology for teaching, phraseology is a fuzzy field of language: Phraseology is a fuzzy part of language [2]. The difficulty of the description of the definition is due to two main reasons: the first attributes this vagueness of definition to the obscuring of fuzzy denominations, as [20] says, the linguistic fact of rigidity has been obscured by fuzzy and very heterogeneous, so that we are in the presence of very often incompatible definitional strata. The second is due to the impossibility of describing the phrase from a single point of view. As [22] observes, the complexity of the phenomenon of locution and the impossibility of describing it from a single point of view.

For years, phraseologists have sought to define phraseology using the following two main approaches [4, 11, 19, 26]: the distributional (statistical) approach and the functional (or traditional). The first is based on the following two principles: the idiom principle and the open choice principle [12]. The first principle emphasizes the context for the choice of a word, according to Sinclair, the choice of one word affects the choice of others in its vicinity [37], but the second principle emphasizes free choice for the combination of words. Frequency is the main criterion in statistical phraseology [36, 37]. While the functional approach refers to other criteria, such as syntactic criteria, semantic criteria and pragmatic criteria [11]. The selection of criteria is made according to the intended didactic objective: the length of the phraseological units is retained in the typology of [14]; fixation in the typologies of [20, 23, 35]; the pragmatic criterion in the typology of [28]; etymology in the typology of [24]. We are going to detail the following criteria which seem to us to be priorities for our project in FOS with foreign learners: frequency, fixation and pragmatic criterion.

2.1 Frequency

Phraseme frequency is an indicator for identifying phraseological units, because phrasemes often have a significant frequency. [41] confirms it in this sense: statistics do not define collocations but are a means of evaluating their significance threshold. Thus, they can help in their extraction. This identification criterion has been adopted in the works of phraseologists, such as [2, 15, 18, 23, 27, 31]. Knowing that a low frequency can hide a high relevance for the field. For example, in his quest for collocations from a corpus of texts in the field of information science and technology, [10] identifies the following units as having a very low frequency: first and foremost, diskette drive, ticket booth, etc.; [15], in turn, also encounters this weakness of studies based exclusively on statistical analyzes of the corpus. In order to overcome the neglect problem, lexicologists usually rehabilitate low frequency expressions in their study lists by choosing other necessary criteria. For our study, we also choose fixation et pragmatic criterion as classification criteria.

2.2 Fixation

Fixation is one of the properties most often mentioned to describe phrasemes in relation to other lexical elements of the language [34]. It is made up of a set of syntactic and semantic characteristics affecting a polylexical unit [33], for example *idée reçue* is a fixed group, but *idée stupide* is not. [7] finds that Fixation poses problems for foreign learners. According to [25], fixation is an extremely complex, polyfactorial phenomenon, which explains why it escapes any attempt to provide a simple and unequivocal definition. Indeed, there is no dichotomy between not being fixed and being fixed. As confirmed by [33], the fixation can only be partial, which supposes degrees in the process. In addition to the fixation by itself, it is also its degree that poses a problem for foreign learners: indeed, the latter are not able to judge whether the phrase *initier à la conception de circuits* is more or less fixed than the phrase *fournir de l'information dans le cas d'un flux d'entrée*.

2.3 Pragmatic Criterion

The third criterion which seems interesting to us in the professional environment is the pragmatic criterion, because certain free expressions can provide pragmatic value. [5] take the word *porte* as an example: in reality, one can only *ouvrir* or *fermer* a door. In fact, the pragmatic criterion is widely taken into account in the classification of phraseology in French (*pragmatèmes* by [28]; linked statements by [13]; road formulas by [16] and in that in English (linguistic routines by [8]; social discursive units by [9]; situational units by [29, 30]; lexical sentences by [32]; socio-interactional units by [1] and conventional expressions of [3]. To identify pragmatic expressions, apart from the experiences accumulated in the electrical energy field, the pragmatic criterion can manifest itself by the high frequency of use [5, 21].

These three criteria seem relevant to us for the identification or classification of phrases from the professional field for foreign learners. The electrical energy domain includes energy sources and electrical projects. Our corpus is made up of end-of-study research projects in electricity. The abundant presence of phrasemes [verb + nominal group or not + preposition + nominal group] (for example, *contrôler les installations sur l'emprise, faire des applications sur l'écoulement de puissance, fournir de l'information dans le cas d'un flux d'entrée*) exists in the field of electrical energy and these phrases pose many problems for non-native engineer-learners. Our problem is to extract this type of phrasemes for teaching. In fact, modeling is often presented as an effective method for easily accessing text. [40] also underlines that the use of a finer linguistic model (…) makes it possible both to systematize syntactic and semantic associations and to propose a less ad hoc computer processing, by class of phenomena.

3 Language Description Software: NOOJ'S Approach

As a language formalization software, NooJ can theoretically describe all the natural languages of the world through four grammars: unrestricted grammar, contextual grammar, algebraic grammar, rational grammar [38, 39]. The four types of generative grammars have a hierarchical relationship: the set of rational grammars is included in the set of algebraic grammars, itself included in the set of contextual grammars, itself encompassed in the set of non-restricted. We will then see the use of this tool by type of grammar: we will first present each type of grammar, for which we will see what NooJ can do or examples of the application. Being able to describe all-natural languages, the unrestricted grammar is more powerful than the first three. Our presentation has therefore focused on the first three grammars: rational grammar, algebraic grammar and contextual grammar.

3.1 Rational Grammar

This type of grammar is composed of two members: the left member consists of an auxiliary symbol and the right member can be either a terminal symbol (example, N → table), or a single terminal symbol followed by a single auxiliary symbol, or the empty word. Rational languages can also be described by finite state graphs (The finite state machine is the machine that can then analyze texts automatically). Indeed, several software can build a finite state machine in the TAL (automatic language processing), but unfortunately, the proposed grammars are not always displayed "graphically". NooJ offers real graphs to be structurally readable as shown in Fig. 1 below.

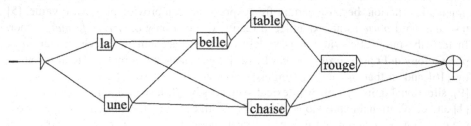

Fig. 1. Finite state graph.

A finite state graph consists of a set of nodes connected and oriented between them and the first and the last node are called the initial node and the terminal node respectively.

Each node represents an atomic linguistic unit (ALU) or stopword. Figure 1 above can output all eight sequences, such as: {la belle table; la belle table rouge; la chaise; la chaise rouge; une belle table; une belle table rouge; une chaise; une chaise rouge} It rejects incorrect sequences like: {la belle chaise; la belle chaise rouge; une table belle; …}. After seeing the applications in NooJ at the level of rational grammar, we will see a more powerful grammar: algebraic grammar.

3.2 Algebraic Grammar

The left member of this type of grammar contains a single auxiliary symbol and the right member is a combination of terminal symbols and auxiliary symbols. The advantage of this type of grammar is to involve the recursion of rules, that is to say that the rules are defined from themselves. For example, in rule S below:

$$S = a : Sb;$$

In the right member, we find the rule "S" (the auxiliary symbols introduced by the character ":" in NooJ), that is to say that it makes self-referential rules. The results produced may be, depending on the frequency of application of rule S:

$$S \rightarrow ab, aabb, aaabbb, aaaabbbb, \ldots$$

We can't have this language $a^n b^n$ in the rational rule, but algebraic grammar can cause this recursion. For the application of rule recursion, NooJ offers colored nodes (prefixed by the ":" character) which allow you to nest another grammar (or another graph). As Silberztein explains, the colored nodes, which correspond to the auxiliary nodes of the rewrite rules, are references to nested graphs [38, 39]. For example, in the sentence grammar in Fig. 2 below:

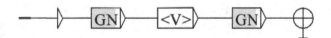

Fig. 2. Sentence grammar graph.

The GN nodes are in color, i.e. the GN is explained by a nested graph (cf. Fig. 3 below).

In this nested graph there is also a GN which will refer to a nested graph (itself), so this grammar can be recursive. In terms of algebraic grammar in NooJ, grammar rules can be recursive. And what do contextual grammar do?

3.3 Contextual Grammar

A context can be added to both members of this grammar. Grammars can be written by an auxiliary or terminal symbol in any member of this grammar, for example:

PLURAL SENTENCE $\rightarrow$ PLURAL GN see GN

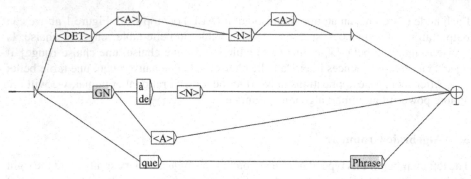

Fig. 3. Nominal group grammar.

Contextual grammars are generative grammars limited by linearly bounded automata which present the conditions of application of the rules by taking into account the context. It is impossible to present what contextual grammars can do, because the contexts are so varied that we cannot present them on a case-by-case basis. But, in order to contextualize each grammar, the use of variables seems unavoidable. Therefore, in this part, we have every interest in presenting three variables in NooJ.

In Fig. 4 below, we depict the match (in gender and number) of the Noun + Adjective structure with algebraic grammars. In the first way, a singular masculine noun (N+m+s) recognizes a singular masculine adjective (A+m+s) and it could have an insertion element (WF), for example an adverb. In order to describe this single structure of two elements, we are obliged to construct at least four paths (cf. Algebraic grammars above).

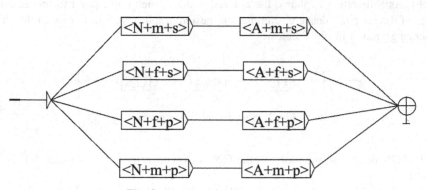

Fig. 4. Match of the N+A structure.

Imagine that we will have many more paths for a more complex structure. This is one of the reasons why we resort to other solutions. Indeed, it only takes one path in Fig. 5 below to describe the N + A structure using variables in NooJ.

In this grammar, two types of variables are used: $THIS variable and local variable. The first type in NooJ always has the current ALU as its value, the current ALU in Fig. 5 below denotes adjectives. The value of the second type can be obtained in the same graph or a nested graph. Figure 5 assigns the variable $N the names. Two constraints

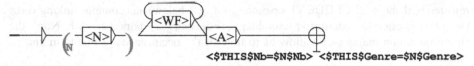

Fig. 5. Match of the N+A structure with variables.

<$THIS$Nb = NNb> and <$THIS$Genre = NGenre> are used to check that
the adjectives agree in gender and number with the nouns: the first constraint checks that
the 'adjective ($THIS) and noun ($N) have the same value for the "Nb" property and
the second constraint verifies that they have the same value for the "Gender" property.

We realize that NooJ is more flexible than other developed programs: at the level of
rational grammar, we can describe a word, a grammatical category, a lexical disjunc-
tion and a lexical concatenation and we can also do lexical disambiguation with the +
EXCLUDE operator; at the level of algebraic grammar, the rules of the grammar can
be realized recursively; at the level of contextual grammar, the three types of variables
($THIS, local variable and global variable) can facilitate a certain description.

4 Modeling and Implementation in NooJ

After observing our corpus and dictionaries in electricity (for example, engineering et
technique francais-chinois), the phrasemes [Verb + Nominal Group or not + Preposition
+ Nominal Group] can be modeled in Fig. 4 below,

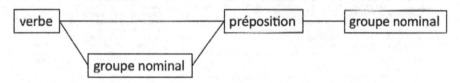

Fig. 6. Modeling of the phrasemes.

Once the modeling is done, we can continue the implementation. In NooJ, V stands
for the verb and PREP stands for the preposition. As explained in Sect. 3.2 Algebraic
Grammar, the GN is explained by a nested graph (cf. Fig. 3 above). So we can establish
this grammar in Fig. 5 below,

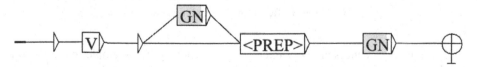

Fig. 7. Implementation of the phrasemes.

At the end, in order not to extract useless sequences, for example, *soit dans les
cours, sont sur le parcours de la route de ceinture*. Unnecessary sequences can be

rejected with the + EXCLUDE VL operator (cf. Fig. 6 below) that contains linking verbs (<être>, <rester>, <paraitre>, <sembler>, <devenir>, <demeurer>). In NooJ, the single quotation marks (<>) allow us to find all the occurrences of this term and its variants.

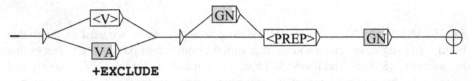

Fig. 8. Disambiguation of the phrasemes.

Once the implementation is in NooJ, we can run our extraction.

5 Results

Thanks to NooJ, we managed to extract 1389 phrase sequences shown in Fig. 9.

Concordance for Text projet en électricité.jnot		

Reset   Display: 5   ○ characters   before, and   5   after. Display: ☑ Matches   ☐ Outputs
                              ● word forms

Before	Seq.	After
variantes de ce projet...	insistons sur les points communs	et différences d'approche entre
premier projet présen...	tirons les conclusions de notre expérience	des projets dans le cadre
expérience des projet...	cadre de la formation	en électricité des étudiants ingénieurs
spécialisation en élec...	A ce stade de leurs études	, les étudiants ont déjà une
notions élémentaires ...	soumis à des courants	et tensions sinusoïdaux. Ils ont
sinusoïdaux. Ils ont d...	abordé les équations de Maxwell dans le vide	. Au cours du semestre, ces
ces notions théorique...	soit dans les cours	où des dispositifs particuliers seront
un circuit électroniqu...	effectuer la mesure d'une grandeur physique	. 3 Le projet, qui représente un
compte le semestre, l...	représente un poids important dans ce début de...	en électricité et en électromécanique
spécifique du projet ...	faire le lien entre la théorie	des circuits et l'électromagnétisme
'aider l'étudiant à se	familiariser avec les opérations simples de trait...	(amplification, sommation, filtrage) ; • d
(amplification, somm...	initier à la conception de circuits électriques	en développant ses capacités d
des outils de simulati...	vue de la validation d'un schéma	(construction a priori d'une
(construction a priori ...	idée de la réponse d'un circuit	, comparaison avec le résultat de
groupes sont ainsi fo...	disposent d'une dizaine de semaines	en moyenne pour mener à
plage de deux heures...	prévue chaque semaine par l'équipe	pour répondre aux questions des
aux questions des étu...	suivre l'évolution de leurs travaux	. Certains étudiants exploitent beaucoup
l'ensemble des group...	faire le point sur leur avancement	, à produire des résultats et
l'équipe enseignante ...	encourager dans la direction choisie	ou de les faire réfléchir
'est enfin une opportu...	stimuler les groupes à la traîne	. Ce n'est qu'après
présentent les résulta...	pratiques de leur projet	, qui doit être fonctionnel. Ils
à l'équipe enseignant...	comparent leur solution finale avec leur solution	d'avant-projet et tirent
pas été suffisamment...	assimilés par les groupes	concernés. Ceux-ci sont alors
rapport d'étude comp...	permettra à l'équipe enseignante	de rendre un avis final

Query   1389/1389

Fig. 9. Result of our extraction.

The extract sequences are very interesting for teaching, for example, *contrôler les installations sur l'emprise, faire des applications sur l'écoulement de puissance, perturber les autres applications par ses pointeurs, comparaison leur solution finale avec leurs solutions d'avant-projet, disposés à différents points du hall machines, situerai ce projet dans son contexte économique, servira à la rémunération.* Despite the lexical disambiguation carried out in our extraction, the phrasemes [Verb + Nominal Group or not + Preposition + Nominal Group] extracted will not all be selected for our study, for example, *a ce stade de leurs études*. According to the statistical approach, frequency is the main criterion for the identification of phrasemes. Concerning our study in FOS, the verification of the low frequency phrasemes allows us not to ignore the relevant phrasemes.

6 Conclusion

The teaching of phrases is necessary for foreign learners. The corpus is a database constituted according to the choice of text genres and can help to specify and memorize the meaning of phrases. Such a database also makes it possible to select phrases to be taught. Based on algebraic grammar, rational grammar and contextual grammar, NooJ, as a corpus processing system, can perfectly meet our modeling expectations. After implementing and launching our grammar in NooJ, we can successfully extract the phrases [Verb + Nominal Group or not + Preposition + Nominal Group]. Inspired by previous projects [42, 43], we have implemented two steps to identify and select relevant phrasemes for teaching: frequency of phrasemes in our corpus, search for relevant phrasemes of low frequency. Following this lexical extraction, we can proceed to teaching.

References

1. Aijmer, K.: Conversational Routines in English: Convention and Creativity. Longman, New York (1996)
2. Altenberg, B.: On the phraseology of spoken English: the evidence of recurrent wordcombinations. In: Cowie, P.A. (ed.) Phraseology: Theory, Analysis, and Applications, pp. 101–122. Oxford University Press, Oxford (1998)
3. Bardovi-Harlig, K.: Conventional expressions as a pragmalinguistic resource: recognition and production of conventional expressions in L2 pragmatics. Lang. Learn. **59**, 755–795 (2009)
4. Bolly, C.: Phraséologie et Collocations. Peter Lang, Berne (2011)
5. Bossé-Andrieu, J., Mareschal, G.: Trois aspects de la combinatoire collocationnelle. TTR: Trad. Terminol. Rédaction **11**(1), 157–171 (1998)
6. Carras, C., Tolas, J., Kohler, P., Sjilagyi, E.: Le Français Sur Objectifs Spécifiques et la Classe de Langue. CLE International, Paris (2007)
7. Cavalla, C.: La phraséologie en classe de FLE. Les Langues Modernes 1, en–ligne (2009)
8. Coulmas, F.: On the sociolinguistic relevance of routine formulae. J. Pragmat. **3**, 239–266 (1979)
9. Cowie, A.P.: Stable and creative aspects of vocabulary use. In: Carter, R., McCarthy, M. (eds.) Vocabulary and Language Teaching, pp. 126–139. Longman, London (1988)
10. Curado, F.A.: Lexical behaviour in academic and technical corpora: implications for ESP development. Lang. Learn. Technol. **5**(106), 129 (2001)
11. Edmonds, A.: Une approche psycholinguistique des phénomènes phraséologiques : le cas des expressions conventionnelles. Langages **189**, 121–138 (2013)
12. Erman, B., Warren, B.: The idiom principle and the open choice principle. Text **20**(1), 29–62 (2000)
13. Fónagy, I.: Figement et changement sémantique. In: Martins-Baltar, M. (eds.) La Locution Entre Langue et Usages, pp. 131–164. ENS Éditions, Fontenay/Saint-Cloud (1997)

14. Gläser R., The grading of idiomaticity as a presupposition for a taxonomy of idioms. In: Hüllen W., Schulze R. (eds.) Understanding the Lexicon, pp. 264–279. Max Niemeyer, Tübingen (1988)
15. Gledhill, C.: Collocations in Science Writing. Gunter Narr Verlag Tübingen, Tübingen (2000)
16. Rey, I.G.: La didactique du français idiomatique. E.M.E. Fernelmont, Belgique (2007)
17. Rey, I.G.: La phraséodidactique en action: les expressions figées comme objet d'enseignement. La Culture de l'autre: l'enseignement des langues à l'Université – Actes (2010)
18. Granger, S.: Prefabricated patterns in advanced EFL writing: collocations and formulae. In: Cowie A. P. (eds.) Phraseology: Theory, Analysis, and Applications, Oxford University Press, pp. 145–160 (1998)
19. Granger, S., Paquot, M.: Disentangling the phraseological web. In: Granger, S., Meunier, F. (eds.) Phraseology: An Interdisciplinary Perspective, pp. 27–49. John Benjamins, Amsterdam/Philadelphia (2008)
20. Gross, G.: Les Expressions Figées en Français: Noms Composés et Autres Locutions. Ophrys, Paris/Gap (1996)
21. Grossmann, F.: Didactique du lexique: état des lieux et nouvelles orientations. Pratiques **149–150**, 163–183 (2011)
22. Heinz, M.: Les Locutions Figurées Dans le Petit Robert: Description Critique de Leur Traitement et Propositions de Normalisation. Max Niemeyer, Tübingen (1993)
23. Howarth, P.: Phraseology in English Academic Writing: Some Implications for Language Learning and Dictionary Making. Niemeyer, Tübingen (1996)
24. Jernej, J.: O klasifikaciji frazema. Fililogija. Hrvatska akademija znanosti i umjetnosti **20–21**, 191–197 (1992)
25. Lamiroy, B., Klein, J.R.: Le problème central du figement est le semi-figement. Linx **53**, 135–154 (2005)
26. Legallois, D., Tutin, A.: Présentation : Vers une extension du domaine de la phraséologie. Langages **189**, 3–25 (2013)
27. Lewis, M.: There is nothing as practical as a good theory. In: Michael, L. (ed.) Teaching collocation: Further developments in the lexical approach, Language Teaching, pp. 10–27. Publications, Hove (2000)
28. Melčuk, I.: La phraséologie et son rôle dans l'enseignement-apprentissage d'une langue étrangère. Études linguistique appliquée **92**, 82–113 (1993)
29. Moon, R.: Textual aspects of fixed expressions in learners dictionaries. In: Arnaud, P., Béjoint, H. (eds.) Vocabulary and Applied Linguistics, pp. 13–27. Macmillan Academic and Professional, Ltd (1992) https://doi.org/10.1007/978-1-349-12396-4_2
30. Moon, R.: There is reason in the roasting of eggs: a consideration of fixed expressions in native-speaker dictionaries. In: Tommola, H., Varantola, K., Salmi-Tolonen, T., Schopp, J. (eds.) Euralex 92 Proceedings, Series Translatologica A, vol. II, pp. 493–502. University of Tampere, Tampere (1992)
31. Moon, R.: Frequencies and forms of phrasal lexemes in English. In: Cowie, A.P. (ed.) Phraseology: Theory, Analysis, and Applications, pp. 79–100. Oxford University Press, Oxford (1998)
32. Nattinger, J., DeCarrico, J.: Lexical Phrases and Language Teaching. Oxford University Press, Oxford (1992)
33. Neveu, F.: Dictionnaire des Sciences du Langage. Armand Colin, Paris (2004)
34. Pecman, M.: Phraséologie Contrastive Anglais-Français: Analyse et Traitement en vue de l'aide à la Rédaction Scientifique. Thèse de doctorat, Université de Nice Sophia Antipolis (2004)
35. Polguère, A.: Lexicologie et sémantique lexicale. Notions Fondamentales. 3rd edn. Les presses de l'Université de Montréal (2016)

36. Römer, U.: Corpus research and practice: what help do teachers need and what can we offer?. In: Aijmer, K. (eds.) Corpora and Language Teaching, pp. 83–98. John Benjamins, Amsterdam/Philadelphia (2009)
37. Sinclair, J.M.: Corpus Concordance Collocation. Oxford University Press, Oxford (1991)
38. Silberztein, M.: La formalisation des langues : l'approche de NooJ. International Society for Technology in Education (2015)
39. Silberztein, M.: Formalizing Natural Languages: The NooJ Approach. Wiley, Hoboken (2016)
40. Tutin, A.: Pour une modélisation dynamique des collocations dans les textes. Actes d'Euralex, Lorient, 207–221 (2004)
41. Williams, G.C.: Les réseaux collocationnels dans la construction et l'exploitation d'un corpus dans le cadre d'une communauté de discours scientifique. Thèse de doctorat, Université de Nantes (1999)
42. Yang, T.: Automatic extraction of the phraseology through NooJ. In: Mbarki, S., Mourchid, M., Silberztein, M. (eds.) NooJ 2017. CCIS, vol. 811, pp. 168–178. Springer, Cham (2018). https://doi.org/10.1007/978-3-319-73420-0_14
43. Yang, T.: Automatic extraction of verbal phrasemes in the culinary field with NooJ. In: Mauro Mirto, I., Monteleone, M., Silberztein, M. (eds.) NooJ 2018. CCIS, vol. 987, pp. 83–94. Springer, Cham (2019). https://doi.org/10.1007/978-3-030-10868-7_8

A Linguistic Approach for Automatic Analysis, Recognition and Translation of Arabic Nominal Predicates

Hajer Cheikhrouhou(✉) and Imed Lahyani

LLTA, University of Sfax, Sfax, Tunisia
cheihkkrouhou.hager@gmail.com

Abstract. The machine translation of nominal predicates from Arabic into French requires a judicious and analytical description in both the source language (SL) and target language (TL). The main interest of the present research work is to define the nominal predicates and support verbs. To do so, we firstly translated from Arabic into French two types of nominal predicates, namely the category <نُصْح> "advice" and the category <نظرة> "look", whose linguistic characteristics were then studied. Next, we downloaded these linguistic data on the NooJ platform to show the efficiency of machine translation and its limits.

Keywords: Arabic nominal predicate · Support verbs · Automatic translation · NooJ

1 Introduction

Our study of **Nominal Predicates** lies within the theory of **Object Classes** by **Gaston Gross**, emanating from that of Z.S. Harris and **Maurice Gross**. We will discuss the automatic identification of Nominal Predicates in Arabic and their translation into French through NooJ platform. To this end, we will briefly define the concept of Nominal Predicates and the Support Verbs. Then, we will study the linguistic characteristics of two types of Nominal Predicates taken from a contemporary Arabic corpus[1], namely, the advice <نصح: conseil> category and the look <regard:نظرة> category. Later, we use these linguistic data in machine translation in the NooJ platform.

---

[1] Ibrahim Al Koni (The Eclipse Of The Well) (الخسوف، ج 1، البئر :(إبراهيم الكوني)) , Ahlam Mosteghanemi: أحلام مستغانمي: (ذاكرة الجسد) (The Memory of the Body) (The Black Suits You) (Delicious as Departure) (شهيّا كفراق (الأسود يليق بك)) , Gerji Zaidan: (The Al Amin and Al Ma'moun) (الأمين والمأمون (جرجي زيدان:) , Rashad Abu Shawar: (The Lovers) (العشّاق :(رشاد أبو شاور) , Abd al-Rahman al-Sharqawi: (The Earth) (نجيب محفوظ: (الأعمال الكاملة) , Naguib Mahfouz: (The Complete Works) (عبد الرحمان الشرقاوي: (الأرض) , Youssef Al-Qaid: (Just Twenty-Four Hours) (يوسف القعيد: (أربع وعشرون ساعة فقط).

M. González et al. (Eds.): NooJ 2022, CCIS 1758, pp. 100–111, 2022.
https://doi.org/10.1007/978-3-031-23317-3_9

2 Nominal Predicates, Support Verbs and Translation

According to the theory of object classes, the simple sentence in Arabic and French consists of a Predicate ~ Argument. The predicate can be a verb, a noun, an adjective, or a preposition. As for the Arguments, they are non-nominal predicates or sentences [1]. Gaston Gross believes that the predicate is the essence and nucleus of the sentence, the carrier of the basic information and the one responsible for selecting the arguments. If the verbal predicate has its own tense, inflection, and aspect, then the nominal predicate, unlike the verbal predicate, needs external support. The latter is done with the nominal predicates through Support Verbs that determine tense, inflection, and aspect [2]. In addition to the actualization of the nominal predicates, some transitive verbs or their alternatives may carry aspectual values, including Inchoative Aspect, Terminative Aspect, Iterative Aspect and Durative Aspect… [3].

Translating the nominal Predicates from the Source Language into the Target Language requires a thorough and comprehensive linguistic study. Beshir Al-Warhani points out that there are three cases in translating the nominal predicates from Arabic into French [4].

- **The first case** is the translation of the nominal predicate and the support verb with the same nominal predicate and the same support verb in the target language. These combinations of transitive verbs do not result in many problems during translation. Example: طرح سؤالا Poser une question. Ask a question.
- **The second case** is the translation of the nominal predicate and the support verb with the same nominal predicate and a different support verb from those found in the source language. The translation is more complicated than the first case. Example: أسدى خدمة Offrir un service. Offer a service.
- **The third case** is the absence of the nominal predicate and the support verb in the target language. That is why we resort to translating the structure into the nominal predicate with a verbal predicate. Example: إسْتَحَم *أخذ حمّاما Prendre un bain. Have a bath/ to bathe.

Based on these concepts that are mainly inspired by the theory of object classes, in what follows, we will mention the linguistic characteristics of the nominal predicate: advisce <نصح: conseil> and look <regard:نظرة>, then we will download these linguistic data in the NooJ platform and show the results.

3 Linguistic Characteristics of the Nominative Predicate: Advice

The category of nominative predicate <نُصْح: conseil:advice> belongs to the category of actions, and it includes the predicate nouns: lessonعِبْرَة, exhortationعِظَّة, counselمَشُورَة, sermonمَوْعِظَة, advice نصيحة, advising نُصْح, pieces of advice نصائح. But we restricted our choice to the nominal predicates, advice, advising and pieces of advice ونصح ونصيحة ونصائح.

3.1   The General Support Verbs: أفعال ناقلة عامة

These nominal predicates in Arabic represent four argumentative schemas, which are:

- **Schema 1:** ف ـ ن 0| [بشر] 1| <نصح> إس | [بشر]>

  Vsupp N0Hum N1Hum Npred <advice>

  → *FR:* N0HumVsupp Npred <conseil> PREP N1Hum

  Example:. هبني نصيحة مبتكرة Would you mind giving me a creative piece of advice.

  Il m'a donné un conseil innovant.

- **Schema 2:** ف ـ ن 0| [حرف] بشر] 1| <نصح> إس | [بشر]>

  Vsupp N0Hum Npred <نصح> PREP N1Hum

  → *FR:* N0Hum Vsupp PREP N1Hum Npred <conseil>

  Example: بعض زبائن أبي قدّموا له نصائح ثمينة

  Some of my father's customers gave him valuable pieces of advice.

  Certains clients de mon père lui ont donné des conseils très précieux.

- **Schema 3:** ف ـ ن 0| [حرف] بشر] 1| <حرف> إس | [بشر] 2ج

  Vsupp N0Hum PREP N1Hum Npred <نصح> PREP Prop

  → *FR:* N0Hum Vsupp PREP N1Hum Npred <conseil> PREP Vinf

  Example: ليتك تستطيع أن توجّه هذه النصيحة إلى ياسين

  I wish you could give such advice to Yassin.

  J'aimerais que tu puisses adresser ce conseil à Yassin.

- **Schema 4 :** ف ـ ن 0| [حرف] بشر] 1| [حرف] <نصح> إس | [بشر] 2ج

  Vsupp N0Hum PREP N1Hum Npred <نصح> PREP Prop

  → *FR:* N0Hum Vsupp PREP N1Hum Npred <conseil> PREP Vinf

  Example: فأسدينا إليه النصيحة بأن يحافظ على سمعة العائلة.

  Hence, we gave him the advice to preserve the reputation of the family.

  Nous lui avons donné un conseil de protéger la réputation de la famille.

It can therefore be deduced that the nominal predicate of "advice" <نُصح: conseil> select a human subject who gives advice and a human object argument as well, and it is possible to select a third object that determines the nature of the advice. The support verb may pass directly (Schema 1) or by a preposition ((لـ وإلى) for and to) (Schemas 2, 3, 4).

Although the basic support verb of actions is " قام: do" in Arabic and (faire) in French, we did not find this verb with the category of nominal predicate "advice". Actually, the basic verbs are "provide"أسدى, "present"قدّم and "give" أعطى. We find other alternatives such as "provide" وجّه and "offer" وهب.

3.2   The Aspectual Support Verbs: أفعال ناقلة مظهريّة

The predicates of "advice" < نُصح > do not coincide with the support verbs that denote the inchoative aspect, the durative aspect and the terminative aspect, because they are punctual, i.e. non-continuous [5].

Example:	شرع في نصحه؟*	*Started advice	*Commence le conseil
	انتهى من نصحه*؟	*Finished advice	* Termine le conseil

These predicates occur with support verbs that denote the repetitive aspect (return to عاود, return back ولّى) and with aspectual reciprocal verbs (receive, agree, accept, respond تلقّى، وقبل، تقبّل، استجاب):

Example: renouveler/répéter un conseil: repeat/renew advice جدّد/ عاود النصح.
I followed/ pursued my friend's advice

3.3 Determiners of Predicate "Advice"

The predicates of <نُصْح> <advice> occur as indefinite or definite by "the" (the alif and the lam: ال) or by complementation:

Example:

إذن قدّم لي نصيحة مبتكرة and then could you give me a creative piece of advice.
وهل نجحت في نصحك لأسدي النصائح لغيرك؟

Have I succeeded in advising you to give advice to others?

قدّم لي أغلى نصائحه He gave me one of his most valuable pieces of advice.
تسدي لي النصائح you give me some advice.

3.4 The Verbal Predicate "نَصَحَ" "Conseiller" " to Advise"

In Arabic, the verbal predicate "advise:conseiller" "nasaha" <نَصَحَ> is synonymous to "give advice" <قدّم نصيحة>. Besides, the verb "advise" "nasaha" <نَصَحَ> has a similar argumentative schema to the nominal predicate, advice نُصْح:

Example: Why didn't you **give me this piece of advice** before?
Why didn't you **advise** me before? (Table 1)

Table 1. The difference between nominal and verbal predicates.

The nominal predicate	The verbal predicate
إلى أحمد من قبل توجّه هذه النصيحة لماذا لم ؟	أحمد من قبل لماذا لم تنصح؟
Pourquoi tu n'as pas **adressé ce conseil** à Ahmed auparavant ?	Pourquoi tu n'as pas **conseillé** Ahmed auparavant ?
Why didn't you **give this advice** to Ahmed before?	Why didn't you **advise** Ahmed before?
بأن يحافظ على سمعة العائلة إليه النصيحة أسدينا.	بأن يحافظ على سمعة العائلة نصحناه.
Nous lui **avons donné un conseil** de protéger la réputation de la famille.	Nous lui **avons conseillé** de protéger la réputation de la famille.
We **advised** him to protect the family's reputation.	

4 Creation of a Bilingual French-Arabic Dictionary

According to Imed Lahyani's classification of Arabic nominal predicates, so far, there exist thirty classes of nominal predicates, such as the example of (Fig. 1):

"(aids, help, advice, look) مساعدات, مساعدة, نصح, نظرة". At this level, we will create two bilingual dictionaries: one for nominal predicates **"Nompredicatifar"** and another for support verbs **"Verbessupportar"**.

```
File  Edit  Lab  Project  Windows  Info  DICTIONARY

#
# Special Characters: '\' ''''' ','' '+' '-' '#'
#use paradigmenomar.nof
#use paradderivnom.nof

#صنف مساعدات
إعانة,N+NPRED+f+FLX=NF3+DOM=AIDE
دعم,N+NPRED+f+FLX=NF4+DOM=AIDE
مساعدة,N+NPRED+f+FLX=NF3+DOM=AIDE
مساندة,N+NPRED+f+FLX=NF3+DOM=AIDE

#صنف اهتمام
اغتناء,N+NPRED+f+FLX=NF5+DOM=INTERET
اكتراث,N+NPRED+f+FLX=NF5+DOM=INTERET
اهتمام,N+NPRED+f+FLX=NF1+DOM=INTERET
عناية,N+NPRED+f+FLX=NF1+DOM=INTERET

#صنف نصح
مشورة,N+NPRED+f+FLX=NF1+DOM=CONSEIL+FR="conseil"
نصيحة,N+NPRED+f+FLX=NF+DOM=CONSEIL+DRV=Dev1+FR="conseil"
####
#صنف نظرة
نظرة,N+NPRED+f+FLX=NF2+DOM=REGARD+FR="regard"
```

Fig. 1. Extract from the «Nompredicatifar.dic» dictionary.

Example: Class of « advice: نصيحة»

```
#صنف نصح
مشورة,N+NPRED+f+FLX=NF1+DOM=CONSEIL+FR="conseil"
نصيحة,N+NPRED+f+FLX=NF+DOM=CONSEIL+DRV=Dev1+FR="conseil"
#####
#صنف نظرة
نظرة,N+NPRED+f+FLX=NF2+DOM=REGARD+FR="regard"
```

نصيحة,N+NPRED+f+FLX=NF+DOM=CONSEIL+DRV=Dev1+FR="conseil".
For example, the nominal predicate <conseil: نصيحة> is:

- a feminine nominal predicate N+NPRED+f
- The inflectional paradigm FLX=NF
- The derivational paradigm DRV=Dev1 to form the deverbal «نصح»
- This noun belongs to the domain CONSEIL
- +FR=conseil (Fig. 2).

```
NooJ - [C:\Users\Hajer CHEIHKROUHOU\Documents\NooJ\ar\Lexical Analysis\Verbesupportar.dic]
File  Edit  Lab  Project  Windows  Info      DICTIONARY
Dictionary contains 102 entries
# NooJ V5
# Dictionary
#
# Language is: ar
#
# Alphabetical order is not required.
#
# Use inflectional & derivational paradigms' description files (.nof), e.g.:
# Special Command: #use paradigms.nof
#
# Special Features: +NW (non-word) +FXC (frozen expression component) +UNAMB (unambiguous lexical entry)
#          +FLX= (inflectional paradigm) +DRV= (derivational paradigm)
#
# Special Characters: '\' ''''' ','' '+' '-' '#'
#use Verbes Arabe.nof

قام,V+Supp+CONS=V+N0Hum+PREP+NPRED+N1Hum+MoutalAin+FLX=V_faàaka51+FR="faire"
قدم,V+Supp+CONS=V+N0Hum+NPRED+N1Hum+FLX=V_allama4+FR="donner"
تلقى,V+Supp+CONS=V+N0Hum+NPRED+PREP+N1Hum+FLX=V_tarajjaàn62a+FR="recevoir"
شرع,V+Supp+CONS=V+N0Hum+PREP+NPRED+N1Hum+Correct+Salem+FLX=V_dhahaba3+FR="commencer"
أخذ,V+Supp+CONS=V+N0Hum+PREP+NPRED+N1Hum+Correct+MahmouzFa+FLX=V_akhatha18+FR="prendre"
بدأ,V+Supp+CONS=V+N0Hum+PREP+NPRED+N1Hum+Correct+MahmouzLam+FLX=V_khabaàa37+FR="commencer"
واصل,V+Supp+CONS=V+N0Hum+NPRED+N1Hum+FLX=V_badaara4+FR="continuer"
استنز,V+Supp+CONS=V+N0Hum+PREP+NPRED+N1Hum+FLX=V_estakhafa10a+FR="continuer"
جدّد,V+Supp+CONS=V+N0Hum+NPRED+PREP+N1Hum+FLX=V_allama4+FR="renouveler"
توقف,V+Supp+CONS=V+N0Hum+NPRED+PREP+N1Hum+FLX=V_tafakaada6+FR="cesser"
أبدى,V+Supp+CONS=V+N0Hum+NPRED+PREP+N1Hum+N1Conc+FLX=V_asmaàa61a+FR="exprimer"
مارس,V+Supp+CONS=V+N0Hum+NPRED+PREP+N1Hum+FLX=V_badaara4+FR="exercer"
```

Fig. 2. Extract from the «Verbesupportar.dic» dictionary.

Example:
قَدَّمَ,V+Supp+CONS=V+N0Hum+NPRED+PREP=«لِ»+PREP=«إِلَى»+N1Hum
+FLX=V_allama4+FR="donner".

The support verb <donner: قَدَّم > is:

- a support verb V+Supp
- The subject is Human followed by a nominal predicate V+N0Hum
- The indirect complement is N1Hum introduced by «إِلَى»/«لِ»
- For the conjugation, we used the inflectional paradigms of "VerbesArabes.nof" created by Hela Fehri+FLX=V_allama4
- + FR=« donner»

Fig. 3. The request <V+Supp><N+NPRED>|<V+Supp><WF>*<N+NPRED>.

Fig. 4. The extraction of the Arabic predicative nouns.

By applying these two dictionaries to our corpus consisting of Arabic literary novels from Nagib Mahfoudh, Ahlem Moustaghanmi…, we got these results (Figs. 3 and 4):

The obtained results show the extraction of the Arabic predicative nouns with the appropriate «Vsupp+NPRED » type: « تبادل مع, أسدى إليه النصح, يتبادلون النظرات, ترسلان نظرة. كمال نظرة...».

After the first step in our investigative procedure of automatic translation, we proceed to the second step which consists in the automatic recognition of different syntactic and semantic schemas of Arabic nominal predicates.

5 The Creation of Grammars for the Analysis and Recognition of Syntactic Patterns

In this phase, we will try to create formal grammars able to analyze the sentences with the aim of recognizing the different arguments found in a corpus or a text and sorting the suitable syntactic constructions without any ambiguity. So far, for each semantic class, we conducted a formal grammar of analysis and recognition, which takes into account the semantic-syntactic specificities of each class of Arabic nominal predicates (Fig. 5).

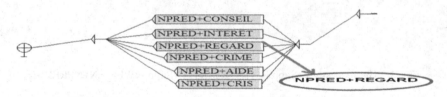

Fig. 5. The transduces of predicative nouns.

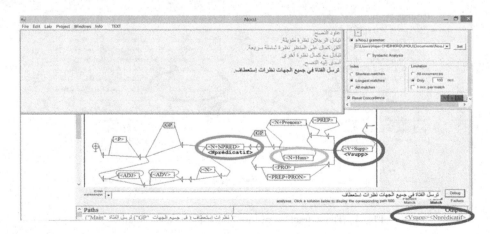

Fig. 6. The transduces of predicative nouns <Regard: نظرة>.

Example: ‏ترسل الفتاة في جميع الجهات نظرات إ ستعطاف.‏

La fille envoie dans toutes les directions des regards de compassion.

The girl sends sympathetic glances in all directions.

The nominal predicate «‏نظرات‏» (regards) functions with the support verb "‏أَرْسَلَ‏" "envoyer" when the subject is N0Hum with a prepositional group that indicates the direction of the look «‏في جميع الجهات‏» «dans toutes les directions» [6] (Fig. 6).

When applying these grammars of syntactic disambiguation [7], we noticed that sentences were properly analyzed by adequate syntactic and semantic schemes (Fig. 7).

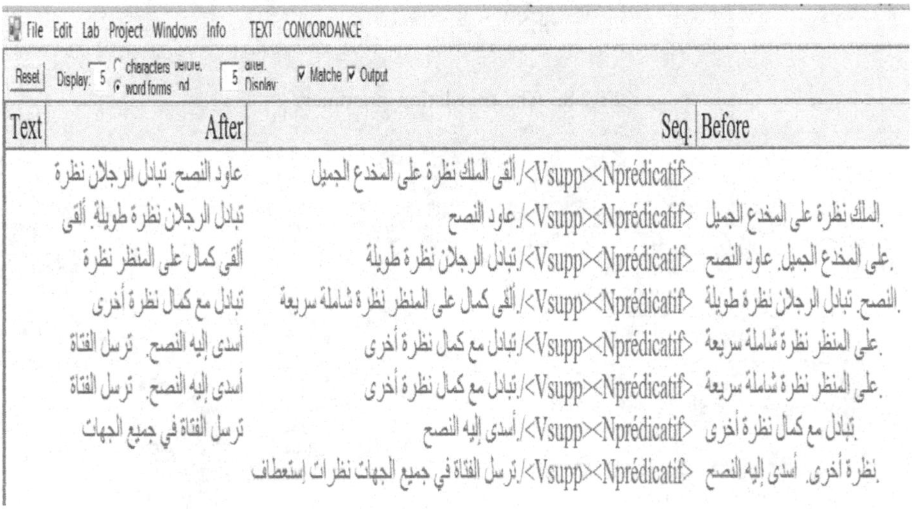

Fig. 7. The table of concordance.

For example, the sentence: ‏تبادل مع كمال نظرة أخرى.‏ is properly analyzed and annotated by <Vsupp> <Nprédicatif> when "‏تبادل‏" is a support verb and "‏نظرة‏" is a nominal predicate.

6   The Creation of Translation Grammars

The last phase of our machine translation process of Arabic nominal predicates is to create Arabic-French translation grammars. By adding the translation grammar, we find adequate translations that respect the word order in the French language [8] (Figs. 8 and 9).

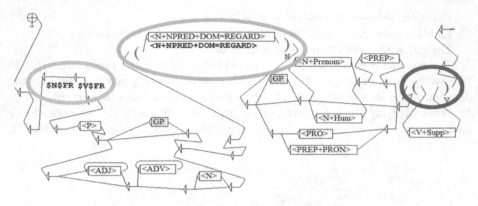

Fig. 8. The translation grammar.

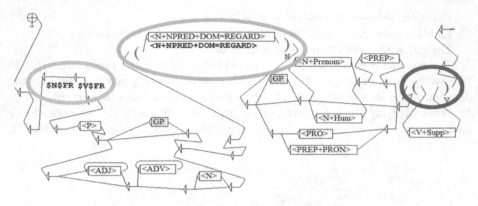

Fig. 9. The primary results of the translation.

It can be noted that the determiners (definite/indefinite) of the nominal predicates are not added. Example: Répéter conseil. Partager regard. Donner conseil.

Hence, the insertion of a grammar indicates whether the adequate determiners is necessary or not. It is trusty to note that although the French nominal predicate "regard" accepts only indefinite determiners; the Arabic nominal predicate accepts both types.

Example [9]: Marie a jeté un regard sur le tableau.

* Marie a jeté le regard sur le tableau.

Marie a jeté des regards sur le tableau. * Marie a jeté les regards sur le tableau.

Regarding the nominal predicate «conseil», it accepts two types of determiners in Arabic and French.

To solve this problem, for each predicate, we have created its own translation grammar to remove all ambiguities [10] (Fig. 10).

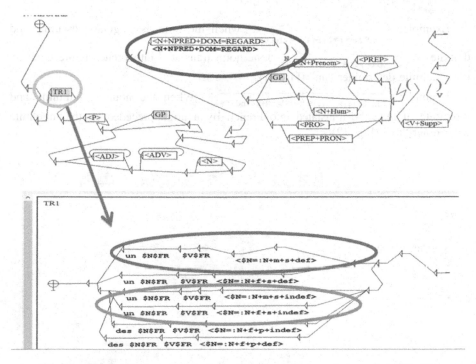

Fig. 10. Filters added to resolve the ambiguities of the nominal predicate "look".

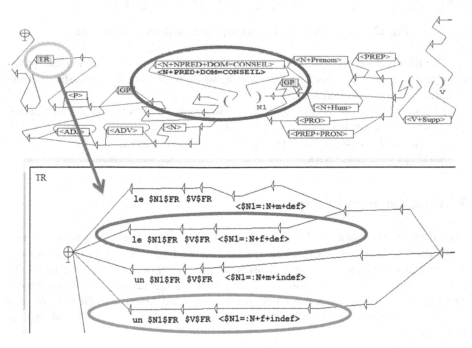

Fig. 11. Filters added to resolve ambiguities in the nominal predicate "advice".

Example: 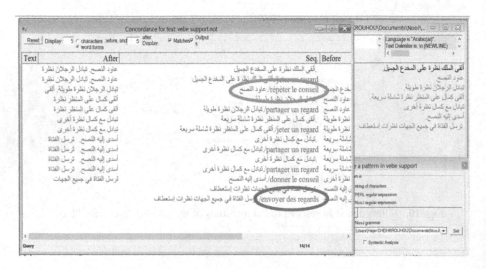 when the noun is singular masculine and
definite `un $N$FR    $V$FR`, the noun translated into French is preceded by
the indefinite determiner "un" (Fig. 11).

Example: `un $N1$FR $V$FR <$N1=:N+f+indef>` When the noun is feminine and
indefinite, it must be translated into French by a noun preceded by the indefinite
determiner "un" (Fig. 12).

Fig. 12. The obtained results after applying the disambiguation filters.

The obtained results are encouraging as the support verbs and the nominal predicates are appropriately translated into French, while respecting the linguistic and distributional properties of each use.

Example: ترسل الفتاة في جميع الجهات **نظرات** إستعطاف./ envoyer des regards./ send glances.
عاود النصح./répéter le consei./repeat the advice.
Example:ترسل الفتاة في جميع الجهات نظرات إستعطاف./send glances.
عاود النصح./repeat the advice.

7   Conclusion and Perspectives

The machine translation of the nominal predicates and support verbs raises several
problems. The latter can be overcome by developing a linguistic approach that includes
the structural, semantic, and lexical aspects, i.e., the theory of object classes. An
exploratory description of the nouns in the source and target language is also necessary.
Through translating two types of nominal predicate from Arabic into French, we have
shown the importance of the NooJ platform in machine translation of natural
languages.

However, we still have a lot to do. As a follow-up to this work, we will consider the automatic translation of other nominal predicate classes into Arabic/French and the creation of other bilingual French-Arabic/Arabic-French dictionaries.

References

1. Buvet, P., Grezka, A: Les dictionnaires électroniques du modèle des classes d'objets. Langages (176), 63–79 (2009)
2. Gross, G.: Manuel d'analyse linguistique : Approche sémantico-syntaxique du lexique. Presses Universitaires du Septentrion, Lille (2012)
3. Gross, G.: Prédicats nominaux et compatibilité aspectuelle. Langages (121), 54–72 (1996)
4. Ouerhani, B.: Les problèmes linguistiques de la traduction automatique des prédicats nominaux entre l'arabe et le français. Meta 2(53), 407–419 (2008)
5. Jaozandry, M.: Les prédicats nominaux du Malgache : étude comparative avec le français. Thèse Doctorale. Université Paris-Nord - Paris XIII (2014)
6. Lahyani, I.: ألفاظ الإدراك البصريّ في العربيّة: مقاربة تركيبيّة دلاليّة. Edition CONTACT, Tunisie (2022)
7. Silberztein, M.: La formalisation des langues l'approche de NooJ. Collection Science Cognitive et Management des Connaissances. ISTE Editions (2015)
8. Cheikhrouhou, H.: The automatic translation of french verbal tenses to arabic using the platform NooJ. In: Mbarki, S., Mourchid, M., Silberztein, M. (eds.) NooJ 2017. CCIS, vol. 811, pp. 156–167. Springer, Cham (2018). https://doi.org/10.1007/978-3-319-73420-0_13
9. Grezka, A: La polysémie des verbes de perception visuelle. Le Harmattan, Paris (2009)
10. Cheikhrouhou, H.: Arabic translation of the french auxiliary: using the platform NooJ. In: Barone, L., Monteleone, M., Silberztein, M. (eds.) NooJ 2016. CCIS, vol. 667, pp. 74–86. Springer, Cham (2016). https://doi.org/10.1007/978-3-319-55002-2_7

Corpus Linguistics and Discourse Analysis

Processing the Discourse of Insecurity in Rosario with the NooJ Platform

Andrea Rodrigo[1]($\boxtimes$), Silvia Reyes[1]($\boxtimes$), and Mariana González[2]($\boxtimes$)

[1] Centro de Estudios de Tecnología Educativa y Herramientas Informáticas de Procesamiento del Lenguaje, Facultad de Humanidades y Artes, Universidad Nacional de Rosario, Rosario, Argentina
andreafrodrigo@yahoo.com.ar, sisureyes@gmail.com

[2] Centro de Estudios de Tecnología Educativa y Herramientas Informáticas de Procesamiento del Lenguaje, Instituto de Eduación Superior N°28 "Olga Cossettini", Rosario, Argentina
marianagonzalez826@gmail.com

Abstract. The CETEHIPL (Centro de Estudios de Tecnología Educativa y Herramientas Informáticas de Procesamiento del Lenguaje) has been working on the pedagogical application of computer tools to language teaching [8]. Today we took a small turn towards discourse analysis and chose to analyze a recurring topic in post-pandemic Argentina: insecurity. Here we intended to record what impact insecurity had and still has on the linguistic domain. We built a corpus of journalistic texts published in December 2021 in the main newspapers in Rosario, Santa Fe, Argentina. We drew our attention to expressions referring to the victim, to the role of the State and to the perpetrator. We created tags to account for terms referring to the discourse of insecurity and included some lexical items provided by *lunfardo*, a Rioplatense slang originally created by immigrants, but which later became a colloquial and informal language variety still in use in our country. We tackled this issue of insecurity with the Rioplatense Spanish resources developed by the IES_UNR team with NooJ. To complete our analysis, we developed grammars to show how the impact of insecurity is made visible from a syntactic viewpoint.

Keyword: NLP · Spanish language · Discourse analysis · Insecurity · NooJ

1 Introduction

1.1 The Aim of Our Paper

With the use of Nooj as our software platform, the aim of the Argentine IES_UNR research team (CETEHIPL, Centro de Estudios de Tecnología Educativa y Herramientas Informáticas de Procesamiento del Lenguaje, UNR) is to take a small turn towards discourse analysis and to study a partly exacerbated and recurring topic in post-pandemic Argentina: insecurity. We believe it is important to contribute this angle of analysis to our project involving the pedagogical application of NooJ, since our work is directly related to discourse analysis, which in turn contributes to the development of critical thinking

© Springer Nature Switzerland AG 2022
M. González et al. (Eds.): NooJ 2022, CCIS 1758, pp. 115–126, 2022.
https://doi.org/10.1007/978-3-031-23317-3_10

among students. Working with a software tool helps us to reflect metalinguistically upon language and generate knowledge, because we are "teaching" what we say, how we say it and why we say what we say to a robot. And in the process, we achieve language learning and capitalize on it.

Here we intended to record what impact insecurity had and still has on the linguistic domain. Consequently, we cannot ignore that the media influences public opinion and how journalism discourses on insecurity. However, we will not discuss here the very complex phenomenon of insecurity, since we consider that the media are exposed to a specific logic, as it is well stated by Guemureman et al. [3 p. 3]:

The structure the media system takes in a country is partly determined by a correlation of forces between various political actors. A tour around the "media map" in Argentina today allows us to affirm that the media system in our country pursues a commercial logic, not a public service one.[1]

The concept of news is influenced by the construction of a piece of merchandise generating profits and participating in consumption. This always occurs within the process of dismantling a protective State, where the notion of punishment is often erased in order to focus on "the victim". Guemureman et al. say [3 p. 3]:

The news cycle as merchandise reproduces the merchandising cycle of any product, the news as merchandise is consumed, its consumption fosters demand, demand fosters production, circulation and consumption, all merchandise generates demand and a consumer market (see footnote 1).

1.2 Why Do We Use NooJ?

From our role of researchers and taking an NLP perspective, we can provide an interesting analysis of insecurity and its linguistic impact. We tackled this issue with the Rioplatense Spanish resources [14] developed by the IES_UNR team with NooJ (created by Silberztein [9]). We use NooJ because it offers a computing environment that provides linguistic resources in many different languages. It is an open access platform where different researchers interact and that enables us to create our own dictionaries and grammars by defining specific processing properties for Rioplatense Spanish. Therefore, we are able to form a module that is constantly being improved. We will now include new tags for new terms in our dictionaries and will develop new grammars about the discourse of insecurity in an attempt to conceptualize it through NLP.

1.3 The Corpus

We compiled a corpus of journalistic texts published in December 2021 in the main newspapers in Rosario: *La Capital* [10], *Rosario12* [11] and *El Ciudadano* [12]. *La Capital*, which was founded in December 1867, is the oldest newspaper in Rosario. *El Ciudadano y la región* is run as a cooperative by its workers since 2017. *Rosario12* is the supplement of *Página 12* since 1983. We took a temporal cut, December 2021, which constituted a retreat of the pandemic and a moment of great economic instability before

---

[1] The translation is ours.

the agreement with the IMF. The compiled texts that allude to insecurity episodes have 80,932 tokens. They were randomly selected one by one, according to the subject matter. Images and links were removed in order to preserve only the journalistic texts, which are available online.

2   General Considerations

2.1   New Tags

To account for the discourse of insecurity, we distinguished three different types of expressions referring to the victim, to the role of the State and to the perpetrator. In this first approach, we can notice that victim-related expressions occupy a predominant place, while State-related expressions are very scarce. This comes into line with what is called the weakening of the role of the State as an immediate consequence of the "media construction of insecurity" [3 p. 5] (see footnote 1). We noticed that expressions referring to the perpetrator come up when texts retake this type of discourse. After various tests, we decided not to create specific tags for each role, for it is not always possible to differentiate terms.

We modified the Properties' Definition file of our Spanish Module Argentina available at the NooJ platform and added the colloquial language variety *lunfardo* [LUNF] to the existing varieties.

In this way, we were able to incorporate *lunfardo* terms marked by a specific tag. *Lunfardo* constitutes an interesting element in our Spanish Module Argentina, which we have not considered up to now. Defined as a slang of socially marginalized people, which intersects with the language spoken by immigrants in the Rio de la Plata area, *lunfardo* appears in journalistic texts referring to insecurity when we pay attention to the speech of perpetrators. In Argentina, *lunfardo* has a strong connection with our culture and is present in music and poetry, particularly in *tango* lyrics. Thus, for example, *Mi noche triste*, 'My sad night', whose lyrics was written by Pascual Contursi [13], shows the presence of *lunfardo* in its first verses:

Percanta que me amuraste en lo mejor de mi vida.
Dejándome el alma herida y espina en el corazón.
'(Beloved beautiful) Woman who tacked ('left') me in the best part of my life.
leaving my soul wounded and a thorn in my heart'.

Consequently, expressions such as *luca,* 'thousand' (relating to money), or *gilada,* 'naive people', are introduced into our dictionary of insecurity terms. In this context, however, *gilada* refers to *droga,* 'drugs', attaining a new meaning, this time related to drug trafficking activities. These semantic changes are typical of *lunfardo.* To determine whether these terms really belonged to *lunfardo,* we looked them up in Gobello's dictionary [2], for he is an authority in *lunfardo.* The adding of *lunfardo* constitutes a true advantage for our NooJ resources, since in the RAE (Royal Spanish Academy) Dictionary [4] some words are labeled as typical of Argentina and/or Uruguay, but not classified as belonging to *lunfardo.*

Some *lunfardo* lexical items were entered into our dictionaries. In order to enrich the semantic meaning of each dictionary, we added the meaning of *lunfardo* words after the numeral or hash sign #, which is not read by NooJ, but only by the human user.

boletear, V+FLX=AMAR+LUNF#matar
chabón, N+FLX=ANFITRIÓN+LUNF#persona desconocida, tonto, torpe
cumpa, N+FLX=ACCIONISTA+LUNF#compañero, compañera
falopa, N+FLX=HAMBRE+LUNF+RIOP#droga, algo de mala calidad
gilada, N+FLX=MESA+LUNF#tontos, droga en lenguaje del hampa
luca, N+FLX=MESA+LUNF#mil pesos, mil unidades de dinero
laburo, N+FLX=ABRIGO+LUNF#trabajo
laburante, N+FLX=ACCIONISTA+LUNF#trabajador
morfar, N+FLX=AMAR+LUNF#comer
mufar, N+FLX=AMAR+LUNF#dar o traer mala suerte
piba, N+FLX=MESA+LUNF#chica
pibe, N+FLX=ABRIGO+LUNF#chico

The Linguistic Analysis of some new *lunfardo* lexical items are shown in Fig. 1.

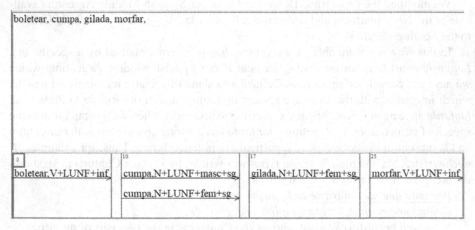

Fig. 1. Linguistic analysis of some new *lunfardo* [LUNF] lexical items.

We continued including new lexical items in our dictionaries. We added neologisms such as *gatillero,* 'shooter', and *balacera,* 'shooting', which are used in Latin America, and added new meanings for already existing words, e.g. *juguete,* 'toy', also refers to 'weapon'. It should be noted that many of these meanings are explicitly mentioned in journalistic texts in an attempt to familiarize the reader with the slang used by criminals. We added the tag [AMER][2] to account for terms related to the Spanish spoken in Latin American countries (Mexico, Colombia, Bolivia, Argentina, etc.):

balacera, N+FLX=MESA+AMER#tiroteo.

---

[2] This tag was previously added to our Properties' definition file.

gatillar, N+FLX=AMAR+AMER#oprimir el gatillo de un arma de fuego.
gatillero, N+FLX=PERRO+AMER#persona que gatilla.
juguete, N+FLX=ABRIGO+AMER#arma.
tranki, ADJ+RIOP#apócope de tranquilo.
soldadito, N+FLX=ABRIGO#persona joven que vende drogas.
pierna, N+FLX=MESA#compañero en el delito.
famunchú, N+RIOP+masc+sg+conc#adicto a la marihuana.

The verb *lavar*, 'wash', also appears in the sense of *blanquear*, 'launder', i.e. to legalize illegal money, and this meaning is stated in the RAE (Royal Spanish Academy) Dictionary as the third sense of *lavar*:

lavar, V + FLX = AMAR#blanquear, ajustar a la legalidad dinero negro.

2.2 Grammars for the Discourse of Insecurity

To complete our analysis we developed grammars to show how the impact of insecurity is made visible from a syntactic viewpoint. As it is our first approach to this phenomenon, we can only offer partial conclusions. For this reason, our research will go on by enlarging the sample in order to progressively achieve a greater coverage of insecurity expressions with the resources of the Spanish Module Argentina designed by our team on the NooJ platform.

We must first put forward the theoretical viewpoint from which our grammars are defined. Relying on Bès assumptions [1], we identified larger phrases [5, 6] such as the noun phrase SINNOM, the adjective phrase SINADJ, or the verb phrase SINVERB, which contain smaller phrases, such as nucleus noun phrases SNN, nucleus adjective phrases SADJN, or nucleus verb phrases SVN respectively. Nucleus phrases are considered minimum processing units involving segments identified with natural intonation patterns. Nucleus phrases facilitate nucleus recognition because the nucleus is always in a fixed position at the end of the nucleus phrase. The only exception is the nucleus preposition phrase, since the preposition always stands at the beginning of the phrase.

2.2.1 Grammar for Noun Phrases

Following Bès [1], in the noun phrase *un ataque a balazos ejecutado por gatilleros*, 'an attack with bullets performed by shooters', we distinguish the nucleus noun phrase SNN *un ataque*, followed by the nucleus preposition phrase SPN *a balazos*. The whole expression *un ataque a balazos* is a (large) noun phrase SINNOM containing two small nucleus phrases. The corresponding grammar is shown in Fig. 2:

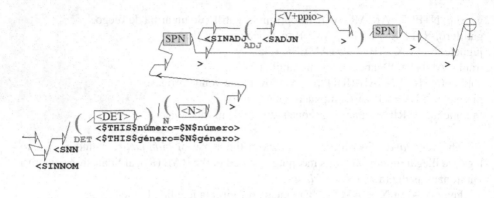

un ataque a balazos ejecutado por "gatilleros"

Fig. 2. Grammar for the SINNOM *un ataque a balazos ejecutado por gatilleros*

The grammar has two identical embedded graphs corresponding to the nucleus prepositional phrase SPN, made up by a preposition and a nucleus noun phrase in the plural. The agreement relationship between determiner and noun is specified by using the variable $THIS, which states that both determiner and noun must agree in number and gender. We apply Show Debug to see if the grammar is validated (Fig. 3):

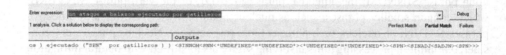

Fig. 3. Validation of the SINOM grammar in Fig. 2

However, to be sure that the grammar created for this phrase did not only apply to an isolated occurrence, we checked it with the corpus and obtained match results that reached a data accuracy level of 75%. We define accuracy level as the percentage of lemmatized expressions that match our grammar. The 25% of inaccurate matching results were connected to ambiguities referring to PREP+N+masc+pl (preposition+noun+masculine+plural), mostly regarding the feminine determiner *la*, which can also be a masculine noun, the musical note A. Our grammar analyzed occurrences such as (*en*) *las*, (PREP+) DET+artdet+fem+pl, as similar to (*a*) *balazos*, (PREP+) N+masc+pl, as if *las* was the plural of the musical note A, instead of a feminine plural determiner. Even though the Pan-Hispanic Dictionary of Doubts indicates that musical notes adopt masculine gender and produce the plural by adding -s or -es, we changed the inflectional paradigm of the whole set of musical notes, because they are used only in the singular, because there is no evidence that they have a plural form in real texts.[3] After modifying our dictionary of nouns, we get a 96% margin of matching (Fig. 4):

Asesinaron en su casa a	la jefa de compras	del Correo Argentino de Santa
pueda aportar datos acercarse a	la Unidad de Homicidios	Dolosos en el Centro de
común. "El agresor sometió a	la víctima con amenazas	constantes y otras demostraciones de
otras demostraciones de poder, como	la exhibición de armas	de fuego", aseveró la funcionaria
después otra comunicación señaló que	un grupo de personas	le estaba propinando una golpiza
Fabbro. La funcionaria delegó a	la División de Homicidios	de AIC realiza tareas investigativas
diciembre de 2021 - 19:46 El cuerpo de	un hombre de unos	70 años fue hallado maniatado y
Gabinete de Criminalística y de	la Brigada de Homicidios	de la Agencia de Investigación
moradores, de 60 años, repelió a	los intrusos a balazos	y logró herir a uno
años, que terminó internado en	el hospital de emergencias	Heca fuera de peligro. La
de robo al 911. Una ambulancia	del servicio de emergencias	Sies trasladó al muchacho hasta
el lugar y ello generó	un encontronazo entre ambos	. Lo acusaron de mandar a
culminación, el punto final de	una sucesión de ataques	de distinta índole contra la
justicia". Este viernes personal de	la Brigada de Homicidios	de la AIC con colaboración
debe investigarse el homicidio y	la aplicación de torturas	). "Estamos hablando del aparato represivo
esa trama y les dictó	el sobreseimiento a ambos	. Sin embargo, la Cámara Federal
el martes pasado frente a	su casa por unos	300 manifestantes antivacunas que rechazan la
falleció poco más tarde en	el Hospital de Emergencias	Clemente Alvarez. Además, la fiscal
de un homicidio calificado por	la función de agentes	de la fuerza. Ante el
fue condenado esta mañana a	la pena de tres	años de prisión efectiva y
Comando Radioeléctrico, cuando agentes de	la brigada de homicidios	de la AIC estaba apostado
la AIC estaba apostado en	la zona desde horas	de la tarde de ayer
reducir al guardia de seguridad,	un grupo de desconocidos	ingresó durante la madrugada de

245/245

Fig. 4. Search with Locate when applying the grammar of Fig. 2

2.2.2 Grammar for Sentences

We will now analyze two sentences related to the discourse of insecurity.

Gianfranco le había ofrecido un trabajo que consistía en "ir a matar a alguien".

'Gianfranco had offered him a job that consisted in "going to kill someone"'.

The grammar[4] of this first sentence is shown below (Fig. 5):

---

[3] The Dictionary itself makes clear that in conventional use musical notes are not marked for plural number and remain invariable.

[4] The inverted commas and full stop punctuation marks are alluded by < P > at the end of the graph.

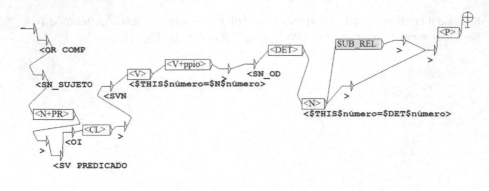

Gianfranco le había ofrecido un trabajo que consistía en "ir a matar a alguien"

Fig. 5. Grammar of the first sentence

This grammar describes a complex sentence comprising a (subordinate) relative clause—which is introduced by the relative pronoun *que*—inside the direct object *un trabajo que consistía en "ir a matar a alguien"*. It is interesting to note that inside the relative clause there is a non-finite noun clause governed by the preposition *en*, which can be perfectly analyzed by NooJ's grammar editor. The *trabajo*, 'job', consisted in *ir a matar a alguien*, 'going to kill someone'. *Alguien*, 'someone', is an indefinite pronoun that refers to the victim, whose name is not disclosed. The important thing is that there is a job to be done and therefore money to be received later. The indefiniteness of the victim contrasts with the explicit allusion to whom orders the job, *Gianfranco*, who does have a name and is the real perpetrator, the intellectual author of the murder, who orders the job to someone else.

Now, in order to process the second sentence:

Les iba a hacer unos laburos y se la re mandó.

'(He) was going to do some jobs and (he) made a mistake'.

we first added the intransitive verbal periphrasis *ir a hacer* to our dictionary of verbs.

ir a hacer, V + FLX = < P2 > IR.

With the <P2> operator (go to the previous word-form, twice) NooJ understands it has to inflect the verb *ir* and leave in a fixed position the sequence *a hacer* (preposition + infinitive). However, in the case of the sequence *la re mandar*, which is a pronominal phrase preceded by a feminine personal pronoun (clitic) *la*, and in order to enter it into our dictionary, we have to tell NooJ not to inflect the two words preceding the verb *mandar*, i.e., *la re* (clitic + adverb). To do so, we relocate the operator <P2> and place it after the inflectional paradigm AMAR, so that the sequence *la re* stays in a fixed position before the verb *mandar*:

la re mandar, V+FLX=AMAR+RIOP <P2> #equivocarse.

We are now in a position to create our grammar and complete it with a PRO-DROP (pronoun dropping) subject [6, 7], which can be defined as a null or implicit subject easily retrievable from verbal agreement morphology in finite clauses, by adding a

SNN_PRO_DROP, as we have already done in previous work [6]. The main grammar is displayed in Fig. 6:

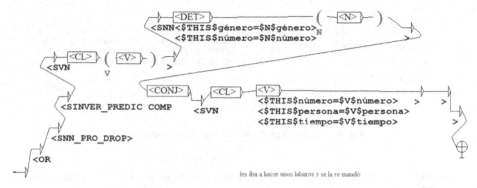

les iba a hacer unos laburos y se la re mandó

Fig. 6. Grammar of the second sentence

Attention must be paid, on the one hand, to the number and gender agreement between determiner and the noun, *unos laburos*, 'some jobs', and on the other hand, to the singular number and third person agreement of the finite verbs *iba* (imperfect past tense) and *mandó* (simple perfect past tense) with the third person singular null pronoun subject.

When we apply this grammar to the corpus, it finds echo in other similar constructions, and the outputs are displayed in Fig. 7:

que ya no tenía vigencia.	Le dieron la libertad pero se dispuso	el secuestro de la moto
con una gente de acá.	Les iba a hacer unos laburos y se la re mandó	. Lo van a boletear", le
sus dos hermanas cuando se	le acercó un hombre que le disparó	directamente a la cabeza. El
era cariñoso, hincha de Central,	le gustaba la fotografía y la escritura	. Características de una vida que
las inmediaciones del lugar donde	se concreto el arresto y se comprobó	que se habría registrado una
parte de atrás, salió acelerando,	se golpeó la cabeza y se murió	desnucado". "Los policías lo hicieron
tapado, me tira el papel,	se toca la cintura y me dice	«No te mato porque no
causándole una grave lesión. Además	le dio una paliza y la estranguló	. De todo ello Laura fue
edificio. 'Le taparon la cara,	le ataron los pies y lo golpearon	', dijo el encargado en LT

Fig. 7. Search with Locate when applying the grammar in Fig. 6

In row four, there is an ambiguity, since the phrase *la escritura*, may have a structure of determiner+noun, 'the writing', but it might also be analyzed as a pronominal clitic (direct object), which in Spanish precedes the verb, plus the present tense third person singular of the verb *escriturar*, 'to register the deed (of a property)'. This ambiguity forces us to add more constraints to our grammar, that is, not to include only a generic clitic CL, but to specify what clitics can precede pronominal transitive verbs. Second-sentence modified grammar[5] is displayed in Fig. 8:

---

[5] We also added the full stop at the end of the graph through <P>.

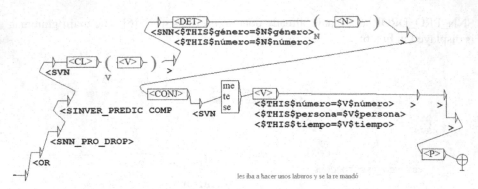

les iba a hacer unos laburos y se la re mandó

Fig. 8. Modified grammar for the second sentence

Thanks to this correction, we achieved search results with a 100% accuracy level of match (Fig. 9).

que ya no tenía vigencia.	Le dieron la libertad pero se dispuso	el secuestro de la moto
con una gente de acá.	Les iba a hacer unos laburos y se la re mandó	. Lo van a boletear", le
las inmediaciones del lugar donde	se concreto el arresto y se comprobó	que se habría registrado una
parte de atrás, salió acelerando.	se golpeó la cabeza y se murió	desnucado". "Los policías lo hicieron
tapado, me tira el papel,	se toca la cintura y me dice	«No te mato porque no

Fig. 9. Search with Locate when applying the modified grammar of Fig. 8

3 Conclusions

This paper is concerned with analyzing the phenomenon of insecurity at a discourse level in a corpus made up of journalistic texts. We distinguished two semantic fields and noted how the expressions referring to the victim prevail over those referring to the role of the State, and consequently, how the idea of criminal "punishment" fades and produces a "feeling" of insecurity. Thus, in a certain way, there is a media construction of insecurity. This does not mean that insecurity events do not occur, but alludes to how the linguistic viewpoint from which they are discoursed produces an impact on the readers. Such impact is due to the fact that the role of the State is almost not discoursed, for journalistic texts only discourse on the perpetrator and the victim.

We cannot assure that the discourse of insecurity has been conceptualized as a whole, since we are giving a first approach to this complex phenomenon. Thus, we can only offer partial conclusions and provide some of its most relevant features:

- It focuses on the victim and the perpetrator as its main discursive figures;
- It presents specific terms, most of them coming from *lunfardo*, which as a marginal jargon attains a point of identification with the discourse of the perpetrator;
- It presents specific syntactic characteristics, since it recovers colloquial expressions, most of which are connected with orality.

In this paper we tried to gradually show the process of our analysis. First, we dealt with the selection of the corpus, and the enlargement of our dictionaries, by including new terms and tags. For instance, we have added some terms and idioms typical of Latin America and also some Rioplatense neologisms to our dictionaries, and tagged them accordingly. We have given a special place to *lunfardo*, whose cultural richness provides a more significant value to the Rioplatense Spanish linguistic resources available in our Spanish Module Argentina. Next, we designed grammars to account for idioms, taking into account Bès's [1] notion of nucleus verb phrase and validated the newly created grammars.

We would like to close our conclusions with a short reflection upon the aim of our research project undertaken by our Study Center (CETEHIPL) and concerned about the pedagogical application of NooJ. We would like to highlight the importance of creating new resources from dictionaries to grammars for the study of language use and of applying them to real texts, and to underline the opportunity to actively interact with real texts. NooJ becomes a useful tool to study Spanish in a language class, which is sometimes mostly influenced by outdated linguistic rules, or which mostly deals with traditional texts sometimes unknown to students. NooJ becomes useful when there is a disassociation between the language taught in class (at an institutional level in a broad sense) and the language used in everyday exchanges. Metaphorically speaking, we would say that students "do not feel they are spoken by the educational institution." The class methodology we propose here focuses on taking the language of students and turning it into our subject matter through its interaction with NooJ, by listening to what students say and how they say it, and on reflecting upon these issues. And above all, our class methodology focuses on banishing notions like "That is wrong" or "That is right", typical of an obsolete modernist paradigm that does not understand the circumstances and interests of the students. We propose inclusion and discussion, rather than suppression and ignorance.

References

1. Bès, G.G.: La phrase verbal noyau en français. Rech. Sur Le Fr. Parlé **15**, 273–358 Université de Provence (1999)
2. Gobello, J.: https://surdelsur.com/es/lunfardo-tango/
3. Guemureman, S., et al.: Rol de los medios de comunicación en el despliegue de los mecanismos de control social, proactivos y reactivos. Legitimación de la violencia estatal contra los jóvenes pobres y su vinculación discursiva con la "delincuencia". In: VI Jornadas de Sociología de la UNLP, 9 y 10 de diciembre de 2010, Ensenada, Argentina. Memoria Académica (2010). https://memoria.fahce.unlp.edu.ar/trab_eventos/ev.5699/ev.5699.pdf
4. Diccionario de la real academia española. https://dle.rae.es/
5. Rodrigo, A., Reyes, S., Bonino, R.: Some aspects concerning the automatic treatment of adjectives and adverbs in Spanish: a pedagogical application of the NooJ platform. In: Mbarki, S., Mourchid, M., Silberztein, M. (eds.) NooJ 2017. CCIS, vol. 811, pp. 130–140. Springer, Cham (2018). https://doi.org/10.1007/978-3-319-73420-0_11
6. Rodrigo, A., Monteleone, M., Reyes, S.: A pedagogical application of NooJ in language teaching: the adjective in Spanish and Italian. COLING 2018, Santa Fe, New-Mexico, USA, 20–26 August 2018 (2018). http://aclweb.org/anthology/W18-3807

7. Rodrigo, A., Reyes, S., Mota, C., Barreiro, A.: Causal discourse connectors in the teaching of spanish as a foreign language (SLF) for portuguese learners using NooJ. In: Fehri, H., Mesfar, S., Silberztein, M. (eds.) NooJ 2019. CCIS, vol. 1153, pp. 161–172. Springer, Cham (2020). https://doi.org/10.1007/978-3-030-38833-1_14

8. Rodrigo, A., Bonino, R.: Aprendo con NooJ: de la Lingüística Computacional a la Enseñanza de la lengua. Editorial Ciudad Gótica, Rosario (2019)

9. Silberztein, M.: Formalizing Natural Languages: *The NooJ Approach*. ISTE-Wiley, London (2016)

10. https://www.lacapital.com.ar/

11. https://www.pagina12.com.ar/suplementos/rosario12

12. https://www.elciudadanoweb.com/

13. Contursi, P.: Mi noche triste. https://www.musixmatch.com/es/letras/Carlos-Gardel/Mi-Noche-Triste

14. Spanish Module Argentina. http://www.nooj4nlp.org/resources.html. Accessed 01 Sep 2022

Analyzing Political Discourse: Finding the Frames for Guilt and Responsibility

Krešimir Šojat[1] and Kristina Kocijan[2]

[1] Department of Linguistics, Faculty of Humanities and Social Sciences, University of Zagreb, Zagreb, Croatia
ksojat@ffzg.hr
[2] Department of Information and Communication Sciences, Faculty of Humanities and Social Sciences, University of Zagreb, Zagreb, Croatia
krkocijan@ffzg.hr

Abstract. This paper deals with the analysis of political discourse in Croatia, more precisely, it aims to determine how dissatisfaction is expressed with the attitudes represented by political rivals. We focus on the detection of linguistic means used to show disagreement with decisions or actions taken by parties or individuals considered political and/or ideological opponents. We are particularly interested in the means used by speakers to indicate that someone has failed to do something that is under his/her responsibility and is, therefore, guilty of this omission. In other words, we want to determine how the concept of responsibility is lexicalized, how it is signaled that there is a failure in someone's responsibility, and, finally, that someone is therefore to be blamed for that omission or even transgression. For this purpose, we use a large corpus of texts, with over 127 million tokens, consisting of transcripts of plenary debates from the Croatian Parliament since 2003. We use NooJ for the construction of a set of rules that aim to detect the usage of the Croatian lexemes *odgovornost* [responsibility] and *krivnja* [guilt] in this corpus. Since Croatian is rich in terms of word formation, a set of rules is designed to capture the usage of derived words morphologically related to these nouns. In data analysis, we take into account the political orientation of MPs, i.e. their affiliation with left, right, or centrist parties, the usage of various linguistic constructions/frames related to responsibility and guilt as well as periods in which they were used.

Keywords: Guilt vs responsibility · Language patterns · Political discourse · Linguistic approach · Croatian parliament · Syntactic grammar · Croatian · NooJ

1 Introduction

The analysis of various forms of communication that explicitly or implicitly convey political ideas has long played a prominent role in social sciences and humanities. In the last thirty years, such research has received significant impetus from the development of methods that enable more exact and formal approaches.

M. González et al. (Eds.): NooJ 2022, CCIS 1758, pp. 127–138, 2022.
https://doi.org/10.1007/978-3-031-23317-3_11

In this work, we deal with the analysis of political discourse in Croatia. We are interested in the way in which members of the Croatian Parliament express their dissatisfaction with certain opinions, decisions, or moves made by other members of the Parliament. More precisely, we want to determine how dissatisfaction is expressed with the attitudes represented by political rivals. We focus on the detection of linguistic means used to show disagreement with decisions or actions taken by parties or individuals considered political and/or ideological opponents.

We start from the assumption that it is within the domain of someone's responsibility to conscientiously and properly perform a certain duty or task. Deliberate or accidental omissions in such actions provoke a revolt among speakers and they blame political opponents for these omissions or failures. This game of blaming and blame denying seems to be at the center of most political talks, thus it is expected to find it in parliamentary speeches as well. We are particularly interested in the linguistic means (for a more philosophical approach to this question, cf. Zimmerman 1985) used by speakers to indicate that someone has done or has failed to do something that is under his/her responsibility and is, therefore, guilty of this omission. In other words, we want to determine how the concept of responsibility is lexicalized, how it is signaled that there is a failure in someone's responsibility, and, finally, that someone is therefore to be blamed for that omission or even transgression.

The remainder of this chapter is presented in five sections. We first provide additional context in this area of research and then give more information on the Croatian language to bring this issue closer. Language descriptions are then followed by a graphical representation of a language model design and examples that the model detected in the corpus. We conclude with a short discussion of our findings and plans for some future work.

2   Previous Work

The topic of responsibility and guilt attribution within the political arena has been widely addressed from several different angles. To demonstrate the importance of the topic and provide a context in which NLP can facilitate similar future research, we will mention a few of these angles. While our approach will consider how politicians attribute responsibility and guilt among themselves, Tilley and Hobolt (2011) were interested in political responsibility attribution (regarding economy and healthcare) from the perspective of a **voter**. Their results show that partisanship influences voters' interpretation of guilt/responsibility and that they will mostly adjust their perception to be in line with their party preferences.

A few years later, Nielsen and Moynihan (2017) were more interested to learn how **politicians** attribute responsibility to the bureaucrats under their supervision. Their findings suggest that judgment on what bureaucrats may be held accountable for is dependent on the party preference of a politician, in their case, conservative vs liberal. Furthermore, they emphasize that guilt in the context of blaming someone, is the extension step i.e. the step that follows the responsibility attribution. What seems to be the common understanding for both groups (voters and politicians) is that they are more generous to individuals or parties that share the same ideological beliefs as them. This is in support of a theory that partisanship acts as what Tilley and Hobolt (2011) term a *perceptual screen* that shapes the final assessment of responsibility/guilt attribution.

A similar observation was made by Damstra *et al.* (2021) who reported on how readers were influenced by the exposure to **news** that blamed the government for a specific economic situation vs the news where the government was credited for the situation. Interestingly, only the readers from the first scenario adopted the frame of blame and as a result gave more negative evaluations of the government, while the second scenario did not affect the readers' opinion. Such behavior is attributed to the (easier to change) external influences of news on those exposed to it compared to one's (more stable) personal political values which are characterized as the internal factor. In addition, Damstra *et al.* (2021) find an explanation of this phenomenon in the theory of negativity effect which states that negative information carries more weight than positive one of the same extreme.

3   About the Language and the Corpus

3.1   Croatian Language Specifics

As in other Slavic languages, Croatian morphology is rich both in terms of inflection and word-formation processes (cf. Babić 1991; Šojat *et al.* 2013). Whereas inflection is almost exclusively based on suffixation, word-formation processes consist of compounding, derivation, and various combinations of compounding and derivation. The main difference between compounding and derivation is that the former involves at least two stems, whereas the latter is based on only one stem. Affixes used in derivational processes are prefixes and suffixes. As mentioned, word-formation processes can also consist of simultaneous combinations of compounding and affixation.

In this research, we primarily focus on word formation, i.e. the rules constructed in NooJ are based on derivation. To detect how the concepts of *blame* and *responsibility* are lexicalized, we designed one set of rules that are based on the noun *odgovornost*, and the other set that is based on *krivnja* (and its synonym *krivica*). These nouns are derived via suffixation from adjectives: *odgovornost* from *odgovoran* [responsible], and *krivnja* from *kriv* [guilty]. The noun *krivac* [culprit, lawbreaker, wrongdoer] is also derived from the adjective *kriv*, whereas there is no similar noun derived from the adjective *odgovoran*.

Syntactically, nouns appear mostly as subject, predicate nominatives with copula *to be* and object as well as subject complements. There are seven cases in Croatian. Generally, subjects and predicate nominatives appear in the nominative case, whereas other syntactic functions take oblique cases. The nouns we mentioned can be:

a)   subjects, e.g.: *Krivac za taj propust dolazi iz vaše stranke.* [The **culprit** for that omission comes from your party.],

b)   nominative parts of predicates, e.g.: *Vi ste krivac za taj propust.* [You are the **culprit** for that omission.],

c)   subject complements, e.g.: *Vi ste postali jedini krivac za taj propust.* [You became the only **culprit** for that omission.],

d)   object complements, e.g.: *Ja vas smatram krivcem za taj propust.* [I find you **guilty** of that omission. Literally: I find you to be the **culprit** for this omission.].

Although Croatian is basically an SVO (subject-verb-object) language, due to its inflectional morphology word order can vary, especially in spoken language (see examples (1) through (6)).

*Vi ste **krivac** za taj propust.—* You are the **culprit** for this omission.   (1)

*Za taj propust vi ste **krivac**.—* For this omission, you are the **culprit**.   (2)

*Za taj ste propust vi **krivac**.—* literally: For this omission are you the **culprit**.   (3)

*Za taj propust **krivac** ste vi.—* literally: For this omission the **culprit** are you.   (4)

*Za taj ste propust **krivac** vi.—* literally: For this are omission the **culprit** you.   (5)

***Krivac** za taj propust ste vi.—* literally: The **culprit** for this omission are you.   (6)

There are even more possible combinations that could be constructed or invented within this simple sentence, but these examples will suffice to illustrate our point: in spoken discourse, the order of words or constituents can vary and constituents can frequently be discontinuous. These facts are taken into account in the construction of the final algorithm.

Semantically, all derivatives of the adjective *odgovoran* [responsible] refer to the concept of responsibility. As mentioned, these derivatives are the noun *odgovornost* [responsibility] and the adverb *odgovorno* [responsibly].

On the other hand, the adjective *kriv* [guilty] is a polysemous lexeme that, apart from this sense, also has senses such as "bent", "wrong", "sorry" etc. However, the meaning of its derivatives that are here taken into consideration – *krivnja* and its synonym *krivica* [guilt] as well as *krivac* [culprit, lawbreaker, wrongdoer] – refer solely to the concept of guilt.

Further in this work, we primarily concentrate on the nouns *krivnja* [guilt] and *odgovornost* [responsibility]. Detailed analysis of the use of adjectives *kriv* and *responsible* within the same Corpus is given in Kocijan and Šojat (2022).

3.2 Croatian Parliament Corpus

For our research, we use a large corpus of texts, with over 127 million tokens consisting of transcripts of plenary debates from the Croatian Parliament from 2003 up to 2021. These debates are freely available on the Croatian Parliament website[1] under the Open Government Data policy. Each speech includes information on the legislative term (hr. *Saziv*), meeting (hr. *Sjednica*), date, the agenda item number (hr. *točka dnevnog reda*), the full title of an agenda item (hr. *Naslov točke dnevnog reda*), MP's name and party affiliation, and the text of his/her speech (Kocijan and Šojat 2022).

---

[1] Hrvatski Sabor, informacijsko-dokumentacijska služba - https://edoc.sabor.hr/

We find similar corpora for other languages like the TAPS-fr corpus of French parliamentary speech (Diwersy *et al.* 2018), the Bundestag corpus of German parliament speech (Biessmann *et al.* 2016), the Hansard corpus of English speeches in the UK House of Commons (Abercrombie and Batista-Navarro 2018), the Hansard corpora of English spoken in the Canadian, Australian, and New Zealand parliaments, as well as the EuroParl corpus, which, in addition to English, provides parallel data on the European Parliament in 24 official languages (Proksch and Slapin 2009; Nanni *et al.* 2021, *inter alia*) or the most recent one, the ParlaMint[2] Corpora that includes 17 European national parliaments annotated after Universal Dependency formalism (Erjavec *et al.* 2022). All this data facilitates a diversity of research questions in political science, sociology, and as of recently, in linguistics as well. The existing corpora are also prepared in different formats, including TXM, CWB, TAPS, XML, and others depending on the approach each study takes.

Although the language is a multi-layered system, non-linguistic dimensions (e.g., gestures, pauses, facial expressions) were not taken into account for this specific research (although such an investigation would further contribute to our understanding of political space). The full Croatian Parliament Corpus – CroParlCor contains 127,263,579 tokens and is constructed out of six files, each corresponding to one full legislative term from 2003 up to 2021. Each legislative term has a different length in months and size i.e. number of tokens (Kocijan and Šojat 2022).

For the purpose of this paper, members of the Parliament are divided into three groups. These groups consist of speakers that are, according to their political orientation, grouped into left, centrist, or right parties[3].

4   Design of the Language Models

In order to determine how we express that something is within the domain of someone's responsibility and/or that someone has failed to do something or has done something wrong, we use the NooJ platform (Silberztein 2016) to create rules designed to detect linguistic constructions used for this purpose. More precisely, we use NooJ for the construction of a set of rules that primarily aim to detect the usage of the Croatian lexemes *odgovornost* [responsibility] and *krivnja* [guilt] in this corpus.

The rules are designed to take into account derivationally related lexemes to Croatian nouns *odgovornost* [responsibility] and *krivnja* [guilt] and relatively free word order in sentences characteristic of spoken language, as recorded in parliamentary debates.

---

[2] ParlaMint includes a subset of Croatian Parliament, specifically the 9th term dating from November 2016 to May 2020, with a total of 20.65 million words (Erjavec *et al.* 2022).

[3] **Left** (ASH, DA, Demokrati, HRLaburisti, HSD, IDF, IDS, ISDF, MB365, Možemo!, NL, Orah, Pametno, RF, SDAH, SDH, SDP, SDSH, SDU, SMSH, Snaga, SNS, SSH, ŽZ); **Right** (Blok za hrvatsku, Domovinski pokret, HČSP, HDS, HDSSB, HDZ, HGS, HIP, HKDS, HKDU, HKS, HNDL, HRAST, HRID, Hrvatski Suverenisti, HSP, NHR); **Center** (Abeceda, BDSH, BUZ, Centar, DC, Fokus, GLAS, HND, HNS, HSLS, HSS, HSU, LIBRA, LS, MDS, MOST, Naprijed Hrvatska, NLM, Novi val, NP, NS-R, Promijenimo Hrvatsku, Reformisti, SDSS, SIP, Stranka s imenom i prezimenom, Stranka rada).

To sum up, rules are designed to take into consideration:

- relatively free word order in Croatian
- syntactic functions such as subject and object are marked morphologically
- subject and object can appear in various positions in sentences – although SVO is a normal order
- phrases can be discontinuous - e.g. with complex verb tenses – subjects can appear between auxiliary and main verbs, etc.

4.1 Language Model for 'Responsibility'

The meaning of *odgovornost* is a state of being responsible i.e. conscientiously fulfilling one's duty and doing the work for the results for which one takes responsibility. To learn what verbs *responsibility* co-occurs with, we have designed a preliminary syntactic grammar allowing us to detect different patterns i.e. the distance between a verb and a noun may range from 0 up to 4 words (see Fig. 1).

In Fig. 1. There is a node marked **V** that holds a set of verbs found in the vicinity of the noun *odgovornost* [responsibility] in our corpus. These verbs have been grouped into categories marking different levels of behavior or one's perception towards *responsibility* (e.g. it is marked as different if someone is **demanding** responsibility from someone *vs* if it is **calling for** it, or if it is **sharing** responsibility *vs* **turning** it **over to** someone else, or if one was **relieved from** it *vs* it was **taken away from** someone). However, we have not explored this option further at this time due to the length restrictions, but we plan to build upon it in future projects.

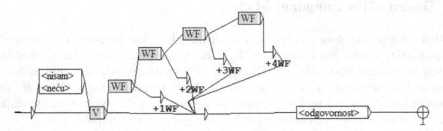

Fig. 1. Preliminary syntactic grammar for detecting the closest verb to the noun '*odgovornost*' [responsibility].

The simple design of the preliminary graph (Fig. 1) allowed us to recognize examples like those given in (7) through (10) that demonstrate different numbers of words that can be found between the verb and a noun *odgovornost*.

[*Vlada*] **nosi odgovornost** . . . - [Government] **carries responsibility**   (7)

[ne može] **umanjiti** *njihovu* **odgovornost**... - [can not] **reduce** their **responsibility**   (8)

[*mi*] **snosimo** *svoj dio* **odgovornosti** . . . - [we] **bear** our share of **responsibility**   (9)

[trebala bi] **postojati** *ista razina financijske* **odgovornosti** ... - [there should] **exist** the same level
of financial **responsibility**   (10)

After a thorough analysis of the results obtained with the preliminary grammar
(Fig. 1), including the false positive ones, we were able to redesign it with more complex
but also better-suited patterns (Fig. 2). With this new design, we were additionally able to
detect a set of prepositions that are found after the noun *responsibility*. This information
gives us better insight into the direction of responsibility, i.e. who/what is it for, from
whom it is expected, or for which reason it is expected of someone (for more details see
the section on *Discussion of results*).

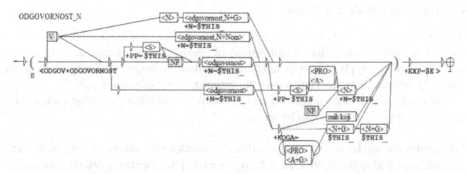

Fig. 2. Augmented syntactic grammar for *'odgovornost'* [responsibility].

Figure 2 shows two main paths of which the first must start with a verb and the other
one excludes it completely. If the graph starts by first recognizing a verb, it can branch
out into 5 possible paths marked with letters *a* through *e*, each of which can have one or
more endings marked with letters *i* through *iv*. However, if the graph excludes the verb,
it can only branch out through paths marked with letters *c* through *e* as defined in the
following list:

a. any noun + *odgovornost*_Genitive
    i.   empty
b. *odgovornost*_Nominative
    i.   empty
    ii. prepositional phrase
c. preposition + *odgovornost*
    i.   empty
    ii. prepositional phrase
d. preposition + Noun Phrase + *odgovornost*
    i.   empty
    ii.   prepositional phrase
    iii. *onih koji*
    iv.   Noun Phrase_Genitive
    v.   Noun Phrase_Genitive + Noun Phrase_Genitive

e. *odgovornost*
   i.   prepositional phrase
   ii. *onih koji*
   iii. Noun Phrase_Genitive
   iv. Noun Phrase_Genitive + Noun Phrase_Genitive

All the recognized examples are annotated with a tag <**ODGOV**>. Similarly, the examples for guilt will be tagged as <**KRIV**>. These annotations will allow us to perform statistical comparison of their usage within each prepared corpus (see section on *Discussion of results*).

4.2 Language Model for 'Guilt'

We have decided to mark occurrences of 3 nouns *krivnja, and krivica* but also *krivac* (culprit, malefactor) as different realizations of 'guilt'. As mentioned, analysis of the adjective *kriv* [guilty] is given separately (cf. Kocijan and Šojat 2022) since it requires a slightly different approach due to its polysemic structure of meaning.

All three nouns that are dealt with in this research are defined within the node named '**krivci**' (Fig. 3) and they can be found:

(a) between a modal verb (defined within the **ModVerbs** node) and the main verb (defined within the **K_Verbs | K_O_Verbs | O_Verbs | Verb** nodes),
(b) after the main verb or
(c) just in front of the main verb (but not including the modal verb).

In all of these cases, there can be 0 up to 4 words (defined within the **WF** node) in between.

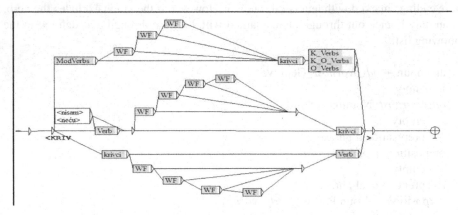

Fig. 3. Main syntactic grammar for '*krivnja, krivica, krivac*'.

Syntactic grammar (Fig. 3) recognizes examples as found in (11) through (13) responding to the patterns (a) through (c) as described in the previous paragraph. All the recognized examples are annotated with a tag <**KRIV**>.

(a) *mora nečiju* **krivnju** *dokazati* – literally: must someone's **guilt** prove   (11)

(b) *govori o ukidanju* **krivnji** – literally: talks about suppressing **guilt**   (12)

(c) **krivaca** *za to nema* – literally: **culprits** for that aren't   (13)

5 Discussion of Results

Our data reveals that the most used preposition after the noun 'responsibility' is *za* [for]. This preposition appears in almost 48% of detected cases (for the comparison, the same preposition is used 71.3% after the adjective 'responsible' in the same corpus, which makes it the most used preposition in this case as well). Preposition *for* is followed by preposition *na* [at] with almost 16% occurrences, *u* [in] with almost 11%, and *prema* [towards] with almost 8%. Other prepositions are found in 3% of cases or less and they are *sa, pred, nad, kao, zbog, po, kod, do, nakon, od, kroz, glede*.

The most frequently used verb with the noun 'responsibility' is the verb *preuzeti* [to take over], followed by *imati* [to have], *snositi* [to carry the weight of], and *govoriti o* [to talk about]. The distribution of these verbs is somewhat different depending on the party orientation (Fig. 4 – top three graphs).

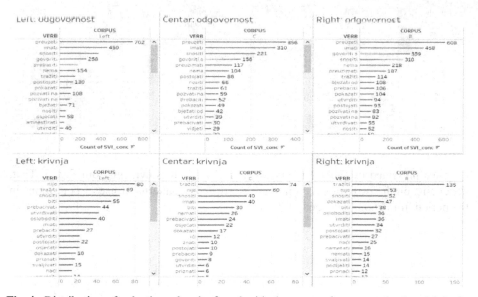

Fig. 4. Distribution of selection of verbs found with the noun *odgovornost* (top) and *krivnja* (bottom) in the left *vs* center *vs* right party orientation.

The top 3 verbs appearing with 'guilt' are *nije* [is not], *tražiti* [to ask for], and *snositi* [to bear] in all three sets of data, although their order is different for the center and right-oriented parties (Fig. 4. - bottom section).

The preliminary results reveal that, in general, there are more occurrences of *responsibility* (83%) than *guilt* (17%) in the corpus, but also that the right-oriented parties subset uses both terms slightly more frequently than either left or centrist subsets. Interestingly, the distribution of both terms (*responsibility* and *guilt*) in all three corpora is 39% (right-oriented parties), 38% (left-oriented parties), and 23% (center-oriented parties).

Further analysis shows that, throughout the given timeline and within each subset, there are periods in which *blame* is used more frequently than in other periods and that there are parties that look for whom to *blame* rather than for those who are *responsible*. While the center-oriented parties talked dominantly more about responsibility only during one time period (see Table 1 Middle section, a period marked C_2016_9), left-oriented MPs have done so during 10 periods (Table 1, left section) and right-oriented 11 periods (Table 1, right section). Both left and center-oriented MPs have talked dominantly more about *guilt* during 5 time periods and right-oriented MPs during 9 time periods. The year 2017 is especially interesting since both left and center-oriented parties have statistically significant [SS] score for talking about *guilt*, while at the same time, right-oriented parties have SS score for talking about *responsibility*.

Table 1. Measures[4] on blame vs guilt usage for each corpus per year.

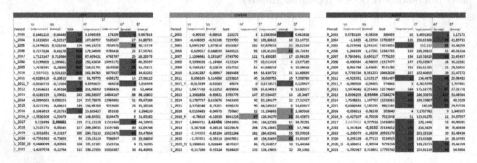

Data presented in Table 1 is visualized in Fig. 5. It is evident from Fig. 5. That, depending on the party orientation, there are different patterns of use of both terms in the period from 2003 to the end of 2021.

---

[4] SS – standard score; AF – absolute frequency in the section; EF – expected frequency in the section.

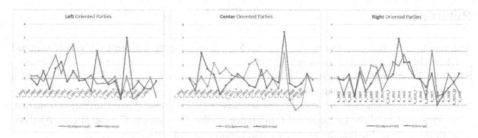

Fig. 5. Distribution of *responsibility* vs *guilt* usage within each corpus (Left vs Center vs Right Oriented Parties) per year.

The area between positive and negative value 2 is considered to be within the expected or normal distribution while statistically significant occurrences cross that line in either position. A positively high SS score for *responsibility* is detected only once for left-oriented parties (during the year 2010), and once for right-oriented parties (during 2017) while the high SS for *guilt* is detected once in each corpus (in 2017 for left and center-oriented parties and 2013 for right-oriented parties).

Although it is not our intention to provide answers as to why is the guilt/responsibility term dominantly used in specific periods or by specific parties, we believe that by detecting these occurrences we provide valuable data for further investigations in communicology but also in philosophy, sociology, and psychology (cf. Shaver 1985).

6 Conclusion

This project is based on the assumption that it is within the domain of someone's responsibility to conscientiously and properly perform a certain duty or task. Deliberate or accidental omissions in such actions provoke a revolt among speakers and they blame political opponents for these omissions or failures. A subset of rules is designed in order to capture the usage patterns related to nouns *odgovornost* (responsibility) and *krivnja* (guilt) within the large corpus consisting of transcripts from the Croatian Parliament but taking into account the MP's party orientation (Left vs Center vs Right).

In general, our results reveal that there are more occurrences of **responsibility** than **guilt** in the entire corpus and that the right-oriented party subset uses both terms more than the left or centrist subsets. However, the analysis also shows that within each subset, there are parties that look at who should feel the guilt rather than the responsibility, that there are periods in which guilt is used significantly more frequently than responsibility, but also vice versa. Answers as to why we detected such patterns we leave to those more versed in providing sociological, psychological, communicational or philosophical answers.

Acknowledgments. We are indebted to several student assistants at the Faculty of Humanities and Social Sciences who participated in the various phases of this study.

References

Abercrombie, G., Batista-Navarro, R.: 'Aye' or 'No'? Speech-level sentiment analysis of Hansard UK parliamentary debate transcripts (2018)

Babić, S.: Tvorba riječi u hrvatskom književnom jeziku [nacrt za gramatiku]. Hrvatska akademija znanosti i umjetnosti. Globus, Zagreb (1991)

Biessmann, F., Lehmann, P., Kirsch, D., Schelter, S.: Predicting political party affiliation from text. In: Proceedings of the International Conference on the Advances in Computational Analysis of Political Text (PolText 2016), Dubrovnik, Croatia, pp. 14–19 (2016)

Damstra, A., Boukes, M., Vliegenthart, R.: To Credit or to blame? The asymmetric impact of government responsibility in economic news. Int. J. Public Opin. Res. **33**(1), 1–17 (2021). https://doi.org/10.1093/ijpor/edz054

Diwersy, S., Frontini, F., Luxardo, G.: The parliamentary debates as a resource for the textometric study of the French political discourse. In: Proceedings of the ParlaCLARIN@LREC2018 Workshop 2018, Miyazaki, Japan (2018). https://hal.archives-ouvertes.fr/hal-01832649/document

Erjavec, T., Ogrodniczuk, M., Osenova, P., et al.: The ParlaMint corpora of parliamentary proceedings. Lang. Resour. Eval. (2022). https://doi.org/10.1007/s10579-021-09574-0

Kocijan, K., Šojat, K.: Negation usage in the Croatian parliament. In: Bigey, M., Richeton, A., Silberztein, M., Thomas, I. (eds.) Formalizing Natural Languages: Applications to Natural Language Processing and Digital Humanities. CCIS, vol. 1520, pp. 101–113. Springer, Cham (2021). https://doi.org/10.1007/978-3-030-92861-2_9

Kocijan, K., Šojat, K.: Who is guilty and who is responsible in the Croatian parliament: a linguistic approach. In: Misuraca, M., Scepi, G., Spano, M. (eds.) Proceedings of the 16th International Conference on Statistical Analysis of Textual Data, Naples, Italy, pp. 503–510. Vadistat Press (2022)

Nanni, F., Glavaš, G., Rehbein, I., Ponzetto, S.P., Stuckenschmidt, H.: Political text scaling meets computational semantics (2021). https://arxiv.org/pdf/1904.06217.pdf

Nielsen, P.A., Moynihan, D.P.: How do politicians attribute bureaucratic responsibility for performance? Negativity bias and interest group advocacy. J. Public Adm. Res. Theory **27**(2), 269–283 (2017). https://doi.org/10.1093/jopart/muw060

Proksch, S.O., Slapin, J.B.: Position taking in European parliament speeches. Br. J. Polit. Sci. **40**(3), 587–611 (2010). http://www.jstor.org/stable/40930601

Shaver, K.G.: The Attribution of Blame: Springer Series in Social Psychology. Springer, New York (1985). https://doi.org/10.1007/978-1-4612-5094-4

Silberztein, M.: Formalizing Natural Languages: The NooJ Approach, Cognitive Science Series. Wiley-ISTE, London (2016)

Šojat, K., Srebačić, M., Štefanec, V.: CroDeriV i morfološka raščlamba hrvatskoga glagola. Suvremena lingvistika, Zagreb, Croatia, pp. 75–96 (2013). https://hrcak.srce.hr/clanak/155178

Tilley, J., Hobolt, S.B.: Is the government to blame? An experimental test of how partisanship shapes perceptions of performance and responsibility. J. Polit. **73**(2), 316–330 (2011). https://doi.org/10.1017/S0022381611000168

Zimmerman, M.J.: Sharing responsibility. Am. Philos. Q. **22**(2), 115–122 (1985). https://www.jstor.org/stable/20014087

Creation of Parallel Medical and Social Domains Corpora for the Machine Translation and Speech Synthesis Systems

Mikita Suprunchuk[1]([✉]), Nastassia Yarash[2], Yuras Hetsevich[2],
Valery Varanovich[3], Siarhey Gaidurau[2], Yauheniya Zianouka[2],
and Palina Sakava[2]

[1] Minsk State Linguistic University, Zakharov Str. 21, Minsk, Belarus
ssrlab221@gmail.com
[2] United Institute of Informatics Problems, Surhanava Str. 6, Minsk, Belarus
[3] Belarusian State University, Nezavisimosti Av. 4, Minsk, Belarus

Abstract. This paper represents the procedure of creating medical and social domains corpora in NooJ. It illustrates a primary analysis of the corpora. Based on the research, the Belarusian NooJ module has been supplemented and thematic dictionaries of medical and social areas in NooJ format have been prepared. Automatic text processing emphasized words' linguistic peculiarities (mainly morphological) that the main module of Belarusian language for NooJ did not recognize. In addition, the article shows how the corpora help to improve the quality of translation, to identify heterogeneous translation options.

Keywords: Automatic language processing · Corpus of a medical domain · Corpus of a social domain · Dictionary · NooJ · Concordance · Belarusian · Russian · English

1 First Section Introduction

In the Republic of Belarus, Belarusian and Russian have the status of official languages. Since there is bilingualism at the legislative level, it is necessary to provide the availability of texts for different purposes in both official languages. O7ne of the important purposes is public education in medical and social fields.

Medical and social texts contain essential information. The first are intended to convey information between health professionals and scientists (for example, in articles, research papers) or to educate and inform the population about public and personal health. Meanwhile, the second group represents the historical and cultural heritage of Belarus and is aimed at acquainting country visitors with it.

Therefore, the need for a system of machine translation and speech synthesis in Belarusian and Russian is still relevant. Based on the above, there is a data layer of mentioned domains poorly covered with such systems, which, in turn, require large parallel corpora for their training [3, 7]. At the moment, there are no large parallel corpora, which include Belarusian, on open access. As a result, the first step in the machine translation and speech synthesis development may be the creation of

© Springer Nature Switzerland AG 2022
M. González et al. (Eds.): NooJ 2022, CCIS 1758, pp. 139–150, 2022.
https://doi.org/10.1007/978-3-031-23317-3_12

corresponding corpora (cf., for example, [5, 8]. Using the existing proofreading and word processing services and NooJ corpora processor [6], it is possible to work with big data to further use it to train machine translation systems and the speech synthesis systems as well. Thus, the access to texts of medical and social domains in both official languages in Belarus and English, a language of global communication, will be obtained by a significant number of people.

Currently, Speech Synthesis and Recognition Laboratory of the United Institute of Informatics Problems (further on—Laboratory; https://ssrlab.by/en/) works at creating corpora of medical and social domains. At this stage, a medical corpus consisting of 848 parallel texts in Belarusian (303,469 word forms), English (373,709 word forms) and Russian (330,996 word forms) has been compiled. In addition, a corresponding parallel corpus of social domain based on parallel texts in Belarusian, English and Russian from the KrokApp travel audio guide [4] was created (cf. Table 1).

2   Compilation of a Medical and Social Domain Corpus

For the corpora of medical and social domains, original texts from Internet resources and online programs were collected. First of all, materials provided on the websites of polyclinics and hospitals in Minsk. They are:

- 1st Central district clinical polyclinic of the Central district of Minsk, http://www.1crp.by/en/home (Fig. 1);
- 4th City clinical hospital named after Mikalaj Saŭčanka, https://4gkb.by;
- Health Department of the Minsk City Executive Committee, https://komzdrav-minsk.gov.by/en/about-committee.

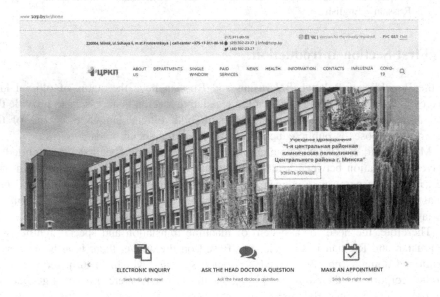

Fig. 1.   The official website of the 1st Central District clinical polyclinic of the Central District of Minsk.

Also the texts from websites and mobile applications KrokApp (https://krokapp.com) and Krokam (https://krokam.com) for tourists and local historians were added [4].

The Laboratory staff work on the content of enumerated medical and travel websites, translate articles, news and maintain them. We received and used these materials for the corpora: current news, instructions, rules, and other information from medical institutions, and essays on the history and interesting objects in different settlements of Belarus from museums and the Institute of History of the Academy of Sciences. Most of the texts were in Russian, some in Belarusian. The texts were translated into Belarusian and English and uploaded to the appropriate platforms. Naturally, the translations were checked by the editor and the person responsible for the project. The medical corpus of 303,469 word forms and history and social corpus of 61,827 word forms were translated.

Figure 2 shows a fragment of parallel texts in Belarusian, English, Russian from the corpus of social texts.

[BE]У горадзе Лунінцы ў 1911–1912 гадах жыў і працаваў Якуб Колас – знакаміты беларускі пісьменнік, паэт і перакладчык. Адзін з класікаў і заснавальнікаў новай беларускай літаратуры. Пра гэта нагадвае турыстам і падарожнікам мемарыяльная дошка, усталяваная на будынку мясцовага краязнаўчага музея. Якуб Колас(Канстанцін Міхайлавіч Міцкевіч) нарадзіўся ў 1882 годзе ў вёсцы Акінчыцы на Стаўбцоўшчыне ў сямі лесніка. У 1902 годзе ён скончыў Нясвіжскую настаўніцкую семінарыю. У 19021906 гадах працаваў настаўнікам на Палессі і на Міншчыне. За ўдзел у нелегальным настаўніцкім зездзе быў звольнены з працы, а ў 1908 годзе асуджаны на тры гады турэмнага зняволення.

[EN]Jakub Kolas, a famous Belarusian writer, poet and translator, lived and worked in Luniniec in 1911–1912. Jakub Kolas is one of the classics and founders of the new Belarusian literature. A memorial plaque installed on the building of the museum of local lore reminds tourists and travelers about this. Jakub Kolas (Kanstancin Michajlavič Mickievič) was born in 1882 in the village of Akinčycy in the Stoŭbcy Region in a family of a forester. In 1902, he graduated from the Niasviž Teacher Seminary. In 19021906 he worked as a teacher in Paliessie and in the Minsk Region. He was dismissed from work for participation in an illegal teachers congress, and in 1908 convicted to three years in prison.

[RU]В городе Лунинец в 1911–1912 годах жил и работал Якуб Колас – знаменитый белорусский писатель, поэт и переводчик. Один из классиков и основателей новой белорусской литературы. Про это напоминает туристам и путешественникам мемориальная доска, установленная на здании местного краеведческого музея. Якуб Колас (Константин Михайлович Мицкевич) родился в 1882 году в деревне Акинчицы на Столбцовщине в семье лесника. В 1902 году он закончил Несвижскую учительскую семинарию. В 19021906 годах работал учителем на Полесье и на Минщине. За участие в нелегальном учительском съезде был уволен с работы, а в 1908 году осуждён на три года тюремного заключения.

Fig. 2. Parallel texts in Belarusian, English, Russian from the corpus of social texts.

The texts described above have become the basis for the creation of the main corpora. Manual text proofreading and correction of errors was accomplished sequentially by some editors, qualified linguists and historians are among them. Before uploading them to NooJ, the following items were additionally checked by means of automatic services provided on the portal *corpus.by* [1]:

- spelling checking,
- analysis of statistical and supplemental information about all symbols in texts,
- analysis of statistics on the use of arbitrary symbolic sequences in an electronic text (counting the frequency of word forms),
- search and correction of errors in the spelling of the Belarusian letters "У" and "Ў",
- recognition and selection of homographs in the text.

Statistical data on the created corpora in NooJ is represented in Table 1.

Table 1. The statistics of medical and social corpora.

Unit	Medical corpus			Social corpus		
	BY	RU	EN	BY	RU	EN
Texts	848	848	848	386	386	386
Tokens	419,165	457,756	481,089	81,481	80,390	101,036
Word forms	303,469	330,996	373,709	61,827	61,085	81,651
Text units delimited by "\n"	32,969	37,398	32,952	4,168	4,172	4,082

The main linguistic peculiarities of the medical and social corpora are:

- There are more complex sentences than simple sentences.
- The noun is the most frequent part of speech.
- Some words are specific for this field, especially in medical texts. They should be added to the dictionary of NooJ. So, it was decided to compose and process the list of medical and social terms.

Slavic languages are flectional synthetic ones (except Bulgarian). Therefore, morphological features require great attention in the development of computer analyzers.

While creating the dictionary of corpora, a list of unknown words was defined. These are words that were not identified by the general_be dictionary of the Belarusian module [2] in NooJ). The list of unknown words was processed manually (Fig. 3). It includes these groups:

- Errors in the original texts. They are misprints, incorrect translations, missing spaces, Latin characters in the Belarusian or Russian texts, etc.;
- 2277 specific medical terms: *дыясталічны* 'diastolic', *колератэрапія* 'color therapy';
- 383 social terms: *лютаранскі* 'Lutheran', *плябанія* 'parsonage';
- Words and word forms that are not included in the Belarusian dictionary general_be.nod: *квартал* 'quarter', *заплечнік* 'backpack';
- English words and symbols: *Sunday, view, html*;
- Roman numerals: *IV, XI, XV*;
- Simple mistakes, punctuation or orthography: *магістарата (магістрата), адзаначыць (адзначыць), вядзяляецца (выдзяляецца)*;

- Words with an apostrophe (the apostrophe divides words into parts): *сур'ёзна*, *аб'ект*. Sometimes the apostrophe is a functional symbol, but in the Belarusian language it has the role of a letter, it does not separate words, it is a part of words;
- Words for which it was not possible to find an appropriate paradigm. For individual words and their categories, it was necessary to supplement the general dictionary of the Belarusian module and add new samples. These are words such as *адзёр* 'measles', *алеін* 'olein', *біскуп* 'bishop', *ваксігрып* 'Vaxigripp', *месціч* 'citizen', *пробашч* 'catholic priest', etc.

```
NooJ - [[Modified] Untitled]
File  Edit  Lab  Project  Windows  Info  DICTIONARY
Unknowns are 30 entries

# NooJ V7
# Dictionary
#
# Language is: be
#
# Alphabetical order is not required.
#
# Use inflectional & derivational paradigms' description files (.nof), e.g.:
# Special Command: #use paradigms.nof
#
# Special Features: +NW (non-word) +FXC (frozen expression component) +UNAMB (unambiguous lexical entry)
#                   +FLX= (inflectional paradigm) +DRV= (derivational paradigm)
#
# Special Characters: '\' '"' ' ' ',' '+' '-' '#'
#
ААН, UNKNOWN
алядашчання, UNKNOWN
врачом, UNKNOWN
г, UNKNOWN
герыятрам, UNKNOWN
герыятры, UNKNOWN
й, UNKNOWN
колькасьці, UNKNOWN
Мінску, UNKNOWN
нетранспартабельных, UNKNOWN
палі клінічнымі, UNKNOWN
паліклінічных, UNKNOWN
т, UNKNOWN
ТЦСАН, UNKNOWN
тэл, UNKNOWN
тэрапіі, UNKNOWN
тэрапія, UNKNOWN
УАЗ, UNKNOWN
устаноеам, UNKNOWN
```

Fig. 3. The list of unknown words in NooJ corpora.

English words, symbols and Roman numerals were omitted as these words should be processed separately in another research. Almost all words with an apostrophe were included in the list of general vocabulary.

3 Creating Medical and Social Trilingual Dictionaries in NooJ

Text corpora are a valuable knowledge source about language peculiarities. They allow monitoring of facts and tendencies that are difficult to notice by common speaking or reading. Lexical and grammatical elements of the Belarusian module in NooJ were used for the lexical and grammar marking of the medical and social corpus which was created by the specialists of the laboratory.

Further work on the dictionaries of medical and social terms consisted in the morphological markup of words selected from the medical corpus. The Paradigm Generator service on the corpus.by platform was used for this purpose [1]. In the processing window you need to enter a word (or several forms) with a part of the language. The Word Paradigm Generator outputs several variants of annotations in NooJ format and a user can choose the right word form with its paradigm. The resulting paradigms have an accent, indicated by the "+" symbol, and special tags separated from the word by an underscore "_". This is semi-automatic processing of unknown words. Thus, each initial form was assigned a morphological class that shows the word change of the lexeme.

The tool is free and available on Computational Platform for Electronic Text and Speech Processing corpus.by (Fig. 4) [1].

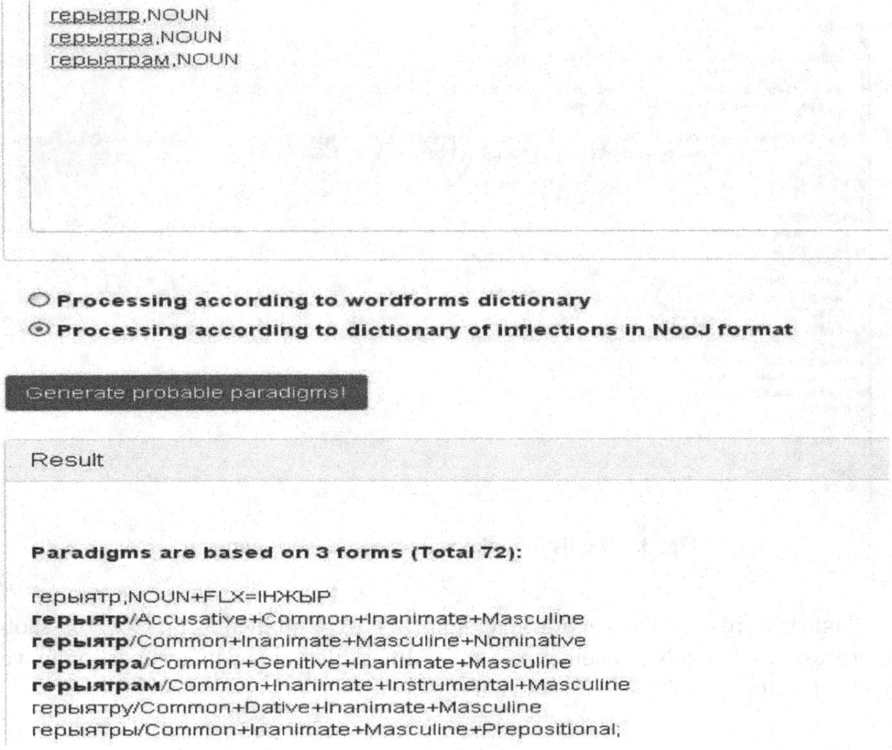

герыятр,NOUN
герыятра,NOUN
герыятрам,NOUN

○ **Processing according to wordforms dictionary**
◉ **Processing according to dictionary of inflections in NooJ format**

Generate probable paradigms!

Result

Paradigms are based on 3 forms (Total 72):

герыятр,NOUN+FLX=IНЖЫР
герыятр/Accusative+Common+Inanimate+Masculine
герыятр/Common+Inanimate+Masculine+Nominative
герыятра/Common+Genitive+Inanimate+Masculine
герыятрам/Common+Inanimate+Instrumental+Masculine
герыятру/Common+Dative+Inanimate+Masculine
герыятры/Common+Inanimate+Masculine+Prepositional;

Fig. 4. An interface of The Word Paradigm Generator service.

Due to unknown reasons, there is no sample in the general_be dictionary for these word groups:

– Feminine words with the suffix -асц-: *самотнасць* 'loneliness', *забудаванасць* 'built - up area', *двухграннасць* 'dihedral', *радасць* 'joy', etc.;
– Masculine singularia tantum common ending with - *інг*: *дайвінг* 'diving', *ліфтынг* 'lifting', *маркетынг* 'marketing'.

These shortcomings are to be corrected.

So, specialized dictionaries (additional for general_be) were created. They are designed for medical (Fig. 5) (*анальгетык, ангіёграф, глюкометр, дыстрэс* 'analgesic, angiography, glucose meter, distress', etc.) or social (*арханёл, біягрупа, брукаванка, дамініканец* 'archangel, biogroup, paving stone, Dominican', etc.) domains. A number of words with paradigms have also been prepared for inclusion in the general dictionary of the Belarusian NooJ module, for example: *агульнасусветны, адсканаваць, бескантактны, аэрагрыль, ірвота* 'worldwide, scan up, contactless, aerogrill, vomiting', etc.

```
# NooJ V7
# Dictionary
#
# Language is: be
#
# Alphabetical order is not required.
#
# Use inflectional & derivational paradigms' description files (.nof), e.g.:
# Special Command: #use paradigms.nof
#
# Special Features: +NW (non-word) +FXC (frozen expression component) +UNAMB (unambi
#                   +FLX= (inflectional paradigm) +DRV= (derivational paradigm)
#
# Special Characters: '\' '"' ' ' ',' '+' '-' '#'
#
герыятр,NOUN+FLX=АВАР
адрэнаблакатар,NOUN+FLX=ІНЖЫР
адыктыўны,ADJECTIVE+FLX=ААЗІСНЫ
акарыцьдны,ADJECTIVE+FLX=ААЗІСНЫ
акрацыяноз,NOUN+FLX=ААГЕНЕЗ
актываваны ,ADJECTIVE+FLX=ААЗІСНЫ
акустыкафобія,NOUN+FLX=ААГАМІЯ
алігаартрыт,NOUN+FLX=ІЎРЫТ
атачаць,VERB+FLX=ЗАВЯШЧАЦЬ
атрафічны,ADJECTIVE+FLX=ААЗІСНЫ
атэрагеннасць,NOUN+FLX=ЭПАКАМІТАСЦЬ
аўтадонарства,NOUN+FLX=АВАВЯЗАЦЕЛЬСТВА
аўтыст,NOUN+FLX=АВАЛІЦЫЯНІСТ
аўтыстычны,ADJECTIVE+FLX=ААЗІСНЫ
бедаквілін,NOUN+FLX=АЛЕІН
біятропія,NOUN+FLX=ААГАМІЯ
```

Fig. 5. Belarusian medical dictionary in NooJ format.

A trilingual dictionary is a perspective phenomenon in the field of Belarusian diplomacy, modern foreign policy, and international relations. The presence of a trilingual dictionary in everyday practice makes it possible to constantly replenish and adjust the lexical stock in three languages. The knowledge of Belarusian and Russian languages, and the spread of English as the "language of international integration" contributes to the creation of extensive interaction between the systems of the three languages in communication. This makes it necessary to compile trilingual dictionaries, especially of medical and social terminology in terms of this research.

All terms of the Belarusian medical and social dictionaries were correlated with their Russian equivalents from the parallel corpora of medical and social domains. The next step was their translation into English which was done by linguists manually. The specialists faced the following difficulties and noticed the following features of trilingual translation into English:

– some of the Belarusian-Russian terms can have more than one terminological equivalent with different meanings in the English language:
абязбольвальны,   ADJECTIVE+TRANS+RU =   "обезболивающий"+TRANS +EN = "anesthetic";
абязбольвальны,   ADJECTIVE+TRANS+RU =   "обезболивающий"+TRANS +EN = "analgesic";
– there is no exact correspondence to a certain term in English, the translation can only be descriptive (in a few words):
вірусаносьбіцтва,   NOUN+TRANS+RU =   "вирусоносительство"+TRANS +EN = "carriage_of_viruses";
маламабільны, ADJECTIVE+TRANS+RU = "маломобильный"+TRANS+EN = "with_limited_mobility".

Trilingual dictionaries can be composed in NooJ format by special command "TRANS+RU" for the Russian equivalent and "TRANS+EN" for English. The whole line of one translated word looks like "шпіталізацыя, NOUN+TRANS+RU = "госпитализация"+TRANS+EN = "hospitalization". In this way, all the terms of the medical and social domain were processed manually by translators and then compiled into NooJ format. The medical dictionary contains 642 words, the social dictionary contains 675 words.

4   NooJ for Proofreading and Translating

4.1   Common Names in the Corpora

Concordances of articles were prepared in the NooJ platform. They made it possible to check uniformity of translation of the same word, to find out the use of synonyms, homonyms, uniformity of names of persons, cities, events. We were able to detect some errors in translations, unify texts.

Here are some examples of how to check compliance during such work. Some interesting cases are connected with the choice of synonyms. For example, the usage of words *city* and *town* and related (Table 2).

Thanks to the work on the corpora and concordance, errors were identified in the translation of this group of words. For example:
The most beautiful manor house in a classicism style with a landscape park became a true decoration of the small city. – Найпрыгажэйшы сядзібны дом у стылі класіцызму з пейзажным паркам стаў сапраўдным упрыгажэннем невялікага гарадка. (*Najpryhažejšy siadzibny dom u styli klasicyzmu z piejzažnym parkam staŭ sapraŭdnym upryhaženniem nievialikaha haradka*).

Here are a few examples that have been found thanks to the NooJ analysis. Thus, the collocation *small city* seems out of place. The word *гарадка* should be translated as *small town*, not *city*.

Or consider the following specific context in the description of *Narowlia*:
У 1840 годзе у сувязі з частым разлівам ракі царква была перанесена на край **мястэчка** *(цяпер гэта цэнтр* **горада**). (*U 1840 hodzie u suviazi z častym razlivam raki carkva byla pieraniesiena na kraj* **miastečka** *(ciapier heta centr* **horada**).

*In eighteen forty the church was transferred to border of the **town** (now its the centre of the **city**).*

Table 2. Translations of *town, city,* etc.

Part of speech	Be	Ru	En
Noun	горад 266 мястэчка 11 (old type of a small urban settlement) гарадок 2 (diminutive)	город 258 местечко 5 (old type of a small urban settlement) городок 9 (diminutive)	town 43 city 384
Adjective	гарадскі 111	городской 108	
Total	390	380	423

The names of the inhabitants of these localities are connected with the words *horad, miastečka, vioska, town, city*. To translate those who live in the city, the words *citizen* and *resident* were used. There was also the word *people*. We analyzed theirs' distribution: *haradžanin* 18, *miescič* 5, *žychar* 18, *citizens* 19, *residents* 17, *people* 5. Here are some examples of variegated distribution of these words:

- *абагульненых вобразах **жыхароў** горада* (abahuĺnienych žycharoŭ horada) – 'generalized images of the **citizens** of the city';
- *Тут праводзіў свае пасяджэнні выбраны **гараджанамі** орган самакіравання - магістрат.* (Tut pravodziŭ svaje pasiadženni vybrany haradžanami orhan samakiravannia - mahistrat.) – 'City Council, which was elected by the **people**, held meetings there'.
- *Парк імя Першага мая ў горадзе Брэсце з'яўляецца не толькі самым папулярным сярод **гараджан** і турыстаў...(Park imia Pieršaha maja ŭ horadzie Brescie zjaŭliajecca nie toĺki samym papuliarnym siarod haradžan i turystaй...)* – 'The First of May Park in the city of Brest is not only the most popular park among the **residents** and tourists...'
- *На гэтай вуліцы пражывалі заможныя **месцічы**-яўрэі.* (Na hetaj vulicy pražyvali zamožnyja miescičy-jaŭrei.) – 'Wealthy **citizens**-Jews lived on this street'.

4.2   Personal Names in the Corpora

Belarusian toponyms have many variants in original and translated texts. Consider the example of the city of Hrodna (Table 3). It is a regional center in the west of Belarus. About 370 thousand people live there.

It appears under the names: *Гродна, Гародня, Горадня*. The following cognate adjectives are possible in the Belarusian language: *гродзенскі, гродненскі, гарадзенскі*. Using NooJ's ability to create concordances, we analyze their applicability. Belarusian and Russian adjectives are translated into English as one word – *Hrodna*.

Deviations from the main variant are associated with the name of Prince David: *Davyd Haradzienski* (1283–1326) (6 cases). In addition, one erroneous translation was detected: *The author of the… monument to Ciotka was the famous* **Grodno** *sculptor Alieś Lipień.*

Different final figures make it possible to identify other deviations, features in translations.

Table 3. Translation variants of the city name *Гродна* (*Hrodna*).

Part of speech	Be	Ru	En
Noun	Гродна 64 Горадня 1 Гародня 0	Гродно 68	Hrodna 154 * Grodno 1 * Grodna 0
Adjective	гродзенскі 75 гарадзенскі 10 Гарадзенскі (Давід) 6	гродненский 89 Давид Гродненский 6	Davyd Haradzienski 6
Total	156	163	161

Another Belarusian city – *Mahilioŭ* – has a similar problem of variability. It is a regional center in the east of Belarus, with 380,000 inhabitants. The following results were obtained (Table 4).

Table 4. Translation variants of the city name *Магілёў* (*Mahilioŭ*).

Part of speech	**Be**	**Ru**	**En**
Noun	Магілёў 36	Могилёв 24 Могилев 13	Mahilioŭ 100 Mahiliou 2
Adjective	магілёўскі 66	могилевский 19 могилёвский 48	
Total	102	104	102

There is also a regular feature of the English language – nouns and adjectives homonyms. And in two cases the translator did not use a special character for the «*ў*» sound.

The peculiarity of the Russian language was also manifested here: the variance of the spelling "*E/Ё*". According to actual rules, the usage of the letter *ё* is not obligatory. So, when automating processes, you need to take into account this detail.

So, while translating and proofreading, NooJ is used:

– to find synonyms;

- to achieve uniformity in the spelling of proper names;
- to accurately and uniformly translate terms and set expressions;
- to detect missing text snippets.

5 Conclusion

The creation of a specialized corpora in the NooJ processor is described in the article. New medical and social corpora contain about 1,6 million tokens. It includes medical and social texts in the Belarusian, English and Russian languages. The texts were taken from specialized websites of medical institutions and from audio guides on historical sights of Belarus. The original texts in Belarusian have been translated into Russian and English. The translation quality was improved due to the combined machine-manual approach: texts were initially translated automatically, after that they were manually proofread and edited, then automatically proofread.

A general dictionary of the Belarusian NooJ module was complemented by new words in the process of corpus preparation; specialized dictionaries of words were compiled: a Belarusian-Russian-English list of medical and social terms. The dictionary is planned to be supplemented.

So, NooJ allows us to achieve uniformity in writing, detect lexical and spelling discrepancies between the original and the translation, facilitates the correction of errors in language or content. There were also several cases when the sentence was omitted during the translation, probably due to the mistake of the translators. Using corpora helped to unify the translation of proper names, too.

References

1. Computational platform for electronic text & speech processing. http://www.corpus.by. Accessed 01 Sept 2022
2. Hetsevich, Y., Varanovich, V., Kachan, E., Reentovich, I., Lysy, S.: Semi-automatic part-of-speech annotating for belarusian dictionaries enrichment in NooJ. In: Barone, L., Monteleone, M., Silberztein, M. (eds.) NooJ 2016. CCIS, vol. 667, pp. 101–111. Springer, Cham (2016). https://doi.org/10.1007/978-3-319-55002-2_9
3. Hetsevich, Y., Kirdun, A.A.: Vykarystannie sistem mashynnaga pierakladu i sintezu mawliennia dlia zabiespiachennia dastupnastsi zakanadawchykh tekstaw na roznykh movakh u Respublitsy Bielarus. Minsk (2018). Гецэвіч, Ю.С., Кірдун, А.А.: Выкарыстанне сістэм машыннага перакладу і сінтэзу маўлення для забеспячэння даступнасці заканадаўчых тэкстаў на розных мовах у Рэспублікі Беларусь. In: Коваленко, Е. И. (ред.). Информационные технологии и право (Правовая информатизация – 2018): матер. VI Междунар. науч.-практ. конф., 17 мая 2018 г.; с. 123–128. Минск (2018)
4. KrokApp – personal audio guide in Belarus. https://krokapp.by/about/. Accessed 01 Sept 2022
5. Michigan Corpus of Academic Spoken English. https://quod.lib.umich.edu/m/micase. Accessed 01 Sept 2022
6. NooJ: A Linguistic Development Environment. http://www.nooj4nlp.org/. Accessed 01 Sept 2022

7. Reentovich, I., et al.: The first one-million corpus for the Belarusian NooJ module. In: Okrut, T., Hetsevich, Y., Silberztein, M., Stanislavenka, H. (eds.) NooJ 2015. CCIS, vol. 607, pp. 3–15. Springer, Cham (2016). https://doi.org/10.1007/978-3-319-42471-2_1
8. The Colorado Richly Annotated Full Text Corpus. http://bionlp-corpora.sourceforge.net/CRAFT/. Accessed 01 Sept 2021

Creation of a Legal Domain Corpus for the Belarusian Module in NooJ: Texts, Dictionaries, Grammars

Valery Varanovich[1]([✉]), Mikita Suprunchuk[2], Yauheniya Zianouka[3],
Tsimafei Prakapenka[3], Anna Dolgova[1], and Yuras Hetsevich[3]

[1] Belarusian State University, Nezavisimosti Av. 4, Minsk, Belarus
ssrlab221@gmail.com
[2] Minsk State Linguistic University, Zakharov Str. 21, Minsk, Belarus
[3] United Institute of Informatics Problems, Surhanava Str. 6, Minsk, Belarus
yuras.hetsevich@newman.bas-net.by

Abstract. This paper represents the procedure of creating a legal domain corpus in NooJ. It illustrates a primary analysis of the corpus including automatic text processing, emphasizing its main linguistic peculiarities, and analyzing prosodic characteristics of legal texts which is necessary for syntagmatic delimitation. It also depicts the compilation composition of three dictionaries in NooJ format: general, legal, and Belarusian English-Russian dictionaries.

Keywords: Automatic language processing · Corpus of a legal domain · Dictionary · Law code · Syntactic grammar · Belarusian · Russian · English

1 Introduction

The current language situation in the Republic of Belarus is characterized primarily as state bilingualism. But despite the state bilingualism, the vast majority of legislative documents are implemented only in Russian. Thus, of the 26 codes of the Republic of Belarus, the texts of which are presented on the National Legal Internet Portal pravo.by 25 are officially adopted in Russian and only one in Belarusian.

To handle the question of translating legislative documents into Belarusian, Speech Synthesis and Recognition Laboratory of United Institute of Informatics Problems of National Academy of Sciences of Belarus in cooperation with specialists from the Faculty of Social and Cultural Communications of Belarusian State University have translated all codes of the Republic of Belarus into the Belarusian language using automatic services of corpus.by [1].

The authors of the article have set several tasks to solve this problem. The first one is to collect all legislative codes of the Republic of Belarus in the Belarusian language for creating a unified text corpus. There are some examples of such corpora in the

---

The original version of this chapter was revised: The affiliation of Anna Dolgova has been corrected as "Belarusian State University". The correction to this chapter available at
https://doi.org/10.1007/978-3-031-23317-3_18

Y. Hetsevich—The authors would like to thank Zmicier Dzenisiuk for his help during the preparation of the article.

M. González et al. (Eds.): NooJ 2022, CCIS 1758, pp. 151–162, 2022.
https://doi.org/10.1007/978-3-031-23317-3_13

world [2–4]. For this, it is very important to perform a primary analysis of the legal domain corpus: to find out the main linguistic peculiarities of this kind of corpus in comparison with the Belarusian literary corpus. Secondly, different types of dictionaries (Belarusian-Russian, Belarusian-English, Belarusian-English-Russian dictionaries) are planned to be composed. This question is very topical for the Belarusian language since there are very few translated Belarusian-foreign and foreign-Belarusian dictionaries of legal terminology (now we are aware of six dictionaries that are different in their merits and significance for the ordering and development of Belarusian legal terminology). The last but not the least task is to develop special morphological and syntactic grammars for further prosodic analysis of legal texts [5, 6]. Automatic syntagmatic delimitation is still not solved for the Belarusian language, either. Therefore, developed NooJ grammars [7] will assist the process of creating a system of prosodic marks (including punctuation and intonation marks) and further automatic segmentation of Belarusian texts of the legal domain [8].

2 Compilation of a Legal Domain Corpus

To create a unified corpus of a legal domain, the specialists have translated all law codes from the Russian language into Belarusian one by one almost independently (Fig. 1).

Назва тэксту і крыніца	Пераклады тэксту	Слоўнікі і дадатковыя матэрыялы
Банковский кодекс Республики Беларусь	БАНКАЎСКІ КОДЭКС РЭСПУБЛІКІ БЕЛАРУСЬ (апрацаваны методыкай вычыткі неафіцыйны пераклад тэксту)	
Бюджетный кодекс Республики Беларусь	БЮДЖЭТНЫ КОДЭКС РЭСПУБЛІКІ БЕЛАРУСЬ (апрацаваны методыкай вычыткі неафіцыйны пераклад тэксту)	Слоўнік замен
Водный кодекс Республики Беларусь	ВОДНЫ КОДЭКС РЭСПУБЛІКІ БЕЛАРУСЬ (апрацаваны методыкай вычыткі неафіцыйны пераклад тэксту)	
Воздушный кодекс Республики Беларусь	ПАВЕТРАНЫ КОДЭКС РЭСПУБЛІКІ БЕЛАРУСЬ (апрацаваны методыкай вычыткі неафіцыйны пераклад тэксту)	

Fig. 1. Law codes in Russian and their translation into Belarusian on the page of the Speech Synthesis and Recognition Laboratory (ssrlab.by).

The translation of each law code undergoes the following stages:

1. The usage of a machine translation system.
2. Proofreading of the obtained translation by the software presented on the corpus.by platform includes:

— spelling checking,
— analysis of statistical and supplemental information about symbols,
— analysis of statistics on the use of arbitrary symbolic sequences in an electronic text (counting the frequency of word forms),
— search and correction of errors in the spelling of the Belarusian letters "У" and "Ў",
— recognition and selection of homographs in the text.

Manual text proofreading and correction of errors was accomplished sequentially by three editors: the first two were qualified linguists, the third was a professional lawyer. In the process of proofreading, a dictionary of the most frequent (regular) substitutions of words and phrases was created. Such a contextual dictionary is also planned to be used when training a machine translation system to improve the quality of the translated text.

Figure 2 below shows an example of the Civil Code of the Republic of Belarus in the Belarusian language obtained by semi-automatic translation from Russian.

ГЛАВА 1
ГРАМАДЗЯНСКАЕ ЗАКАНАДАЎСТВА

Артыкул 1. Адносіны, якія рэгулююцца грамадзянскім заканадаўствам

1. Грамадзянскае заканадаўства вызначае прававое становішча ўдзельнікаў грамадзянскага абароту, падставы ўзнікнення і парадак ажыццяўлення права ўласнасці і іншых рэчавых правоў, правоў на вынікі інтэлектуальнай дзейнасці, рэгулюе адносіны паміж асобамі, якія ажыццяўляюць прадпрымальніцкую дзейнасць, ці з іх удзелам, дагаворныя і іншыя абавязацельствы, а таксама іншыя маёмасныя і звязаныя з імі асабістыя немаёмасныя адносіны.

Прадпрымальніцкая дзейнасць — гэта самастойная дзейнасць юрыдычных і фізічных асоб, якая ажыццяўляецца імі ў грамадзянскім абарачэнні ад свайго імя, на сваю рызыку і пад сваю маёмасную адказнасць і накіраваная на сістэматычнае атрыманне прыбытку ад карыстання маёмасцю, продажу рэчаў, вырабленых, перапрацаваных ці набытых указанымі асобамі для продажу, а таксама ад выканання работ ці аказання паслуг, калі гэтыя работы ці паслугі прызначаюцца для рэалізацыі іншым асобам і не выкарыстоўваюцца для ўласнага ўжытку.

Fig. 2. A fragment of the civil code after semi-automatic translation.

After translating 17 law codes into Belarusian, a group of specialists compiled a unified corpus in NooJ format to create a dictionary of legal terms and expressions. Figure 3 shows the Belarusian corpus of a legal domain that consists of 17 law codes in NooJ format [9]. The total number of word tokens is 1,043,018.

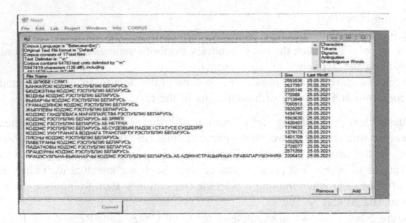

Fig. 3. The legal corpus in NooJ interface.

Characteristics of the corpus are as follows: about 1 million tokens; 731,584 word forms; 64,783 text units delimited by "\n"; 47,219 different annotations; 5,947,419 characters (136 diff): 4,911,529 letters (97 diff), 94,801 digits (10 diff), 724,456 blanks (3 diff), 216,633 other delimiters (26 diff).

The main linguistic peculiarities of the legal corpus are:

- There are more complex sentences than simple ones. Documents should be very clear and precise, that's why reasons, explanations, and repetitions are often included in law articles. Some words are specific for this theme and should be added to the dictionary of NooJ [9].
- The noun is the most frequent part of speech.
- Some words are specific for this theme.
- In the Belarusian language in comparison with the Russian one, the number of words in texts is more but the number of characters is less: for example, in the Civil Code in Russian there are 129,348 word usages, 1,043,572 characters (excluding spaces), and in the Belarusian translation - 132,414 word usages, 1,015,631 characters. So, the average word length in the Russian text is 8.06 characters, in the Belarusian - 7.67 characters.
- Some grammatical forms are not recommended for usage in other styles but could be admitted in the official style, e. g. present participle (passive and active): *суд выращае вынікаючыя*: PTCP.PRES.ACT *з гэтага пытанні* 'the court decides issues that result from it' (Civil Code); *прадаставіць вызваляемае*: PTCP.PRES. PAS *жылое памяшканне* 'to give a living space which is being cleared' (Housing Code).

The results of primary corpus processing show the next data:

- Unknown words, nearly 2,660: *адклікальнага, адпаламу;*
- Unique word forms, nearly 365 words: *бенефіцыярны, сублізінг;*
- Abbreviations, nearly 20: *АН, ФСК*
- Spelling errors, nearly 50: *стаціли, праналежнасць;*

Untranslated words, 20: *скриншот, бербоут.*

The list of unknown words was processed manually (Fig. 4). It includes these groups:

- Words and word forms that are not included in the general Belarusian dictionary_be.nod: *зносіны, нармаванне*;
- English words and symbols: *http, documents*;
- Roman numerals: *IV, XI*;
- Simple mistakes: мажех (межах), сваечасова (своечасова);
- Words with an apostrophe (the apostrophe divides words into parts): *адаб'ецца, аб'яднаць.* Sometimes the apostrophe is a functional symbol, but in the Belarusian language the apostrophe has the role of a letter, it does not separate words, it is a part of words.

English words and symbols and Roman numerals were omitted as these words should be processed separately in another research. Almost all words with an apostrophe were included in the list of general vocabulary.

```
Unknowns are 1345 entries

# NooJ V7
# Dictionary
#
# Language is: be
#
# Alphabetical order is not required.
#
# Use inflectional & derivational paradigms' description files (.nof),
# Special Command: #use paradigms.nof
#
# Special Features: +NW (non-word) +FXC (frozen expression component)
#                   +FLX= (inflectional paradigm) +DRV= (derivational
#
# Special Characters: '\' '"' ' ' ',' '+' '-' '#'
#
asp,UNKNOWN
by,UNKNOWN
document,UNKNOWN
etalonline,UNKNOWN
h,UNKNOWN
H,UNKNOWN
hk,UNKNOWN
Hk,UNKNOWN
HK,UNKNOWN
```

Fig. 4. The list of unknown words in NooJ.

3   Creating Medical and Social Trilingual Dictionaries in NooJ

Text corpora are a valuable knowledge source about language peculiarities. They allow us to monitor facts and tendencies that are difficult to notice by common speaking or reading. Lexical and grammatical elements of the Belarusian NooJ module were used for the lexical and grammar marking of the law corpus which was created by the specialists of the laboratory. In this case, a number of words was not recognized. In the result of their detailed analysis a part of words was included in the general dictionary of the Belarusian NooJ module as they are considerably widespread: e.g. ап'яненне 'intoxication, drunkenness', аўдыявізуальны 'audiovisual', гідрацыкл 'hydrocycle', etc. Unrecognized rare words were collected into a specialized dictionary. It includes law terms апекавальнік 'guardian, caretaker', адпісанне 'refusal', дыспаша 'claims adjustment', контрсталійны 'demurrage'; other sphere terms авердрафт 'overdraft', абвалоўка 'mound', дыспрозій 'dysprosium', супесь 'sandy loam'(according to the law codes themes); regular derivatives сухавяршынны 'stag-headed', перадрамонтны 'pre-repair', непражыванне 'non-residence (they are easily formed by the general word-building rules, so it is unreasonable to include them into the general dictionary); borrowings that are only being adapted into the Belarusian language суббербоўт 'sub-bareboat', ф'ючарсны 'futures', эквайрынг 'acquiring', etc.

After manual analysis of all unknown words, two groups of vocabulary were composed: words of legal terminology and general vocabulary. As the Belarusian NooJ module already had the general vocabulary "general_be.dic" it was decided to create an additional dictionary for general unknown words (nearly 150 word forms in initial form) and a law dictionary (nearly 200 forms).

The principle of creating these dictionaries is the same. All unknown words were originally processed by Word Paradigm Generator. This is an online service that generates the paradigm of a word. At the service input, a word or its word form is given. The service searches for a paradigm in the dictionary. If a ready-made paradigm is absent, the user receives a generated paradigm of the entered word or paradigms created on the basis of words similar in spelling. The resulting paradigms have an accent, indicated by the "+" symbol, and special tags separated from the word by an underscore"_". The main core of this program is processing words in NooJ format. It means that Word Paradigm Generator suggests appropriate variants for an unknown word without any manual correction except choosing the right paradigm. This is semi-automatic processing of unknown words.

The tool is free and available on Computational Platform for Electronic Text and Speech Processing corpus.by (https://corpus.by/WordParadigmGenerator/?lang=en).

Every initial form (lemma) from the list of unknown general words was assigned a morphological class. This class shows the flexion features, i. e. how the word changes. Then the law dictionary in the Belarusian language Law_codes_be.dic was compiled for NooJ format and now is available for further text processing with Belarusian texts of any domains. It is an addition to the main NooJ dictionary for the Belarusian language that has around 200 words in the initial form.

A trilingual dictionary is a perspective phenomenon in the field of Belarusian diplomacy, modern foreign policy, and international relations. The presence of a trilingual dictionary in everyday practice makes it possible to constantly replenish and adjust the lexical stock in three languages. The knowledge of Belarusian and Russian languages, and the spread of English as the "language of international integration" contributes to the creation of extensive interaction between the systems of the three languages in communication. This makes it necessary to compile trilingual dictionaries, especially of legal terminology in terms of this research. The presence of such a dictionary base will help to prevent various mistakes that are possible while translating law codes from Russian and mastering the vocabulary and grammatical structure of Belarusian, Russian and English languages. The use of a trilingual dictionary makes it possible to rely not only on the Russian language but also on other languages being studied, which is important for processing the material in our native language in other spheres of life. This is a good reason to create a Belarusian-Russian-English law dictionary from Law_codes_be.dic (Fig. 5).

Fig. 5. Belarusian law dictionary (Law_codes_be.dic) in NooJ format.

All terms of the Belarusian law dictionary Law_codes_be.dic were correlated with their Russian equivalents from the parallel corpus of a legal domain. The next step was their translation into English which was done by linguists manually. The specialists faced the following difficulties and noticed the following features of trilingual translation into English:

1. some of the Belarusian-Russian law terms can have more than one terminological equivalent with different meanings in the English language:

   падведамаснасць,NOUN+FLX=АСКОМІСТАСЦЬ+TRANS+RU="*подве-домственность*"+TRANS+EN="*subordinate*"
   падведамаснасць,NOUN+FLX=АСКОМІСТАСЦЬ+TRANS+RU="*подве-домственность*"+TRANS+EN="*jurisdiction*"

2. two different Belarusian-Russian nouns (of masculine and feminine gender) are translated by the same word equivalent in English:

   сужонка,NOUN+FLX=АБАДРАНКА+TRANS+RU="супруга"+TRANS +EN="marital partner"
   сужэнец,NOUN+FLX=АБАДРАНЕЦ+TRANS+RU="супруг"+TRANS +EN="marital partner"

3. there are Belarusian-Russian law terms which can be translated by several equivalents with the same or similar meaning:

   паручальнік,NOUN+FLX=АБАГАЧАЛЬНІК2 +RU="*поручитель*"+EN="*fidejussor*"
   паручальнік,NOUN+FLX=АБАГАЧАЛЬНІК2+RU="*поручитель*"+EN= "*surety*"
   паручальнік,NOUN+FLX=АБАГАЧАЛЬНІК2 +RU="*поручитель*"+EN="*guarantor*"
   паручальнік,NOUN+FLX=АБАГАЧАЛЬНІК2+RU="*поручитель*"+EN="*bail bondsman*"
   паручальнік,NOUN+FLX=АБАГАЧАЛЬНІК2 +RU="*поручитель*"+EN="*adpromissor*"

Trilingual dictionaries can be composed in NooJ format by special command "TRANS + RU" for the Russian equivalent and "TRANS + EN" for English. The whole line of one translated word looks like "*Абвалоўка*, NOUN + FLX = ЛЕСНІЧОЎКА + TRANS + RU = "*обваловка*" + TRANS + EN = "*mound*". In this way, all the terms of the legal domain were processed manually by translators and then compiled into NooJ format. A new dictionary consists of 200 notions and is shown in Fig. 6.

```
# NooJ V7
# Dictionary
#
# Language is: be
#
# Alphabetical order is not required.
#
# Use inflectional & derivational paradigms' description files (.nof), e.g.:
# Special Command: #use paradigms.nof
#
# Special Features: +NW (non-word) +FXC (frozen expression component) +UNAMB (unambiguous lexical entry)
#                   +FLX= (inflectional paradigm) +DRV= (derivational paradigm)
#
# Special Characters: '\' '"' ' ' ',' '+' '-' '#'
#
абаратаздольны,ADJECTIVE+FLX=ААЗІСНЫ+TRANS+RU="оборотоспособный"+TRANS+EN="transferable"
абвалоўка,NOUN+FLX=ЛЕСНІЧОЎКА+TRANS+RU="обваловка"+TRANS+EN="mound"
авердрафт,NOUN+FLX=ААЛІТ+TRANS+RU="овердрафт"+TRANS+EN="overdraft"
авізуючы,PARTICIPLE+FLX=АБСЛУГОЎВАЮЧЫ+TRANS+RU="авизующий"+TRANS+EN="advising"
аграхімікат,NOUN+FLX=ААЛІТ+TRANS+RU="агрохимикат"+TRANS+EN="agrochemicals"
аграэкатурызм,NOUN+FLX=АМІНАЗІН+TRANS+RU="агроэкотуризм"+TRANS+EN="agricultural and ecological tourism"
агульнадамавы,ADJECTIVE+FLX=АВЛАЖНЫ+TRANS+RU="общедомовой"+TRANS+EN="whole-building"
агульнанебяспечны,ADJECTIVE+FLX=ААЗІСНЫ+TRANS+RU="общеопасный"+TRANS+EN="whole-dangerous"
ад'юнкт,NOUN+FLX=АВАЛІЦЫЯНІСТ+TRANS+RU="адъюнкт"+TRANS+EN="adjunct"
ад'юнкт,NOUN+FLX=АВАЛІЦЫЯНІСТ+TRANS+RU="адъюнкт"+TRANS+EN="material supply"
адвалорны,ADJECTIVE+FLX=ААЗІСНЫ+TRANS+RU="адвалорный"+TRANS+EN="ad valorem"
```

Fig. 6. Compiling Belarusian-Russian-English dictionary from Law_codes_be.dic.

4 Syntactic Grammars for Searching Legal Terminology and Punctuational Syntagmas

To check the trilingual dictionary, it was decided to create syntactic grammar for searching legal terms. This kind of grammar helps to define all items which are necessary depending on the set goal. It was created to show a concrete example of all nouns in a new corpus and a dictionary application. The grammar structure is presented in Fig. 7. The NooJ module shows not only the found word with its translation but also the left and the right context. It is very convenient when a user wants to check a word translation, find its paradigm, or verify how many times this word occurs in the corpus.

Для мэт гэтага Кодэкса падатковае	рэзідэнцтва/"residence"'"рэзидентство"	фізічнай асобы вызначаецца ў адносінах
замежнай дзяржавы, то яго падатковае	рэзідэнцтва/"residence"'"рэзидентство"	вызначаецца ў адпаведнасці з палажэннямі
годзе, за які вызначаецца падатковае	рэзідэнцтва/"residence"'"рэзидентство"	, мае грамадзянства Рэспублікі Беларусь ці
гражна-наглядальную карту падпісваюць	правяральнік/"verifier"'"проверяющий"	(кіраўнік праверкі) і плацельшчык ці
гражна-наглядальную карту падпісваюць	правяральнік/"controller"'"проверяющий"	(кіраўнік праверкі) і плацельшчык ці
гражна-наглядальную карту падпісваюць	правяральнік/"auditor"'"проверяющий"	(кіраўнік праверкі) і плацельшчык ці
новыя рынкі тавараў (работ, паслуг),	маркетынг/"marketing"'"маркетинг"	, рэклама; захоўванне тавараў: транспарціроўка тавараў
дміністрацыйнага арышту; змяшчэнне ў	карцэр/"punishment cell"'"карцер"	або адзіночную камеру на гаўптвахце
ў пісьмовай форме. 3. Змяшчэнне ў	карцэр/"punishment cell"'"карцер"	або адзіночную камеру ажыццяўляецца на
арыштаваныя могуць быць змешчаны ў	карцэр/"punishment cell"'"карцер"	або адзіночную камеру за: 1) абмежаванне

Fig. 7. Syntactic grammar for searching nouns and their equivalents in Russian and English.

The last step of the research is to define the syntactic peculiarities of legal texts. For this task, the grammar for marking Belarusian phrases at punctuation level was applied. It was previously created by the Belarusian NooJ team to specify prosodic marking that involves the segmentation of sentences into punctuational phrases and the determination of their intonation type. The law texts are very difficult to read because of long sentences with many word combinations and complex structures. Applying this grammar for prosodic (intonation) analysis is a new and promising method to identify the syntactic structure of the official style (Fig. 8 and Fig. 9).

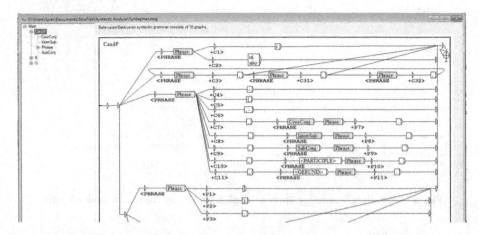

Fig. 8. The Grammar for marking Belarusian phrases at punctuation level.

Fig. 9. The results of applying syntactic grammar in the legal corpus.

After processing and analyzing the concordance of the legal corpus after applying grammar in NooJ, the authors came to the following conclusions:

1. The predominance of complex sentences, especially complex sentences with subordinate conditionals. They are characterized by difficult structures and minimal use of punctuation. For example,

Да таго часу, пакуль палажэнні часткі першай гэтага пункта не дазваляюць вызначыць статус фізічнай асобы, асоба прызнаецца падатковым рэзідэнтам Рэспублікі Беларусь у бягучым каляндарным годзе, калі яна фактычна знаходзілася на тэрыторыі Рэспублікі Беларусь больш за сто восемдзесят тры дні ў папярэднім каляндарным годзе, а ў выпадку, калі фізічная асоба фактычна знаходзілася за границамі тэрыторыі Рэспублікі Беларусь сто восемдзесят тры дні і больш у папярэднім каляндарным годзе, яна не прызнаецца падатковым рэзідэнтам Рэспублікі Беларусь у бягучым каляндарным годзе. (Tax Code).

2. Simple sentences with homogeneous parts of the sentence, and the series of these homogeneous parts can be very common (up to 8–10). For example:

Не дапускаецца ўстанаўленне падаткаў, збораў (пошлін) і льгот па іх выплаце, якія наносяць урон нацыянальнай бяспецы Рэспублікі Беларусь, яе тэрыта-рыяльнай цэласнасці, палітычнай і фінансавай стабільнасці, у тым ліку тых, якія абмяжоўваюць свабоднае перамяшчэнне фізічных асоб, перамяшчэнне тавараў (работ, паслуг) ці фінансавых сродкаў у межах тэрыторыі Рэспублікі Беларусь ці тых, якія ствараюць у парушэнне Канстытуцыі Рэспублікі Беларусь і прынятых у адпаведнасці з ёй заканадаўчых актаў іншыя перашкоды для ажыццяўлення прадпрымальніцкай і іншай дзейнасці арганізацый і фізічных асоб, акрамя забароненай заканадаўчымі актамі. (Tax Code).

3. The presence of numerous passive structures. For example:

Замежныя (міжнародныя) назіральнікі акрэдытуюцца Цэнтральнай камісіяй. Пасяджэнні Цэнтральнай камісіі склікаюцца па меры неабходнасці Старшынёй Цэнтральнай камісіі……скрынкі для галасавання правяраюцца, пламбіруюцца або апячатваюцца старшынёй участковай камісіі… Пратакол падпісваецца старшынёй або намеснікам старшыні і членам камісіі. (Elections Code).

4. The string of nouns, mainly in the genitive case, i.e. the use of the noun combinations in the genitive case.

Тэрмін паўнамоцтваў назіральніка пачынаецца з дня яго акрэдытацыі і заканчваецца ў дзень устанаўлення адпаведнай камісіяй вынікаў падліку галасоў, вынікаў выбараў, рэферэндуму, адклікання дэпутата, члена Савета Рэспублікі. (Elections Code)

Працягжэнне тэрміну карыстання нетрамі для здабычы карысных выкапняў, выкарыстання геатэрмальных рэсурсаў нетраў праводзіцца ў парадку, прадугледжаным артыкуламі 33 і 35 гэтага Кодэкса для давання горных адводаў (Mineral Resources Code).

5 Conclusion

The creation of a specialized corpus in NooJ processor is described in the article. A new law corpus contains 1,043,018 tokens. It includes legal texts in the Belarusian and Russian languages, which are law codes of the Republic of Belarus. One law code was officially introduced by the Parliament in the Belarusian language, the other 25 — in Russian. Laboratory scientists translated Russian-language law codes into

Belarusian. The translation quality was improved due to the combined machine-manual approach: texts were initially translated automatically, after that they were manually proofread and edited, then automatically proofread.

A general dictionary of the Belarusian NooJ module was complemented by new words in the process of corpus preparation; a specialized small dictionary of 200 words was compiled: a Belarusian-Russian-English list of law and professional terms. The dictionary is planned to be supplemented.

Syntactic grammars were constructed for machine translation. These grammars will help to divide long sentences without punctuation marks and provide a better reading of law texts. We also plan to find and describe syntactic and morphological markers and other words in which prosodic indicators influence the way we read law texts.

References

1. Computational platform for electronic text & speech processing. http://www.corpus.by. Accessed 01 Sep 2021
2. Byulaw. Law & Corpus Linguistics. https://lawcorpus.byu.edu. Accessed 01 Sep 2021
3. Monolingual Polish corpus in the law domain. https://elrc-share.eu/repository/browse/monolingual-polish-corpus-in-the-law-domain. Accessed 01 Sep 2021
4. British Law Report Corpus. http://flax.nzdl.org/greenstone3/flax?a=fp&sa=collAbout&c=BlaRC&if=. Accessed 01 Sep 2021
5. Hetsevich, Y., Varanovich, V., Kachan, E., Lysy, S., Reentovich, I.: Semi-automatic part-of-speech annotating for belarusian dictionaries enrichment in NooJ. In: Barone, L., Monteleone, M., Silberztein, M. (eds.): Automatic Processing of Natural-Language Electronic Texts with NooJ: 10th International Conference, NooJ 2016, České Budějovice, June 9–11, 2016, Revised selected papers, pp. 101–111. Springer International Publishing (2016). https://doi.org/10.1007/978-3-319-55002-2_9
6. Hetsevich, Y., Kirdun, A.A.: Vykarystannie sistem mashynnaga pierakladu i sintezu mawliennia dlia zabiespiachennia dastupnastsi zakanadawchykh tekstaw na roznykh movakh u Respublitsy Bielarus. = Гецэвіч, Ю.С., Кірдун, А.А.: Выкарыстанне сістэм машыннага перакладу і сінтэзу маўлення для забеспячэння даступнасці заканадаўчых тэкстаў на розных мовах у Рэспублікі Беларусь. In: Коваленко, Е. И. (ред.). Информационные технологии и право (Правовая информатизация – 2018): материалы VI Междунар. науч.-практ. конф., Минск, 17 мая 2018 г., с. 123–128. Минск (2018)
7. NooJ: A Linguistic Development Environment. http://www.nooj4nlp.org/. Accessed 01 Sep 2021
8. Udaskanaliennie pratsy awtamatyzavanykh sistem pa tekstakh jurydychnaj tematyki = Удасканаленне працы аўтаматызаваных сістэм па тэкстах юрыдычнай тэматыкі. https://ssrlab.by/7804. Accessed 01 Sep 2021
9. Reentovich, I., et al.: The First One-Million Corpus for the Belarusian NooJ Module. In: Okrut, T., Hetsevich, Y., Silberztein, M., Stanislavenka, H. (eds.): Automatic Processing of Natural-Language Electronic Texts with NooJ. In: 9th International Conference, NooJ 2015, Minsk, Belarus, June 11–13, 2015, Revised selected papers, pp. 3–15. Springer International Publishing (2016). https://doi.org/10.1007/978-3-319-55002-2

Natural Language Processing Applications

Construction of an Educational Game "CONJ_NOOJ"

Héla Fehri[1][✉] and Nizar Jarray[2]

[1] MIRACL Laboratory, University of Sfax, Sfax, Tunisia
hela.fehri@yahoo.fr
[2] University of Gabes, Zrig Eddakhlania, Tunisia

Abstract. Learning through play is a concept used in educational science and psychology. It defends the idea that child acquires skills through the activity of play, making sense of the world around him. It can keep kids motivated and more engaged. Indeed, the game would give them social and cognitive skills and self-confidence that would allow him to live new experiences and evolve in unfamiliar environments. It also encourages them to verbalize their thoughts, to argue their choices and, therefore, helps them to improve their language skills and learn from their mistakes.

The aim of this paper is to propose a serious game based on dictionaries and local grammars. This game is developed with the NooJ platform. It improves the player's level in languages. This is done by mastering the conjugation of Arabic, English and French Verbs on the one hand and the inflection of French Nouns and adjectives on the other hand. The obtained results are satisfactory and the developed game can be used as a teaching tool.

Keywords: Educational game · Conjugation · Inflection · Dictionary · Transducer · Learning · Verb · Noun · Adjective

1 Introduction

Traditional teaching and learning methods are not always effective and adapted to all children. That is why some teachers resort to using games as a learning support. In fact, game-based education [1, 2] allows children to stay motivated and more engaged, to verbalize their thoughts, to argue their choice and to perfect their language and learn from their mistakes. However, the development of an educational game is not a trivial task because the game should be simple and straight. Moreover, the interface must be intuitive so the child does not try to understand how the game works.

The aim of this paper is to propose a game developed with the NooJ platform [3, 4]. This game allows its players to master Arabic, English and French verb conjugation. It also allows learners to master French, nouns and adjectives inflection.

Let's note that several linguistic phenomena are not treated in a simple way that helps to learn them. That is why the combination of the serious games and NLP [5, 6] domain can facilitate the development of educational games and promote the understanding and

© Springer Nature Switzerland AG 2022
M. González et al. (Eds.): NooJ 2022, CCIS 1758, pp. 165–177, 2022.
https://doi.org/10.1007/978-3-031-23317-3_14

the learning of linguistic phenomena. For these reasons, the implementation of this game is based on _dm dictionary [5] for the French language, the Verbes Arabes dictionary for Arabic and the _phrasal verb and _Contractions dictionaries for English. It is based also on the transducers that allow the conjugation of the appropriate verb or the infection of the noun or adjective. This game is easy to play and does not require any computer skills.

The remaining part of this paper is structured as follows: Sect. 2 presents the proposed educational games. Section 3 deals with the experimentation carried out to evaluate the games efficiency. Finally, the paper ends with a conclusion and some perspectives.

2 Proposed Method

CONJ_NooJ is a multilingual educational game. It improves skills and competencies of the player in the following languages: French, Arabic and English. In fact, it allows its players to master the conjugation of verbs in different languages and in all tenses. Moreover, it is developed using intuitive and funny interfaces.

The proposed method is divided into three phases (a) *Identification of Resources,* (b) *Construction of Resources* and (c) *Game Steps.* Figure 1 describes this method.

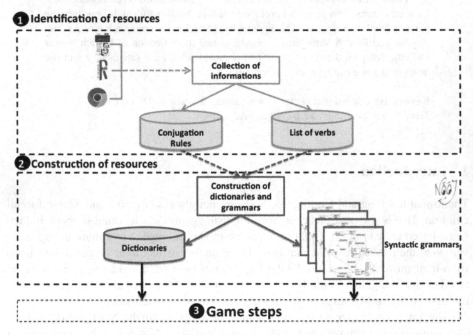

Fig. 1. CONJ_NooJ proposed method.

2.1 Identification of Resources

The phase *identification of resources* is based on a collection of information from Internet and e-dictionaries such as REVERSO[1] and LAROUSSE[2]. This information is about verbs, nouns, adjectives and inflectional rules in the desired language. This phase is important to identify and add the necessary features to the dictionaries. These features will be used by the grammars in the process of conjugating verbs, nouns and adjectives. In our work, three dictionaries are identified for verbs: Arabic, English and French, a dictionary for French nouns and another for French adjectives.

2.2 Building of Resources

The phase *Construction of Resources* consists in building dictionaries and grammars that we need to perform the conjugation of verbs and the inflection of nouns and adjectives. It is based on the information collected in the first phase. This phase is done with NooJ. So, for the dictionaries, two features are required: FLX and DRV. FLX represents an inflectional model to recognize the inflected forms and DRV represents a derivation model to recognize the derived forms.

In the following sections, we present the built resources for different categories.

2.2.1 Arabic Verbs

For the Arabic language, CONJ_NooJ is based on the "Verbes Arabe" dictionary that exists already in the NooJ platform. This dictionary contains 9257 verbs.

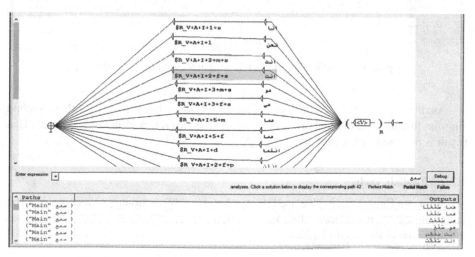

Fig. 2. Conjugation of verbs in the past tense in the active voice.

---

[1] www.reverso.net.

[2] www.larousse.fr.

CONJ_NooJ needs 10 grammars to allow the conjugation of verbs in all tenses of Arabic. Figure 2 represents an extract of a grammar that allows the conjugation of the Arabic verb in the past (I) in the active voice (A).

In the grammar of Fig. 2, the conjugation of the verb "سَمَّعَ"with the second singular feminine person "anti" (*you*) (2 + f + s) in the active voice (A) gives as result "سَمَّعْتِ". This result is obtained by the instruction "$R_V + A + I + 2 + f + s".

Figure 3 represents an extract of the grammar that allows the conjugation of the Arabic verbs in the present tense (P) in the passive voice (K).

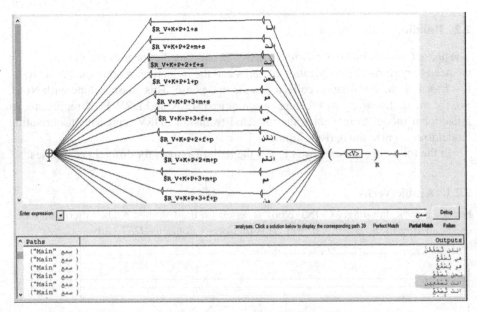

Fig. 3. Conjugation of verbs in the present tense in the passive voice.

As shown in Fig. 3, the conjugation of the verb "سَمَّعَ"in the present (P) with the second singular feminine person "انتِ"(*you*) in the passive voice (K) gives as result "تُسَمَّعِين". This result is obtained by the instruction "$R_V + K + P + 2 + f + s".

2.2.2 English Verbs

To conjugate English verbs, we used the "_phrasal verb" dictionary that contains 1260 verbs and the "_contractions" dictionary, which contains 49 entries. These dictionaries already exist in the NooJ platform.

For English verbs, we built 12 grammars to process all possible combinations of tense, aspect and mood: past tenses, present tenses, future tenses, present perfect tenses, past perfect tenses and future perfect (simple and continuous for each tense). Figure 4 describes the conjugation of verbs in the future perfect with all pronouns.

As shown in Fig. 4, the conjugated form is obtained as follows: will + have + past participle (PP).

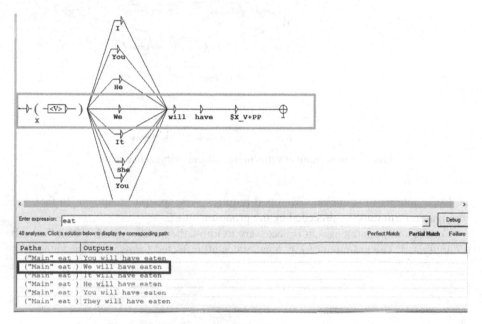

Fig. 4. Conjugation of verbs in the future perfect tense.

2.2.3 French Verbs

To conjugate French verbs, we used as resources the "_dm" dictionary that contains 7842 verbs. This dictionary already exists in the NooJ platform.

For the French language we have treated all tenses, aspects as well as all moods. Figure 5 is a grammar that allows the conjugation of the verb in the present in the subjunctive mood.

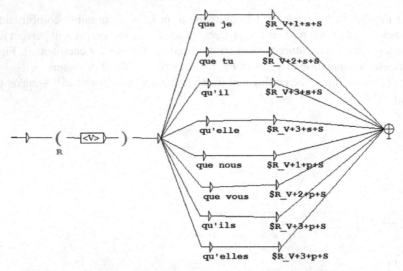

Fig. 5. Conjugation of verbs in the present (subjunctive mood).

Let's note that the subjunctive mood requires very specific treatment. In fact, the conjugated form must be preceded by the pronoun "que".

For the compound tenses, it is necessary to know the auxiliary with which the verb is conjugated. The grammar of Fig. 6 generates all inflected forms in the past tense.

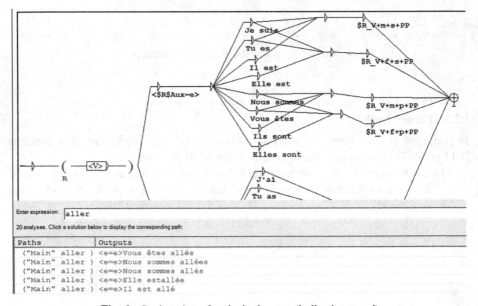

Fig. 6. Conjugation of verbs in the past (indicative mood).

For the past tense, there are verbs that are conjugated with the auxiliary "to be" and others with the auxiliary "to have". Therefore, it is necessary to know with which auxiliary the verb is conjugated to achieve the necessary agreement of the past participle. The constraint "RAux" detects the auxiliary related to the appropriate verb. Indeed, this constraint can take as value "e" for the auxiliary "to be" or "a" for the auxiliary "to have". For example, as shown in Fig. 6., the verb "aller" *(to go)* is conjugated with the auxiliary "to be".

2.2.4   French Nouns and Adjectives

For the inflection of nouns and adjectives, we used 2 dictionaries: one for the adjectives and another for the nouns. The dictionary of adjectives contains 15000 entries and the dictionary of nouns contains 11000 entries. These two dictionaries are extracted from the "_dm" dictionary.

As transducers, we construct 4 graphs: 2 for adjectives and 2 for nouns. For the adjectives, we find two grammars: the first grammar (Fig. 7) allows the agreement of adjectives according to gender and number. In this grammar, all inflected forms for the adjective "petit" *(small)* are generated.

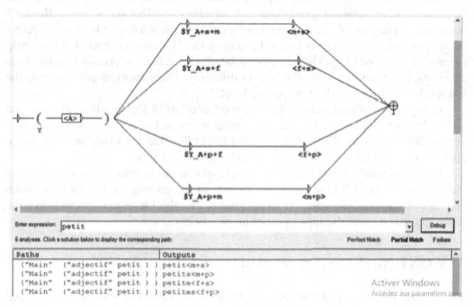

Fig. 7. Agreement of adjectives.

The second grammar (Fig. 8) allows the transformation of an adjective into an adverb.

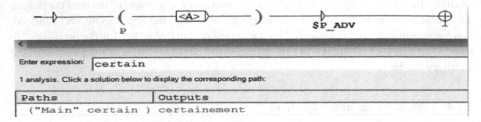

Fig. 8. Transformation of adjective into adverb.

As shown in Fig. 8, the adjective "certain" is transformed into "certainement".

2.3 Game Steps

The phrase "*Game steps*" has two main steps: Review and Evaluation. The first step, labelled "Review," is to recognize the conjugation of appropriate verbs in the chosen language or the inflection of appropriate nouns or adjectives. This step is named "Review" because it can help the player to remember the conjugation of a few verbs or the infection of some nouns and adjectives before beginning the "Evaluation" part. This can help succeed in the second step. The second step, labelled "Evaluation", is composed of three exercises, the difference being the level of difficulty. The player can only move to the last level when he succeeds at the second level.

As regards verb conjugation, the first level consists in learning how to conjugate a verb in a specific tense. The second level consists in learning how to conjugate a verb in different tenses. The third level consists in filling the crossword puzzle with the appropriate conjugated forms of a set of verbs given randomly.

As regards nouns and adjectives, the first level consists in learning the agreement of the appropriate word. The second level consists in recognizing the gender of the noun and how to transform an adjective to an adverb. The third level consists in filling the crossword puzzle with the appropriate noun or adjective.

3 CONJ_NooJ Experimentation

To validate our proposed method, we have implemented a software tool called CONJ_NooJ Educational game that allows the conjugation of Arabic, English and French verbs, and the inflection of French nouns and adjectives. In the following sections, we describe different levels of this game in different languages.

3.1 Conjugation of Verbs

The interface of Fig. 9a contains all tenses to review the Arabic language. If the player chooses "المستقبل"(*future*), the interface of Fig. 9b is displayed. The player introduces a

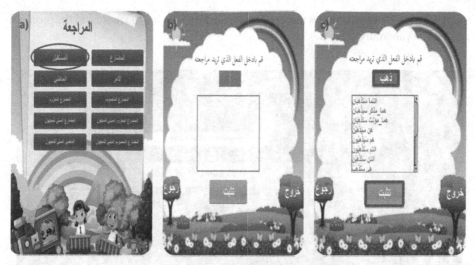

Fig. 9. Review step: arabic language.

verb to review and after clicking on the "validate" button the result is displayed in the desired tense (Fig. 9c).

In Level 1 (Fig. 10), the pronoun and the verb are displayed randomly. The player should introduce the answer in the chosen tense. If the answer is correct, it is displayed in green color and the heart is colored also in green. However, if the answer is wrong, the correct answer and the heart are displayed in red. At the end of this level, the colored hearts in green represent the correct answers while the colored hearts in red represent the incorrect answers and the score is displayed.

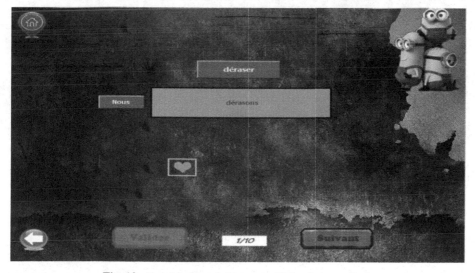

Fig. 10. Level 1: French language (Color figure online).

For Level 2, the principle is the same as Level 1 except that the tense and the pronoun are chosen randomly (Fig. 11).

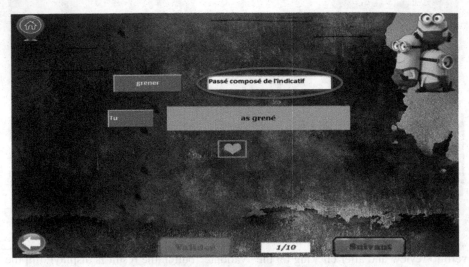

Fig. 11. Level 2: French language.

The third level consists in filling the crossword puzzle with the appropriate conjugated forms of a set of verbs given randomly (Fig. 12). After filling the crossword puzzle, the correct answers are displayed in green and the incorrect answers are colored in red.

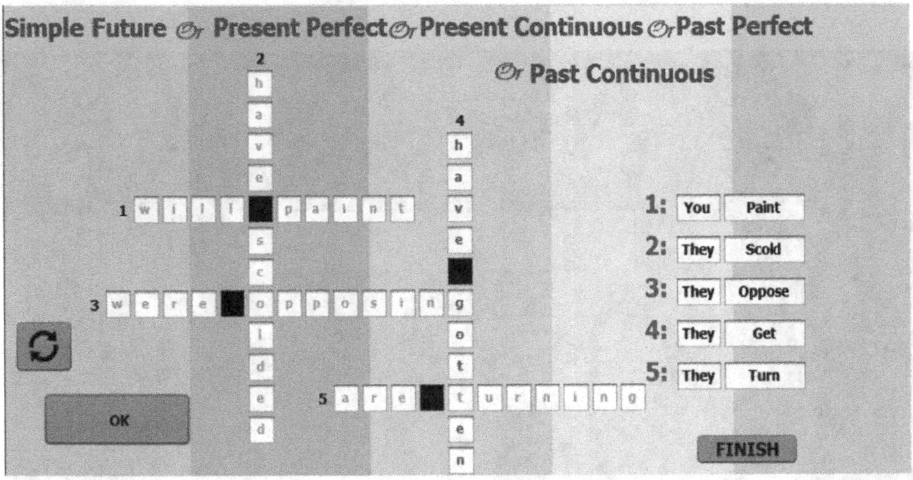

Fig. 12. Level 3: English language (Color figure online).

Let's note that Level 3 has a greater degree of difficulty because the player must remember all the conjugated forms of a given verb whatever the tense and filter those that respect the constraints of the grid.

3.2 Inflection of Adjectives and Nouns

In the first level, the adjective, the number and the gender are displayed randomly (Fig. 13). If the player introduces the correct form, the answer is displayed in green and the circle is also colored green. If the answer is wrong, it will be colored red.

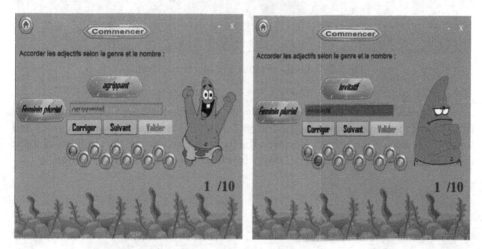

Fig. 13. Adjectives: Level 1 (Color figure online).

The Level 2 consists in transforming adjectives into adverbs. The adjective may not be transformed into an adverb and in this case the player must write "n'existe pas" (*does not exist*) else he tries to introduce the correct adverb (Fig. 14).

Fig. 14. Adjectives: Level 2 (Color figure online).

As regards nouns, in the first level, the noun and the number are displayed randomly (Fig. 15). If the player introduces the correct form, the answer is displayed in green and the circle is also colored green. However, the incorrect answer and the circle are colored red. The player can see the correct answer by clicking on the "Corriger" button.

Fig. 15. Nouns: Level 1 (Color figure online).

The second level (Fig. 16) consists in choosing the appropriate determinant; the player should recognize the gender of the noun.

Fig. 16. Nouns: Level 2.

4   Conclusion and Perspectives

In this paper, we have proposed an educational game named "CONJ_NooJ". This game helps children to learn how to conjugate a verb correctly and can be used as a teaching tool to teach conjugation. The development of this game is based on local grammars and dictionaries, which are built in the NooJ platform. These resources are called in the implementation phase using Java and noojapply.

In the future, we plan to add other levels taking into account the intuitiveness of the interfaces. Furthermore, we plan to exploit the built resources to develop a system that generates texts with well-conjugated verbs in the appropriate language. So, we can parse a text, extract the different infinitive forms of verbs and conjugate them in the desired tense.

References

1. Iten, N., Petko, D.: Learning with serious games: is fun playing the game a predictor of learning success? Br. J. Educ. Technol. **47**(1), 151–163 (2016)
2. Concilio, I.D., Braga, P.H.: Game concepts in learning and teaching process. In: Krassmann, A., Amaral, É., Nunes, F., Voss, G., Zunguze, M. (eds.): Handbook of Research on Immersive Digital Games in Educational Environments, pp. 1–34. IGI Global, Hershey (2019). https://doi.org/https://doi.org/10.4018/978-1-5225-5790-6.ch001
3. Silberztein, M.: The NooJ manual. https://www.nooj4nlp.org/ (213 pages) (2003)
4. Silberztein, M.: La formalisation des langues: l'approche NooJ. Collection Sciences Cognitive et Management des Connaissances. Edition ISTE, London (2015)
5. Fehri, H., Ben Messaoud, I.: Construction of educational games with NooJ. In: Fehri, H., Mesfar, S., Silberztein, M. (eds.) NooJ 2019. CCIS, vol. 1153, pp. 173–184. Springer, Cham (2020). https://doi.org/10.1007/978-3-030-38833-1_15
6. Fehri, H., Arroum, L., Aoun, S.B.: Construction of an educational game "VocabNooJ." In: Bigey, M., Richeton, A., Silberztein, M., Thomas, I. (eds.) NooJ 2021. CCIS, vol. 1520, pp. 124–134. Springer, Cham (2021). https://doi.org/10.1007/978-3-030-92861-2_11
7. Trouilleux, F.: A new French dictionary for NooJ: le DM. In: Automatic Processing of Various Levels of Linguistic Phenomena: Selected Papers from the NooJ 2011 International Conference, pp. 16–28. Cambridge Scholars Publishing (2012). 1–4438- 3711–3 (2011)

Annotation of Procedural Questions in Standard Arabic Using Syntactic Grammars

Essia Bessaies[✉], Slim Mesfar, and Henda Ben Ghzela

Riadi Laboratory, University of Manouba, Manouba, Tunisia
{essia.bessaies, slim.mesfar}@riadi.rnu.tn,
henda.benghezala@ensi.rnu.tn

Abstract. Most question answering systems have been designed to answer short questions (straight answers such as dates, locations), but there are only a few pieces of research about complex questions.

In this paper, we present a method for analyzing complex questions at the syntactic and the morphological levels with a pattern-based structure. These linguistic patterns allow us to annotate the question and its semantic features for extracting the focus and topic.

We start with the implementation of the rules which identify and annotate the various medical named entities. Our Named Entity Recognizer (NER) is able to sift through references to people, places and organizations, diseases, viruses, as targets to extract the correct answer from the user. The NER is embedded in our question answering system.

The task of our system is divided in four phases each of which plays a critical role in the general performance: question analysis, segmentation and passage retrieval, answer validation and, finally, answer extraction. We use the NooJ platform which represents a valuable linguistic development environment. The first evaluations show that the actual results are encouraging and could be deployed for further question types.

Keywords: Information extraction · Medical questions · Arabic language · Local grammar · Named entities

1 Introduction

Nowadays, the medical domain has a high volume of electronic-recorded documents and any search for specific information through large quantities of data can be complex and time-consuming. This is especially evident when we seek a short and straight answer to a human natural language question rather than a full list of documents and web pages. In this case, the user requirement could be a question-answering (QA) system which represents a specialized area within the field of information retrieval.

QA systems are aimed at providing inexperienced users with a flexible access to information allowing them to write a query in natural language and obtain not only the documents which contain the answer but also its precise answer passage from input texts.

© Springer Nature Switzerland AG 2022
M. González et al. (Eds.): NooJ 2022, CCIS 1758, pp. 178–188, 2022.
https://doi.org/10.1007/978-3-031-23317-3_15

However, there are some QA systems which do not square match such statements due to inherent differences and difficulties with the language itself as well as due to lack of tools available to assist researchers. For this reason, this project attempts to design and develop the modules of an Arabic QA system.

For this project, the developed question answering system is based on a linguistic approach, using NooJ's linguistic engine to formalize the automatic recognition rules to then apply them to a dynamic corpus of medical journalistic articles.

We also present a method for analyzing the syntactic and morphological aspects of medical questions. With this method, we seek to examine the linguistic patterns (grammars) of questions which can be made by a speaker in the context of medical procedures.

In Sect. 2, we present a general overview of works related to state-of-the-art question answering systems. In Sect. 3, we describe the generic architecture of the proposed QA system. In Sect. 4, we develop our approach to recognition and analysis of procedural questions and extraction of the right answer.

2 Related Works

There has been a substantial increase in the number of Question Answering systems. This is so because QA systems offer a good solution to retrieve information, discover and share knowledge.

There are many works and research about building factoid QA systems. However, it was during the last years that studies have started to focus also on the creation and development of QA systems for procedural texts.

To our knowledge, there are many research works on procedural texts and QA systems:

- [7]: allows semantic interpretation of procedural texts for answer retrieval and finding a single response from a procedural passage. Benchmark datasets like bAbI, SCoNE and ProPARA have also been created, but they mostly serve the purpose of procedural text comprehension and are not suitable for a guided response.
- [2]: The main aim of the research, apart from its intended contribution to text processing, is to be able to answer procedural questions (How-to? questions). A preliminary structure of a model based on conceptual and linguistic analysis of procedural texts by simple text grammar system in French language.
- [3]: The challenges of answering procedural questions from procedural text have been investigated by Saint-Dizier. Parsing and analyzing argumentative structures in procedural texts have been addressed successfully by Fontan.
- The challenges of answering procedural questions from procedural text have been investigated [8] and procedural title identification and tagging, instructions and instruction arguments have also been investigated and processed. Parsing and analyzing argumentative structures in procedural texts have been addressed successfully.

- A conceptual categorization of procedural questions based on verb categories has also been addressed for French [1]. Also, identification of advice and warning structures from procedural texts has been investigated [4]. A quite large corpus from several domains (basic: cooking, do it yourself, gardening, and complex: social relations, health) and a large number of web sites have been constructed for experiment and it has been found that warnings are basically organized around an 'avoid expression' combined with a proposition

After this investigation, to solve the problem of QA system, the developed question answering system is based on a linguistic approach, using NooJ's linguistic engine in order to formalize the automatic recognition rules and then apply them to a dynamic corpus composed of Arabic medical journalistic articles.

3   The Generic Architecture of the Proposed QA System

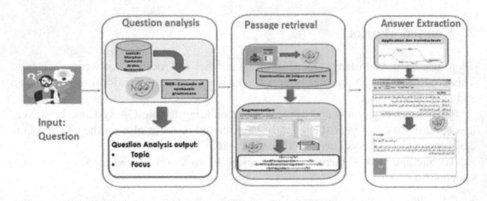

Fig. 1. Architecture of a QA system.

From a general viewpoint, the design of a QA system (Fig. 1.) should include four phases:

1. **Question Analysis:** this module performs a morphological analysis to determine the class of question (procedural question). A question class helps the system to classify the question type to provide a suitable answer. This module may also identify additional semantic features of the question such as the focus and topic.
2. **Passage Retrieval and Segmentation:** the second reason behind question classification is to develop the linguistic patterns for the segmentation of sentences. These patterns are helpful in segmentation and identifying the type of sentences. The main task is to develop the linguistic patterns for the candidate answers. These patterns are helpful in matching in parsing and identifying the candidate answers.

3. **Answer Extraction:** this module selects the most accurate answers among the phrases in a given corpus. The selection is based on the question analysis. The suggested answers are then given to the user as a response to his initial natural language query. We are working on the integration of similarity scores in order to better rank the retrieved passages.

4   Our Approach

4.1   Question Analysis

The system first takes the Arabic question which is preprocessed to extract the query that will be used in the Passage Retrieval module and Text preprocessing segmentation. The question is also classified to identify the type of the question (procedural question) and, consequently, its expected answer, which will then be used in the Answer Extraction module.

Named Entity Recognition (NER):
The Named Entity Recognition (NER) is a critical piece of our QA system to identify such answers and questions associated with the extracted named entities. For this project, we have adapted a rules based approach to recognize Arabic named entities and right answers, using different grammars and gazetteers.

We think that an integration of a NER module will definitely increase the system performance. It is also very important to point out that an NER is required as a tool for almost all the QA system components. The NER module will allow us to extract proper nouns as well as temporal and numeric expressions from raw text [6].

For this purpose, we used our own NER system especially formulated for the Arabic medical domain. We have considered six proper names categories:

1. Organization: named corporate, governmental, or other organizational entity;
2. Location: name of politically or geographically defined location;
3. Person: named person or family;
4. Viruses: names of medical viruses;
5. Disease: names of diseases, illness, sickness;
6. Treatment: names of treatments.

We have considered six proper names categories: organization, location, person, viruses, diseases, and treatment (Table 1).

Table 1. Named entity recognition.

Categories	Definitions	Examples
Organization	Names of corporations, gov. entities or ONGs	بنك ألدم = blood bank
Location	Politically or geographically defined locations	مستشفى الأطفال = Children's Hospital
Person	Names of persons or families	طبيب النساء علي طارق = Gynecologist Tariq Ali
Viruses	Names of medical viruses	فيروس الروتا = Rotavirus
Diseases	Names of diseases, illness, sickness	مرض السرطان = Cancer
Treatment	Names of treatments	علاج طبيعى = Physiotherapist

Then, in order to look for the best answer, the NER provides the maximum amount of information (syntactic, semantic, distributional, etc.) for the given question, such as the expected answer, the type of question and topic of the question. This information will play an important role in the phase of extraction candidate answers (Table 2 and 3).

- Topic: the topic corresponds to the subject matter of the question.
- Focus: the focus corresponds to the specific property of the topic that the user is looking for.

The following example shows the detailed annotation of the identified parts of a question.

Example.

What are the procedures for obtaining a treatment card?

ما هي الإجراءات للحصول على بطاقة علاج؟

ما , What = Interrogative+ ADV

الإجراءات للحصول , the procedures for obtaining = Focus

بطاقة علاج, treatment card = topic

4.2 Segmentation and Passage Retrieval

Sentence segmentation refers to dividing a string of written language into its component.

In this paper, we propose a rule-based approach to Arabic text segmentation, where segments are sentences, our approach relies on an extensive analysis of a large set of lexical cues as well as punctuation marks. Our approach relies on morphological and syntactic information using several dictionaries and orthographic rectification grammar. To this end, we use NooJ linguistic resources [9] in order to perform an abridged morphological and syntactic analysis. Integration of segmentation tool for Arabic texts an enhanced version of [5] (Fig. 2).

- **The sentence style**: + Declarative, + Imperative, + Interrogative OR + Exclamative

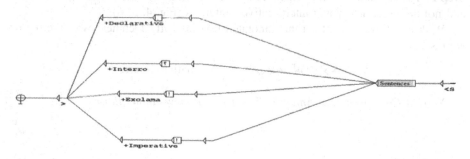

Fig. 2. Segmentation tool for Arabic texts.

This segmentation phase will, on the one hand, reduce the complexity of the analysis and, on the other hand, improve NooJ platform functionalities. Also, we achieved our annotation phase by identifying different types of lexical ambiguities, and then an appropriate set of rules is proposed. These patterns are helpful in segmentation and identifying the type of sentences.

184   E. Bessaies et al.

Example.

ما هي الإجراءات للحصول على بطاقة علاج؟

بطاقة العلاج المجانية هي بطاقة الإعانة الطبية للدولة وتسمح البطاقة لحامليها بالعلاج المجاني. الإجراءات لحصول علي بطاقة علاج الاستظهار بجواز السفر أو شهادة ميلاد أو بطاقة تعريف وطنية وصورة شمسية واستمارة طلب بطاقة العلاج. بعد تكوين الملف تقومون بإيداعه علي مستوي صندوق الاجتماعي القريب من سكناكم.

Step 1: After the application of the grammars on this text we notice that the concordances occur as shown below. The segmentation tool will also identify the type of sentence (Fig. 3).

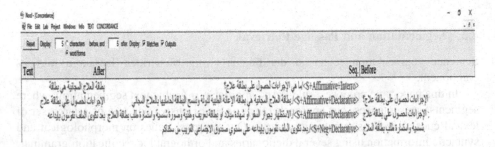

Fig. 3. Concordance using the segmentation tool.

These patterns of segmentation are helpful in matching in parsing and identifying the candidate answers and type of sentence.
Step 2: The annotation of the sentences by the recognition of the declarative sentences and not the exclamatory and interrogative sentences (Fig. 4, 5, 6).

With NooJ, we can extract the annotated text in XML document with the regular expression:

<S+affirmative+Interro> ؟من يدعم الموت الرحيم —

1. *NooJ > Concordance > Annotate Text (add/ remove annotation)*

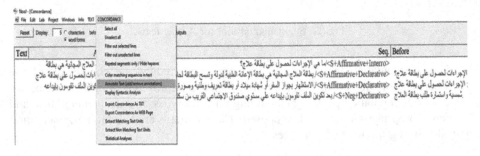

Fig. 4. Result of *Annotate Text*.

2. *Text > Export annotated text as an XML document*

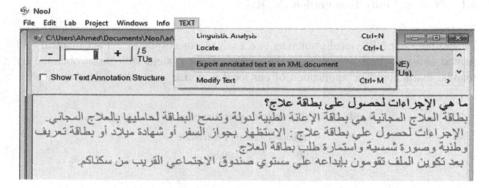

Fig. 5. Exporting text annotation.

After *Export annotated text as an XML document*, we need to add tag annotation < S > (sentence).

3. Add < S >

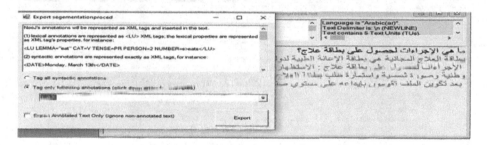

Fig. 6. Result of annotating a text as an XML text.

The segmentation process undertaken in this study will be described. Then the text segments will be discussed, first in general terms, introducing the units of analysis in this study, then in particular terms, examining the paragraph and the sentence as independent units of analysis.

Passage Retrieval is typically used as the first step in current QA systems. In particular, we show how a variety of prior language models trained on correct answer text allow us to incorporate into the retrieval step information that is often used in answer extraction.

Step 3: After analyzing the procedural question, extract the focus and the question topic and segment the text in order to extract the candidate answers.

5 Experiments and Results

5.1 Named Entity Recognition (NER)

Evaluation

To evaluate our NER local grammars, we analyze our corpus to extract manually all named entities. Then, we compare the results of our system with those obtained by manual extraction. The application of our local grammar gives the following result:

Table 2. NER grammar experiments on our corpus.

Precision	Recall	F-Measure
0,90	0,82	0,88

According to these results, we have obtained an acceptable identification of named entities. Our evaluation shows F-Measure 0,88. We note that the rate of silence in the corpus is low, which is represented by the recall value 0,88 because journalistic texts of our corpus are heterogeneous and extracted from different resources (Fig. 7).

Fig. 7. Result of NER NooJ syntactic grammar.

5.2   Recognition and Analysis of Procedural Questions

Evaluation

To evaluate our automatic annotation question local grammars, we also analyze our user's queries to extract manually the question analysis. Then, we compare the results of our system with those obtained by manual extraction. The application of our local grammar gives the following result:

Table 3. Annotation question grammar experiments.

Precision	Recall	F-Measure
0,89	0,81	0,87

According to these results, we have obtained an acceptable annotation of the question.

Our evaluation shows F-Measure 0,87. We note that the rate of silence in the corpus is low, which is represented by the recall value 0,81. This is due to the fact that this assessment is mainly based on the results of the NER module (Fig. 8).

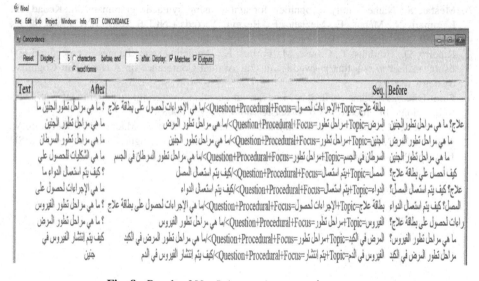

Fig. 8. Result of NooJ *Annotation* syntactic grammar.

6   Conclusion

In this paper, the task of our QA system is divided into three phases: question analysis, segmentation and passage retrieval, and answer extraction. Each of these phases play a critical role in the general performance of QA systems. Our focus of work was chiefly placed on the first phase: question analysis. In the near future, we aim to apply this pattern extraction to a real corpus in order to deal with the answer extraction phase. As a medium-term research, we intend to consider studying the processing of the other type of question (Questions with examples).

References

1. Aouladomar, F., Saint-Dizier, P.: An exploration of the diversity of natural argumentation in instructional texts. In: 5th International Workshop on ComputationalModels of Natural Argument, IJCAI, Edinburgh (2005)
2. Delpech, E., Saint-Dizier, P.: Investigating the structure of procedural texts for answering how-to questions. In: Proceedings of LREC (2008)
3. Fontan, L., Saint-Dizier, P.: Analyzing argumentative structures in procedural texts. In: Nordström, B., Ranta, A. (eds.) GoTAL 2008. LNCS (LNAI), vol. 5221, pp. 366–370. Springer, Heidelberg (2008). https://doi.org/10.1007/978-3-540-85287-2_35
4. Fontan, L., Saint-Dizier, P.: Constructing a know-how repository of advices and warnings from procedural texts. ACM Symp. Doc. Eng. **2008**, 249–252 (2008)
5. Hammouda, N.G., Haddar, K.: Integration of a segmentation tool for arabic corpora in nooj platform to build an automatic annotation tool. In: Barone, L., Monteleone, M., Silberztein, M. (eds.) NooJ 2016. CCIS, vol. 667, pp. 89–100. Springer, Cham (2016). https://doi.org/10.1007/978-3-319-55002-2_8
6. Mesfar, S.: Named entity recognition for arabic using syntactic grammars. In: Kedad, Z., Lammari, N., Métais, E., Meziane, F., Rezgui, Y. (eds.) NLDB 2007. LNCS, vol. 4592, pp. 305–316. Springer, Heidelberg (2007). https://doi.org/10.1007/978-3-540-73351-5_27
7. Ribeiro, D., Hinrichs, T., Crouse, M., Forbus, K.: Predicting state changes in procedural text using analogical question answering. In: 7th Annual Conference on Advances in Cognitive Systems (2019)
8. Saint-Dizier, P.: Some challenges of advanced question-answering: an experiment with how-to questions. In Proceedings of PACLIC **2008**, 65–73 (2008)
9. Silberztein, M.: NooJ's linguistic annotation engine. In: Koeva, S., Maurel, D., Silberztein, M. (eds.), INTEX/NooJ pour le Traitement Automatique des Langues, Cahiers de la MSH Ledoux. Presses Universitaires de Franche-Comté, pp. 9–26 (2006)

Integrated NooJ Environment for Arabic Linguistic Disambiguation Improvement Using MWEs

Dhekra Najar[✉], Slim Mesfar, and Henda Ben Ghezela

RIADI, University of Manouba, Manouba, Tunisia
Dhekra.najar@gmail.com

Abstract. Language resources are a necessary component to language Development in NLP. They are useful for any empirical language study including linguistic analysis, language translation and language disambiguation. The linguistic development environment NooJ (http://www.nooj4nlp.net/) allow formalizing complex linguistic phenomena such as compound words generation, processing as well as analysis. NooJ offers the possibility to use the dynamic library NoojEngine.dll or the command-line program: noojapply.exe. In this study, we will take advantage of the noojapply.exe program that is freely available in the Standard edition of NooJ. Noojapply.exe allows users to apply dictionaries and grammars automatically to texts from external environments.

In this paper, we introduce a module for Arabic MWEs recognition that is based on rules grammar. MWEs module allows recognizing several types of morphosyntactic variations that can occur to a Multi Word Expression. Then, these linguistic resources are compiled to be used as parameters in the command-line noojapply.exe in order to be integrated within an Arabic language processing environment for linguistic disambiguation. Our work is divided into three sections. First, we deal with a literature review on disambiguation tasks in the Arabic language. Then, we give a detailed description of our Integrated NooJ environment for Arabic linguistic disambiguation and the associated grammars. Finally, a set of tests and experiments is carried out to measure the impact of multi- word expression recognition in Word disambiguation.

Keywords: Disambiguation · Natural language processing · NooJ · Arabic language · NLP

1 Introduction

Arabic is a morphologically complex and challenging language. This is due to various specificities that place serious obstacles for the majority of Natural Language Processing applications in this language. In fact, Arabic morphology and syntax provide the ability to add a large number of affixes to each word which makes combinatorial increment of possible words and meanings [1]. Thus, it is only by relying on contextual and semantic features that we are able to understand such words.

© Springer Nature Switzerland AG 2022
M. González et al. (Eds.): NooJ 2022, CCIS 1758, pp. 189–201, 2022.
https://doi.org/10.1007/978-3-031-23317-3_16

Therefore, a disambiguation process is needed to better interpret and understand a text. Automatic lexical disambiguation task is one of the most productive areas of Automatic Language Processing. Several works associate word disambiguation tasks to the identification of their POS (part-of-speech). POS disambiguation is the fact of determining the grammatical category of a word in a particular context to finally obtain an annotated corpus. Note that a disambiguated annotated corpus is a document where each word has only one morpho-syntactic annotation [2].

In this paper, we study the different types of ambiguity levels in Arabic language and present a based-rule method for Arabic text analysis and disambiguation. We take advantage of NooJ's linguistic engine to implement disambiguation syntactic grammars. More specifically, for each ambiguous word, a list of specific syntactic rules is applied in order to specify the correct morphological interpretation of that word.

Our work is divided into three sections. First, we deal with a literature review on disambiguation tasks in the Arabic language. Then, we give a detailed description of our Integrated NooJ environment for Arabic linguistic disambiguation and the associated grammars. Finally, a set of tests and experiments is carried out to measure the impact of multi- word expression recognition in Word Disambiguation.

2   State of Art

2.1   Arabic Specificities

Unfortunately, the lack of Arabic linguistic resources that are publicly available makes the progress of Natural Language Processing (NLP) applications in this language difficult. Arabic language specificities make the analysis of Arabic text complicated. This is due to two fundamental factors:

- The words are characterized by their rich agglutinative structures;
- Arabic texts are generally non-vocalized which results in a high degree of lexical ambiguity.

Other specificities like the high inflectional nature of Arabic language, the dual forms for pronouns and verbs, and the absence of the upper case in the beginning of named entities, represent a challenging problem for Arabic NLP researchers. These Arabic language specificities place difficulties for the majority of Natural Language Processing applications. We illustrate Arabic ambiguities with these examples (Table 1):

Table 1. Arabic ambiguities examples.

	Example 1	Example 2	Example 3
Arabic word	ذهب (1)	عامل (2)	أسد (3)
Meaning 1	gold (n)	employee (n)	Did he block ? (Interrogative agglutination)
Meaning 2	goes (v)	treats (v)	lion (n)
Meaning 3	Make gold (v)	factor (n)	I block (v)

When we see the words in example 1, 2 and 3 in isolation, we cannot determine the exact meaning of each word. As seen in the third example, prefixes and suffixes can be agglutinated to another word so can produce a form that is homographic with another full form word [3].

Example: أسد lion - سد + ا I block.

We also notice the various meanings that can give a polysemic (multi-meaning) word: example 1 and 2. In this case, the meaning can only be interpreted by relying on context and semantics.

2.2 Sources of Syntactic Ambiguity in Arabic

2.2.1 Vocalization Ambiguity

Vocalization, or short vowels, are largely absent in Arabic texts, the matter that makes morphological and syntactic analysis difficult and highly ambiguous [4].

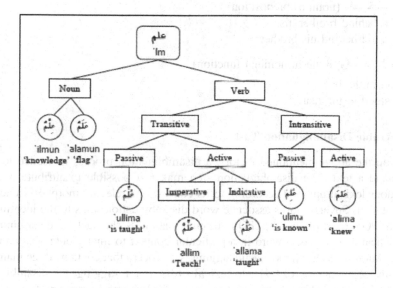

Fig. 1. Vocalization Ambiguity of the word "علم".

In Fig. 1, we illustrate ambiguities of the word "علم" caused by the lack of vocalization. As we can see in the figure below, all lemmas are different only in that one of them has a doubled sound or different vocalization which is not explicit in writing or even in reading.

2.2.2 Word Order Ambiguity

Arabic allows VSO, SVO and VOS constructions. While SVO is easily detected by the parser and usually does not cause an ambiguity problem [5].

- أكل الولد التفاحة: VSO sentence
  The boy ate the apple.
- الولد أكل التفاحة: SVO sentence
  The boy ate the apple.
- الولد أكل التفاحة: VOS sentence
  The boy ate the apple.

A lot of ambiguities are also caused by the relatively free word order in Arabic (VSO, VOS) especially for Automatic identification of POS tasks.

2.2.3 Multifunctionality of Arabic Nouns

Arabic nouns are characterized by their multifunctionality. They are derived from verbs and can take verbal functions in the sentence. Some nouns also can become prepositions, adverbs, adjectives [5].

- وقف خلف أخيه (noun as preposition)
  stood behind brother-his.
  He stood behind his brother.

- وقف في الخلف (noun in nominal function)
  stood in the-back.
  He stood in the rear.

2.3 Arabic Disambiguation Task

Based on the above-mentioned factors, a disambiguation process is needed to better understand a text. The disambiguation step makes it possible to attribute, for each ambiguous lexical unit and according to its context, the relevant morpho-syntactic tag or annotation. Several works associate word disambiguation tasks to the identification of their POS (part-of-speech). POS disambiguation is the fact of determining the grammatical category of a word in a particular context to finally obtain an annotated corpus. Automatic morpho-syntactic tagging is a process that contains three main steps [6, 7]: the segmentation of text into **lexical units**; **prior tagging**; the disambiguation which makes it possible to attribute, for each lexical unit and according to its context, the relevant morpho-syntactic annotation.

Based on the literature, there are three main approaches: linguistic approach that makes use of the rules of the language such as morphological or syntactic information implemented in language specific rules; statistical approach that uses a set of standard statistical scores to estimate the degree of association between its words and hybrid approach that combines statistical calculus and linguistic Filters. The approach we follow for developing our system is mainly based on a linguistic approach. We generally deal with Arabic language ambiguities and specifically with morpho-syntactic ambiguities. The system is mainly based on a local grammar containing various rules for disambiguation. Our approach distinguishes between the problems of morphological analysis (what are all the different readings of a word without regard to context) and morphological disambiguation (what is the correct reading in a specific context).

3 Approach

3.1 Disambiguation Approach

The main concern of our study is to treat the different types of ambiguity levels in Arabic language. We present a based-rule method for Arabic text analysis and disambiguation in order to reduce the number of annotations in a text and determine the relevant morpho syntactic tag. As previously mentioned, we have to follow 3 main steps in order to disambiguate Arabic text:

1. the segmentation of text into lexical units which is ensured by NooJ's morphological analyzer [8];
2. the prior tagging (simple words) using El-DicAr [9];
3. the disambiguation process is based on a local grammar containing various rules for the resolution of Arabic ambiguities.

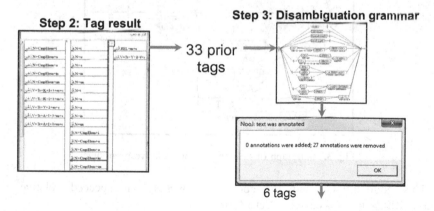

Fig. 2. Disambiguation step.

Applying these steps to this example below (who has gone, الذي قد ذهب), produces the following linguistic analyses. Our approach distinguishes between the problems of morphological analysis (what are all the different readings of a word without regard to context as seen in step 1) and morphological disambiguation (what is the correct reading in a specific context by applying the disambiguation grammar).

As we can see in the example below in Fig. 2 (who has gone, الذي قد ذهب), we have 33 prior tags resulting from applying El-DicAr[1] dictionary resources (step 2). The disambiguation process (step 3) aims to detect the relevant tag for ambiguous words by identifying the correct POS and reducing the number of lexical codes for each word. The number of annotations of this example was reduced to only 6 tags.

ذَهب ´   ⑥   ´V+الذي + قَد´

- The word "الذي" should correspond to a relative pronoun;
- The second word to the adverb «قَد»;
- ذهب should be here annotated as a verb and could not be in the future or Imperative form.

3.2 Disambiguation Grammars

Our approach is mainly based on a local grammar containing various rules for Arabic disambiguation that were manually detected. We have taken some Arabic basic linguistic rules into account to be as efficient as possible (Fig. 3).

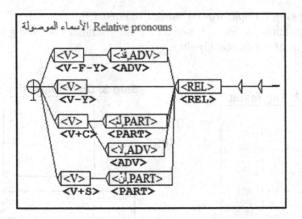

Fig. 3. Subgraph of disambiguation "relative pronouns"

This grammar is used to report that words that succeed relative pronouns <REL> are in accusative Verb form.

In fact, in this example, the word ("الذي", who) should correspond to a relative pronoun, and the second occurrence to the adverb «ذهب» (قد; «ذهب», goes) should be here annotated as a verb and could not be in the future or Imperative (constraint: <V-F-Y>)[2].

This grammar recognizes the sequence "(who has gone, الذي قد ذهب)". In that case, it produces the annotation " <REL>" at the position of the word ("الذي", who), and the

---

[1] "El-DicAr" Electronic Dictionary for Arabic linguistic resources.

[2] Verbs, nouns and adjectives codes in El-DicAr are listed in the Appendix.

annotation " <ADV>" at the position of the word «دَ» and produce 6 tags to the word (ذهب, goes). The left tags are different semantic annotations reading the word (ذهب, goes). All the various morpho-syntactic readings were deleted.

✓ Morpho-syntactic disambiguation.
• Semantic disambiguation.

Note that each of these annotations has a 0- character length; in consequence, NooJ uses them to filter out all the annotations of the Text Annotation Structure that are not compatible with them [10]. In consequence, many morpho-syntactic annotations are deleted, as well as some semantic annotations.

Our goal is to develop a set of rules such as the rule above in order to target frequent ambiguous words and linguistic structures to be as efficient as possible. We should be as specific as possible to avoid producing incorrect results.

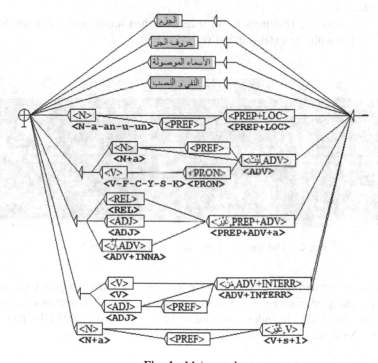

Fig. 4. Main graph.

Initially, we try to collect the maximum of Arabic basic linguistic rules. Then, these rules are used within syntactic grammars to locate ambiguous sequences in text. The grammar rules use information from gazetteers combined with contextual and syntactic information.

As seen in Fig. 4, our grammar contains various subgraphs: Apocopate[3], Genitive[4], Denial/Accusative, Optative and some particular cases that were manually detected and verified by a linguistic expert.

We will use our compiled linguistic resources and modules as parameters in the command-line noojapply.exe in order to be integrated within an Arabic language processing environment for linguistic disambiguation.

- We execute noojapply.exe from the command-line program.
- We launch the command form:

☐ Noojapply language-code result.ind lexicalresources.nom+ syntacticresources. nog+ onequery,og texts,txt+

☐ noojapply ar ORGANISATIONS.ind _ElDicAr.nod CompoundDic.nod Graph_Morpho_Locked.nom Graph_Morpho_AlifToHamza_Locked.nom Graph_ Morpho_HamzaToAlif_Locked.nom Ly_MorphologicalGrammar.nom ENAMEX_ ORG.nog text.txt

This will apply the resources to all texts and then apply and index the query to result in the file with the extension.ind (Fig. 5).

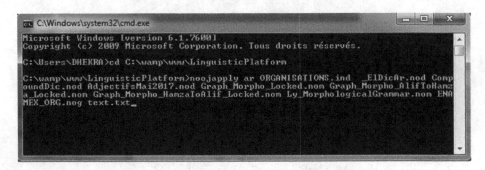

Fig. 5. The command in noojapply.exe command-line.

We executed a number of Noojapply.exe commands from a php code to apply dictionaries and grammars (queries) automatically to texts from our external environment and we were able to index 4 modules: Module for Arabic MWEs recognition; Module for NER recognition (Location, Organizations, Persons) (Fig. 6);

---

[3] Apocopate cutting off the last sound or syllable of a word.

[4] A form of the noun in some languages, which shows the relationship of possession or origin between one thing and another.

```
.ind
256,287,<ENAMEX+PERS+Autre+F=الاتحاد في الصحة مدير+N=إيمانويل+POLIT>
4,17,<ENAMEX+PERS+Autre+F=مدير+N=إيمانويل+POLIT>
5,17,<ENAMEX+PERS+TITRE+N=سوزان>
6,21,<ENAMEX+PERS+Autre+F=سفير+N=إيمانويل+POLIT>
6,31,<ENAMEX+PERS+Autre+F=الاتحاد مُناضل+N=إيمانويل+POLIT>
46,58,<ENAMEX+PERS>
65,82,<ENAMEX+PERS+TITRE+N=سوزان>
350,381,<ENAMEX+PERS+Autre+F=الاتحاد في الصحة مدير+N=إيمانويل+POLIT>
*****
```

Fig. 6. Example of a resulting file.ind.

4 Experimentations and Results

We present preliminary experiments on a corpus containing 150 heterogeneous articles from the web.

- Unvowled corpus;
- 2.202 number of lexical units;
- 20.292 number of prior tags.

Based on our disambiguation grammar we were able to remove about 40,000 thousand.

Beside the real ambiguities, we were faced with some system ambiguities that are due to the interaction of rules and the competition of constraints (priority). So, we were obliged to restructure our grammar so we avoid interaction of rules.

Table 2. Results

	Removed annotations	Added annotations (semantic)
AMBG Genitive حروف الجر	5814	0
AMBG Accusative - النصب	386	0
AMBG Disambig others	221	0
AMBG Verbal Negation لا, لَنْ, ما	167	0
AMBG Personal pronouns الأسماء الموصولة	85	0
AMBG Coordination حُرُوفُ العَطْفُ	10	0
AMBG Demonstrative pronouns - إِسْمُ الْإشارَةِ	10	0
AMBG Apocopate - الجزم	3	0
AMBG Nominal Negation لَيْسَ	0	0
AMBG Vocative النّدَاءُ	0	0
MWEs Grammar	500	58
Organization Grammar	0	58
Persons Grammar	0	45
Locations Grammar	0	5
Total	**7196**	**166**

Based on our disambiguation grammar we were able to remove about 35,47% thousand. We obtain a high accuracy rate as seen in Table 2.

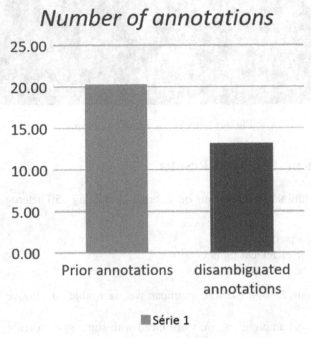

Fig. 7. Number of reduced annotations.

The table above presents the recall and precision obtained by applying disambiguation grammar on the test corpus. The results, as seen in Table 2, indicate that we have reached high quality results of ambiguity recognition in the texts.

Table 3. Results

Precision	Recall
0.97	0.88

We believe that our system has **reduced morpho-syntactic ambiguities** and have ameliorated the precision of the results (Table 3).

There is some silence due to some missing rules in our grammar or to the implementation complexity of some rules but we judge our results as precise because we can see that in most cases the annotations deleted are correct (Fig. 7).

Although, we have some delimitation problems that are related to:

- Some complex rules to implement;
- Lack of some rules in our grammar.

We also have an Arabic character encoding issue that we still work to resolve it in order to correctly get an annotated text.

Fig. 8. Annotated text.

Finally, we are still working on disambiguation's grammar enrichment and enhancement. We aim to reach advanced level of morpho-syntactic disambiguation through the disambiguation platform in order to be able to annotate texts with different semantic annotations as seen in Fig. 8.

5   Conclusion

In this paper, we study the different types of ambiguity levels in Arabic language and present a based-rule method for Arabic text analysis and morpho-syntactic disambiguation. We take advantage of NooJ's linguistic engine to implement disambiguation syntactic grammars. More specifically, for each ambiguous word, a list of specific syntactic rules is applied in order to specify the correct morphological interpretation of that word.

Disambiguation process must be integrated in the preprocessing stages in order to obtain better linguistic analysis with NLP tools.

Further work is needed to remove the compositional analyses of compound nouns using the CompounDic [11] as well as NER grammar [12]. This will reduce the number of annotations of the sentences in text.

Appendix

Verb's codes in El-DicAr	P	Transitive - Indicative
	I	Intransitive - Past
	S	Subjunctive
	C	Apocopate
	F	Future
	Y	Imperative
	A	Active form
	K	Passive form
Noun's and adjective's codes in El-DicAr	a	Accusative
	u	Nominative
	i	Genitive
	an	Tanwin, Nominative
	un	Tanwin, Accusative
	in	Tanwin, Genitive
Noun's and adjective's codes in El-DicAr	1, 2, 3	1st, 2d, 3d person
	M, f	Male, female
	S, d, p	Singular, dual, plural
	S, d, p	Singular, dual, plural

References

1. Ditters, E.: A formal grammar for the description of sentence structure in modern standard Arabic. In: The Proceeding of Arabic NLP Workshop at ACL/EACL (2001)
2. El Jihad, A., Yousfi, A.: Etiquetage morpho-syntaxique des textes arabes par modèle de Markov caché. In: Proceedings of Rencontre des Etudiants Chercheurs en Informatique pour le Traitement Automatique des Langues, pp. 649–65 (2005)
3. Kamir, D., Soreq, N., Neeman, Y.: A comprehensive NLP system for modern standard Arabic and modern Hebrew. In: Proceedings of the ACL-02 Workshop on Computational Approaches to Semitic Languages. Association for Computational Linguistics, pp. 1–9 (2002)
4. Attia, M.A.: Accommodating multiword expressions in an Arabic LFG grammar. In: Salakoski, Tapio, Ginter, Filip, Pyysalo, Sampo, Pahikkala, Tapio (eds.) FinTAL 2006. LNCS (LNAI), vol. 4139, pp. 87–98. Springer, Heidelberg (2006). https://doi.org/10.1007/11816508_11

5. Attia, M.: An ambiguity-controlled morphological analyzer for modern standard Arabic modeling finite state networks. In: Challenges of Arabic for NLP/MT Conference, The British Computer Society, London, UK, vol. 200610, no. 1.72 (2006)
6. Le Minh, P.: Silicon light emitting devices for integrated applications (2003)
7. Paroubek, P., Rajman, M.: Etiquetage morpho-syntaxique. Ingénierie des langues, 131–150 (2000)
8. Silberztein, M.: La formalisation des langues: l'approche NooJ. ISTE, London (2015)
9. Mesfar, S.: Analyse morpho-syntaxique automatique et reconnaissance des entités nommées en arabe standard (Doctoral dissertation, Université de Franche-Comté. UFR des Sciences du langage, de l'homme et de la société) (2008)
10. Silberztein, M.: "NooJ's Dictionaries". In: the Proceedings of the 2nd Language and Technology Conference, Poznan (2005)
11. Najar, D., Mesfar, S., Ghezela, H.B.: A large terminological dictionary of arabic compound words. In: Okrut, T., Hetsevich, Y., Silberztein, M., Stanislavenka, H. (eds.) NooJ 2015. CCIS, vol. 607, pp. 16–28. Springer, Cham (2016). https://doi.org/10.1007/978-3-319-42471-2_2
12. Najar, D., Mesfar, S.: Opinion mining and sentiment analysis for Arabic on-line texts: application on the political domain. Int. J. Speech Technol. 20(3), 575–585 (2017). https://doi.org/10.1007/s10772-017-9422-4

The Digital Text Workshop Cloud, New Solutions for Super Calculation Environments

Ilaria Veronesi[1]([✉]) [iD], Rita Bucciarelli[2] [iD], Francesco Saverio Tortoriello[1] [iD],
Andrea Rodrigo[3] [iD], Marianna Greco[4] [iD], Colomba La Ragione[5] [iD],
and Javier Julian Enriquez[6] [iD]

[1] University of Salerno, Fisciano, Italy
iveronesi@unisa.it
[2] University of Siena, Siena, Italy
[3] University of Rosario, Rosario, Argentina
[4] Ministry of Education, Rome, Italy
[5] University Pegaso of Naples, Naples, Italy
[6] Polytechnic University of Valencia, Valencia, Spain

Abstract. Quantum physics is the basis of scientific thinking and influences the mind. Wendt [1] in Quantum Mind and Social Science argues that the mind and social life are macroscopic phenomena of quantum mechanics and that *the quantum consciousness hypothesis* is the cognitive basis of a quantum social science. In these new scientific parameters of knowledge, our visualization matrix is essentially a holographic projection. Research innovation lies in seeking the point of convergence to describe a formal process that, as a multi-code process, goes from a phase of joined sentences to a data implementation phase, Planat of the Institute of Femto -ST Dep. of Micro Nano Sciences and Systems, Besançon, France. The goal is to find points of contact between quantum physics, computational linguistics, and quantum computing. Planat [2] states that the quality that the linguist must possess beyond courage is… *Competence to transcribe mathematical concepts into grammatical structures.* This assumption is at the basis of our study. The tools are 1) identifying new parameters for the production of fixed structures identified in the Planat model mathematical theories; 2) using Charles Baudelaire's narrative text [3] to clarify the importance of the verb in the sentence through the research and experimentation method into a local grammar; 3) utilizing Max Silberztein's NooJ system [4], for the production of sentence analysis and paraphrases, tools for developing formal dictionaries and grammars, and NLP applications such as semantic annotators; 4) developing the implementation of advanced integrated Machine Learning algorithms for the creation of knowledge from obtained data; 5) applying the BuViTeMS (© 2020) AW Digital Intelligence model for the production of edited, reformulated and translated sentences using a mixed system. Thus, the entire formal process will make use of: 1 Lexicon-Grammatical to transfer the numerical quantum language into a lexicon-grammatical code; 2 The NooJ's environment to generate statistical analysis and graphs.

Keywords: Scientific thinking · Quantum physics · Quantum computing · Computational linguistics, · Multi-code process · Mathematical concepts · Grammatical structures

© Springer Nature Switzerland AG 2022
M. González et al. (Eds.): NooJ 2022, CCIS 1758, pp. 202–213, 2022.
https://doi.org/10.1007/978-3-031-23317-3_17

1 Introduction

Quantum communication with a digital transformation is like in Gloria Bertasi[1] *A drone flying over the city, past and future that are married in a sequence, to summarize in a video, with images, our... Digital, classrooms, coworking.* It is a new didactic model that represents a leading project from the rector Tiziana Lippiello*: «Commitment to the new generations. We are a forge of ideas to face global challenges»* It is a communication that digitalizes signs, symbols and icons, morphs, imprinted in formal techniques, but which scientifically transmits an integral semantics. The idea is born from the collaboration research model with scientists from all over the planet, who meet on a social network dedicated to all scientific disciplines, who work on areas of expertise and who use new tools for comparison, in real time. It is an open dialogue in which the experts by field of experience provide materials and guidance. In other words, collaboration in real time leads the participants to understand the study indicators, the methodology, and a model *of Project quantum computing: quantum models, technologies and validations.* These are products available at Research Gate[2], which offers an open dialogue in collaborative work. The present work focuses, on the DPH text[3] in the field of quantum and literary communication which represents the synthesis of the *digital literary communication project included in Graphic coverings to study non local structures of communication descriptions analysis validations magazén: lieux - méthodologies - processus et validations.*[4] The objective is to create semantic equivalences between quantum mathematics and computational linguistics in the French narrative typology in which the guiding themes are: Entanglement Numbers; experts Corpus Linguistics Grammar Computational Linguistics Morphology Natural Language Processing Lexicography Syntax NooJ. We have conducted and authored searches in these related topics ranging from number theory to the theory of group graphs _ sentence. The present work instead represents the intuition of the passage from literary textuality in the digital one, or from a narrative text in code.[5] The model is Quantum Gravity Research, Los Angeles, and in Raymond Aschheim, Marcelo M. Amaral, Fang and Klee Irwin, who in Graph Coverings for Investigating *Non-Local Structures in Proteins, Music and Poems* [2], Charles Baudelaire, in Les Petits Poèmes en prose [3].

In this way, the mathematical model proposed by French experts is analyzed, in addition to the points of contact and structural equivalences between mathematical theory and computational linguistics, but above all, a new exploration is identified in the research area that generates a new mathematical, linguistic, computer science multi code paradigm, etc. Thus, providing us with points of reflection to reach the equivalences

---

[1] https://corrieredelveneto.corriere.it/venezia-mestre/cronaca/21_dicembre_23/venezia-futuro-ca-foscari-digitale-aule-coworking-studentato-lido-27357a14-6.

[2] https://www.researchgate.net/publication/355491134_Quantum_computation_and_measurements_from_a_space-time_in_fixed_languages.

[3] https://www.researchgate.net/messages/1770891171.

[4] https://www.researchgate.net/publication/355116190_Graphic_coverings_to_study_non_local_structures_of_communication_descriptions_analysis_validations_magazen_lieux_-met ologies_-processus_et_validations.

[5] All books on Research Gate.

between the structures or between the different typologies. The research question is: will we be able to find other points of convergence between quantum theory, mathematics, and linguistics?

Likewise, the research hypothesis is structured with a new methodology with the participation of experts, who meet on a social network and work within areas of expertise, using new tools of comparison. The present work focuses on the formal process of literary production, on its encounter with digital intelligence. The research questions are: -Will the mathematical model succeed in describing formal processes? Will we succeed with scientific theories to elucidate the process of synthesis of languages and still find the points of convergence between quantum mathematics and computational linguistics? With Nagel and Newman [5] the attempts to mechanize the mental processes of reasoning begin, and it should not be forgotten that already Euclid codified geometry, but many centuries will pass before one could have axiomatic reasoning. Mathematicians and logicians first sensed that in formal systems, meaning and form of the knowable and nature could be discerned. Indeed, in the dialogue Caroll [6] poses a profound philosophical problem in Douglas R, Hofstadter Godel, Escher, Bach "do words and thoughts follow formal rules or not?" The answer is to be found in Wendt [1]: we are continually "trapped" through language and communication. As a result, it is inferable that today's communication is formal, that is, made of systems, axioms, methods of validation and theorems and included in a formal grammar (Table 1).

A Mathematical Model: Group Relationship and Analysis

In the first phase, we look for the assumptions that lead us to the primary purpose, which is to verify the applicability of scientific theories, as a correlation tool to literary communication. We analyze and investigate the process that transformed the literary text into a scientific model performed by M. Planat. The conjugation classes of the subgroups in a finitely generated group start from the concept of relationship. Let $rel(x_1, x_2, \ldots, x_r)$ be the relation defining the finitely presented group $fp = \langle x_1, x_2, \ldots, x_r | rel(x_1, x_2, \ldots, x_r) \rangle$ on r letters (or generators). We focus our attention on the classes of subgroups of fp with respect to the nature of the relation rel.

Table 1. Reformulation of the textual tract of C. Baudelaire sequence in Planat et al.

t	$d=1$	$d=2$	$d=3$	$d=4$	$d=5$	$d=6$	$d=7$
1	1	1	1	1	1	1	1
2	1	3	7	26	97	624	4163
3	1	7	41	604	13,753	504,243	24,824,785
4	1	15	235	14,120	1,712,845	371,515,454	127,635,996,839
5	1	31	1361	334,576	207,009,649	268,530,771,271	644,969,015,852,641

The point of convergence between linguistics and mathematics lies in a side-by-side methodology, namely, the transfer of the number group to the phrase group is the French research model ... *Our mathematical theory of the secondary structures in proteins, music and poems relies on the concept of a finitely generated group and the corresponding graph coverings... and LGLI lexicon-grammar methodologies.* The intuition arises that the process of the mathematical model for the reduction of the group just described is filtered through... *The cardinality structure ηd (fp) of the conjugation classes of the subgroups...*[6]*to transform a group into a partition of certain cardinality structures and then... And so the formal reduction process is the same as the linguistic model.*

In the first stage, we identify in the theories of Planat [2] a formal paradigm that is developed in mathematical theories. By then, the assumptions are sought that lead us to the primary purpose, which is to test the applicability of scientific theories, as a correlation tool to literary communication. They focus the studies on the mathematical model on the justifications of formal processes as K. Godel in Douglas R; Hofstadter Godel, Escher [6] *of uses mathematical reasoning to explore mathematical reasoning itself* and this is what happened in the present work in which mathematical theories, such as group theories and their properties, are investigated in search of answers included in mathematical reasoning itself, to motivate, validate and justify: 1- the comparison of parameters in different textual contexts; 2- structuring or validating a guiding formal system, which by serving mathematical reasoning (system of validation of axioms, a method etc.) in Douglas R; Hofstadter Godel pg. 50 [6], theories, theorems to support that activate a synthetic, homologated, fixed formal code embedded in a new formal paradigm; 3- analysis of the Quantum Gravity Research model, in Planat [2], Charles Baudelaire, in Les Petits Poèmes en prose: Le Spleen de Paris, 1869, poème XVI for the narrative text seq. n ᵛ 2 [3]:

[...] *Le gamin du céleste Empire hésita d'abord; puis, se ravisant, il répondit: «Je vais vous le dire.» Peu d'instants après, il reparut, tenant dans ses bras un fort gros chat, et le regardant, comme on dit, dans le blanc des yeux, il affirma sans hésiter: «Il n'est pas encore tout à fait midi.» Ce qui était vrai. [...].*[7]

In wanting to proceed to an analysis, we focus on the text in question and identify the points of convergence, according to Planat [2], our mathematical theory of secondary structures in proteins, music and poems is based on the concept of finitely generated groups and the corresponding coverings of graphs, as explained. A theory in which the authors declare their belonging not only, they explain their similarity points, transformations and code symbols embedded in their own grammar, making use of scientific theories in these focal points: page 1 [2] *Introduction.... In this paper, we show for the first time a remarkable analogy between the structure of the bonds between amino acids of a protein (the secondary structure of proteins) and the nonlocal structures observed in tonal music and poems. We explain the origin of these analogies with finitely generated groups and graph covering theory.*

---

[6] IBIDEM page 3.

[7] Gouvard, J. M. (2017). Le Spleen de Paris de Charles Baudelaire: des «petits genres journalistiques» aux «petits poèmes en prose». Mémoires du livre/Studies in Book Culture, 8(2).

Description: Transformation into finite group: Analysis and partitions into groups (group theory); Homomorphism, Generators, etc (Table 2).

Chosen codes:

– Protein language = alphabet;
– Musical language = letters (tonal analysis -) recursion
– Poetic -narrative language = letters (final analysis) recursion

Categories of 3 symbols: H = (Names and Adj); E = (V); C = (diet and ended).

Categories of 4 symbols: H = (Names and Adds); E = (V); C = (diet and ended); A = Prep.

Categories of 5 symbols: H = (Names and Adds); E = (V); C = (diet and ended); A = Prep; Lawyer.

Table 2. Reformulation of the textual tract of C. Baudelaire sequence in Planat et al. pag 9

Le Gamin du Céleste Empire … Ce Qui était Vrai.	Card. Seq. of cc of Subgroups	r
3 letters: rel=$C^2 H^6 C^2 H^7 H^8 E^8 C^7 CC^4 CC^2 E^8 C \cdots$	[1,3,7,34,131]	2
4 letters: rel=$C^2 H^6 A^2 H^7 H^8 E^8 C^7 CC^4 CC^2 E^8 C \cdots$	[1,7,41,636,14364]	3
5 letters: rel=$C^2 H^6 A^2 H^7 H^8 E^8 B^7 CB^4 CC^2 E^8 C \cdots$	[1,15,235,14376,]	4

. Research conducted so far, thanks to the scientific model and Planat [2] in Quantum Gravity Research, Los Angeles, and in Raymond Aschheim, and Marcelo M. Amaral, Fang and Klee Irwin in Graph Coverings for Investigating "Non-Local Structures in Proteins, Music and Poems" to the support guided in the studies. It has enabled us to describe in the quantum mathematical model a new formal code in a descriptive grammar. The dissertation continues with the transfer into a formal grammar, with a different code, but with the same mathematical axioms.

2 Comparing Models: Language Environments and Lexicon-Grammar as an Elementary Calculation LGLI

Progressing in the exposed sense, let us compare the mathematical pattern in the methodologies of M. Planat [2] with the Lexicon-Grammar methodologies for the transformation of mathematical codes into linguistics.

In this way, if we would like to proceed to one taxonomic classification from the possible sentences from the narrative sequence of the French narrative literary text, it would be convenient to clarify the importance of the verb in the sentence through the research and experimentation method of LGLI [7] and to insert them into a local grammar. Thus, we intend to bring the mathematical paradigm back into linguistic structures in order to produce a formal synthetic code in a formal grammar Lexicon-Grammar L.G.L.I.[8] [7].

During a decade of experimental work carried out in the Department of Communication Sciences of the University of Salerno in collaboration with other research centers and, in particular, with the " Laboratoire d'Autornatique et Linguistique (CNRS - Paris)", new methods for linguistic investigation have been developed. Research has been carried out based essentially on the construction of syntactic lexicons that, taking advantage of the opportunities offered by computerized data processing, point to a description, as exhaustive and formal as possible, of a specific language. The research is part of the project "Lexicon-Grammar of the Italian language (LGLI)". The theoretical reference model is represented by the "Operator-argument Grammar" [8]. *A rigorously analytical approach has been derived in which, despite the centrality of the syntax and the scientific nature of the rules of transformation, the grammar of a language should no longer be interpreted as an abstract model, but be investigated based on concrete statements L.G.L.I* [7].

By associating the first-class code sentence (43) with the class code sentence (41), a multiplicity of sentences with the same characteristics is realized (Fig. 1):

N_0 =: Nhum	N_1 = $V^0\Omega$
N_0 =: Nnr	N_1 = di $V^0\Omega$
N_0 =: il fatto Ch F	N_1 = $N_{1ad}\Omega$
N_0 =: $V^1\Omega$	N_1 = se Fo se F cib
N_0 di V_1 Ω	Ppv = lo
N_0 V	N_1 = Nhum
N_0 V N_1 contro N_2	N_1 = N-hum
N_0 V (presso con) Nhum	N_1 = il fatto ChF
	N_1 di Nhum
N_1 =: Che F	N_1 da N_2
[illegible]	N_1 dal fatto ChF
N_1 =: Aux $V^0\Omega$	ChF a N_2hum
N_1 di $V^0\Omega$ N_1 =: di Aux $V^0\Omega$	Passivo
Neg/interrog = Fcong	N_1 =: N_1 Agg^1
Imp = Fcong	N_1 =: Agg^1ChF
N_1 =: Che Fcong	N_0 V (essere cong)
N_1 =: Fcong	N_1 hum per Aux $V^0\Omega$

Fig. 1. Description of an operator by classes of operators (lexicon-grammar): converging models. Classifying table: Elia 1984 p. 193.

This transformation can occur injectively: if, taken two distinct elements of the first set, two distinct elements of the second set correspond (Monomorphism). It can occur surjectively: if each element of the second set corresponds to at least one element of the first set (Epimorphism).

[8] NooJ, a natural language processing software developed by Max Silberztein (2007, 2008). NooJ and the evolution of Intex (Silberztein 1993, 1999) on which Silberztein worked in the decade 1992–2002 under the guidance of Maurice Gross at LADL. NooJ allows the construction of dictionaries and electronic grammars and their application to large corpora (www.nooj4n 1p.net). NooJ is a linguistic engine that includes some computational devices used both for the formal description of linguistic phenomena and for the parsing of written texts: automata and finite state transducers, recursive networks, regular expressions and context -free grammars [4].

It can occur biunivocally if each element of the first set corresponds to one and only one element of the second set (Isomorphism) F Description of an operator by classes of operators (lexicon-grammar): converging models.

A first reduction in formal code is obtained in the categorization of operators [10] p. 16 according to a lexicon-grammatical classification of verbs and checks the possibility of aggregation with nominal forms. Research on sentence structures involves a lexicon-grammatical classification of verbs and checks the real possibility of aggregation with nominal forms. According to the theories of Harris and Chomsky, through the study of the combinatorial possibilities of sentences, sentences which have ample possibility of commutation of lexical entries within the position N radioactivity of the class of IVs) are considered "free". A second characteristic of simple sentences is characterized by the co-occurrence of a class of operator verbs and support verbs.

It is appropriate to parse sentences according to the theories of Harris and Chomsky [11] through the study of the combinatorial possibilities of sentences, which are considered "free" sentences and that have wide possibility of switching lexical entries within the N position (productivity of the class of N). A second feature of simple sentences is characterized by the co-occurrence of a class of operator and support verbs. The third one, by sentences that are referred to as phrases: As a result, as stated earlier, if we would like to proceed to one taxonomic classification from the possible sentences from the narrative sequence of the French narrative literary text, it would be convenient to clarify the importance of the verb in the sentence through the research and experimentation method and to insert them into a local grammar:[9]

Seq. 2 XVI

[…] *Le gamin du céleste Empire hésita d'abord; puis, se ravisant, il répondit: « Je vais vous le dire.» Peu d'instants après, il reparut, tenant dans ses bras un fort gros chat, et le regardant, comme on dit, dans le blanc des yeux, il affirma sans hésiter: « Il n'est pas encore tout à fait midi.» Ce qui était vrai. […]»*[10]

Analysis of the linguistic mechanisms of the sequence Fs.

1= Verbal operators: *Je vais vous le dire; il reparut; le regardant; il affirma; hésiter; (Ce qui) était vrai. Mechanisms of Pronominalization*
2= Substitute preverbal pronouns: *le dire; il reparut; le regardant; il affirma; hésiter; (Ce qui) était vrai. Pronominal positionality*
3= Polyrematic: *celeste Empire*; M.Word = *(le regardant) dans le blanc des yeux:* Denotative phrase DPH = *comme on dit.*

Parsing and reduction in Fs = Analysis on a sequence.

---

[9] Elia, A., Martinelli, M., D'agostino, E., 1985, "Three components of Italian syntax: simple sentences, supporting verb sentences and idiomatic sentences ", in Proceedings of SLI 24, *Syntax and morphology of the language Italian use. Descriptive theories and applications,* Rome, Bulzoni, pp. 311–325.

[10] The boy of the Celestial Empire at first hesitated; then, changing his mind, he replied: "I'll tell you." A few moments later he reappeared, holding a very large cat in his arms, and looking him, as they say, straight in the eye, said without hesitation: "It is not yet noon." What was true.

Fixed sentences: *le regardant, ..., dans le blanc des yeux*, Ppv V.
Comparative analysis: Mathematical Model – L.G.L.I
3 = Le *gamin hésita* = Det N0 V = HEC.
4 = N0 Det V C = A H E C.
Le gamin. Empire hésita =
5 = N0 V C c = A E H C B.
regardant, comme on dit, dans le blanc des yeux, =N0 V Ppo C loc.
Analysis of the mechanisms of the sentence.

- Pronominal manipulation = analysis of the average such as

  Je vais vous le dire; il reparut; le regardant; il affirma; hésiter;(Ce qui) etait vrai.
  = Ppv V_{supp} V; Ppv V Ppv V.........

- Calculation of the Fibonacci series, homophone iteration[11]

  Le_1 *gamin du* $cé_1le_2ste_3$ E_5mpire_8 $hé_{13}sita$ *d'abord; puis, se ravisant, il répondit*:
  "*Je vais vous le dire*
  1 1 2 3 5 8 13...

- Phrase M. Word or idiomatics = Les Chinois voient l'heure dans l'œil des chats.

  .... *le regardant, comme on dit, dans le blanc des* yeux ... = $N\,0\,V\,as\,C\,1$
  They are found in the seq. 2 A multifrequency of polyrematics as per the title.

3   The Lexicon-Grammatical and Automatic Text Analysis[12]

NooJ is geared towards developing grammars processing large amounts of texts and therefore contains a full-fledged corpus processing module, indexing, annotation and querying of corpora is a basic functionality. Corpora's size is typically ...Text can be imported in a wide variety of formats and a lexical analysis is immediately applied on the basis of a robust dictionary module that has a built-in morphological analyzer. The result of the lexical analysis becomes the initial tier in a set of stand-off annotation levels containing at first POS and morphological codes as well as the result of any morphological grammars that carried out typical pre-processing normalizations of the text.[13]

---

[11] The recursive technique was carried out on the elementary calculation of syllables and on the phonic repetition of a phonal analysis (Silvestri 2014, pag.214).

[12] For the realization analysis textual automatic was used the NOOJ software.package, mainly based on the use of electronic dictionaries, local grammars and state automata and transducers _ finished (hereinafter FST). In the course from the software applications, they are States used the dictionaries electronic developed by the Science Department from the Communication of the University of Salerno, or five dictionaries of the DELA system (dictionaries of simple and compound words) to which it has been flanked a dictionary electronic specialist in the sector from the communication.

[13] Max Silberztein, Tamás Váradi, Marko Tadić, Open source multi -platform NooJ for NLP.

210   I. Veronesi et al.

It is a supercomputing environment in which computations are produced by transformational analysis of feature mechanisms and graphs are produced in the NooJ environment:

One of the most attractive features of the system that immediately appeals to users is the ease with which sophisticated grammars (of various levels of computing power) can be built in graph form and applied to corpora as a query [12] (see, Fig. 2, for an example). This feature alone makes NooJ ideal for teaching and a rapid application development tool alike. The graphs have alternative textual notation in case that mode of definition proves more applicable (Fig. 3).

Fig. 2. Sophisticated grammars of various levels of computing power built in graph form and applied to corpora as a query.

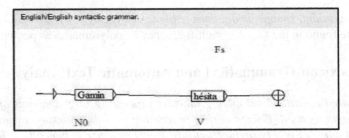

Fig. 3. Analysis and graphs converging in a single local grammar.

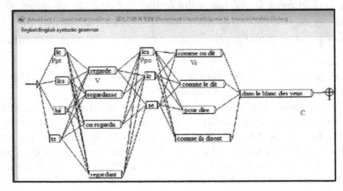

Fig.4. … le regardant, comme on dit, dans le blanc des yeux … = N 0 V as C 1

In accordance with the above, one characteristic of NooJ [13] is that its corpus processing engine uses large-coverage linguistic lexical and syntactic resources, which allows NooJ users to perform sophisticated queries that include any of the available morphological, lexical or syntactic properties. In this way, both Planat and Silberztein methods could serve as a basis for carrying out operations in Linguistic, Physics, and Mathematics settings that would allow users to build broader mathematical, lexical, and semantic structures in these fields of study (Fig. 4).

4   Digital Intelligence W.Tool in NooJ Environment

The DIGITAL INTELLIGENCE W.T language environment (©2020) BiVuTeGMS involves the presence of an "excellent" human mind to control and guide the whole process:

1. taxonomies of phrases, parts of phrases, syntagms or parts of syntagms, reconverted into acronyms that have undergone validations such as: analysis and detection of linguistic mechanisms (manipulations of substitutions, permutations, syntagmatic and phonological calculation according to Silvestri's theories), productions computation of averages, of selected sentences;
2. In linguistic environment Nooj software M Silberztein, production of parts phrases or syntagms reconverted into graphs following the techniques and tools of graph theory (parallel production of the presence of the same phenomenon with the two justifications for linguistic-mathematical domains.

This is the definitive reduction in acronyms, that is, the resultant of fixed sentences. The digital archive is supported by a sheet of editing, reformulation, reconversion of sentences or textual parts. If we would like to describe the formal process, we would say that the data, i.e. sentences, follow the following process of archiving data collection (sentences) and calculation of linguistic mechanisms and averaging - reductions into categories (L.G.L.I) production of formal codes in NooJ environment and transformational and distributional analysis of chosen traits in high computing and scientific validation environments, phrase reductions into acronyms. The central part of the software consists of a digital sheet in which the operator edits, translates, and reconverts using acronyms (i.e. fixed phrases) and free phrases that the digital operator produces as needed. It is called redactor text precisely because it is similar to a paper sheet, it can construct different text types and dependent on human skills, even better on human excellences and therefore their functions are: drafting of a text composed of free sentences and paraphrases; translation and reformulation from one language to another L1 L2 L3 including iconic languages (Fig. 5).

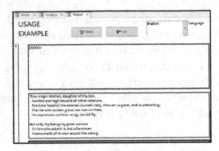

Fig. 5. Example of the digital intelligence W. Tool in NooJ environment.

5 Conclusion and Research Results

Although we have described the Planat's mathematical model with a single text at our disposal and on the basis of their production, we can say that we have compared mathematical theories to the computational linguistic theories of Lexicon-Grammar in the stages and process of similarity between languages and system of reduction in fixed synthetic code and homologated by domains [9, 14–19]. From the concentration on the mathematical concept contents of group, relation and series, it emerged that they are the unequivocal reductions to paraphrase the number group into phrase group, then into validation code from mathematical to linguistic symbols.

In describing the clear stages for the formal description of languages, it is understood that, of course, important stages are missing, such as quantum computing and universal digital writing code.

References

1. Alexander, W.: Quantum Mind and Social Science. Cambridge University Press, Cambridge (2015)
2. Planat, M., Aschheim, R., Amaral, M.M., Fang, F., Irwin, K.: Graph coverings for investigating non local structures in proteins. Music and Poems. Sci 3(4), 39 (2021)
3. Baudelaire, C.: Le Spleen de Paris. A posthumous Cllection of Poems by Charles Baudelaire. BoD-Books on Demand, Petits poèmes en prose) (2019)
4. Silberztein, M.: Joe loves lea: transformational analysis of direct transitive sentences. In: Okrut, T., Hetsevich, Y., Silberztein, M., Stanislavenka, H. (eds.) *Automatic Processing of Natural-Language Electronic Texts with NooJ*. NooJ 2015. Communications in Computer and Information Science, vol. 607, pp. 55–65. Springer, Cham (2015). https://doi.org/10.1007/978-3-319-42471-2_5
5. Nagel, E., Newman, J.R.: Gödel's Proof, Rev New York University Press, New York (2001)
6. Hofstadter, D.R., Trautteur, G., Veit, B.: *Gödel, Escher, Bach: an eternal brilliant garland: a metaphorical fugue on minds and machines in the spirit of Lewis Carroll*. Adelphi (1984)
7. Elia, A., Martinelli, M., D'Agostino, E.: Three components of Italian syntax: simple sentences, support verb sentences and idiomatic sentences. In: Atti della SLI 24, *Syntax and Morphology of the Italian Language of Use. Teorie e applicazioni descrittive*, Roma, Bulzoni, pp. 311–325 (1985)

8. Harris, Z.S.: "The elementary transformations". TDAP 54. Philadelphia: University of Penn-sylvania. (Excerpted in Harris 1970:482–532, & abbreviated in Harris 1981.211–235.) (1964)

9. Bucciarelli, R., Capone, R., Tortoriello, F.S., Greco, M., Savarese, G., Enriquez, J.: Learning analytics-scientific description and heuristic validation of languages NLG. J. e-Learn. Knowl. Soc. **15**(3), 251–261 (2019)

10. Elia, A., Landi, A., Bucciarelli, R.: From grammar to poetic text. *Loffredo editore, Naples* (2000)

11. Elia, A., Monteleone, M., Marano, F.: From the concept of transformation in Harris and Chomsky to the Lexique-Grammaire of Maurice Gross. *Hist. Linguist.* 76–82 (2011)

Online Resources

12. https://www.researchgate.net/messages/61518552
13. https://www.researchgate.net/messages/1770891171
14. https://www.researchgate.net/messages/70162360
15. https://www.researchgate.net/messages/57516656
16. https://www.researchgate.net/messages/701623600
17. Type Race: M. Renda, R. Bucciarelli team del POLO Università di Salerno, Corpus di completamento parole lemmi e frasi e parafrasi di frasi
18. Digital Intelligence Acro–Word; R. Bucciarelli; P. Villari; M. F. Terrone; R. Marcone; F. Santoro: DB ambienti di sviluppo linguistico e riformulatore testo con tecniche cloud delle lingue naturali verbali e non verbali
19. Word–Tool, R. Bucciarelli; P. Villari; F. M. Terrone; M. Greco; R. Marcone; F. Santoro: Redactor text di formulazione testo e di riconversione del linguaggio LIS in codice della lingua naturale (L_1 in L_2), traduttore automatico tedesco-italiano e inglese - italiano, trasmissione in tempo reale

Correction to: Creation of a Legal Domain Corpus for the Belarusian Module in NooJ: Texts, Dictionaries, Grammars

Valery Varanovich, Mikita Suprunchuk, Yauheniya Zianouka,
Tsimafei Prakapenka, Anna Dolgova, and Yuras Hetsevich

Correction to:
Chapter "Creation of a Legal Domain Corpus
for the Belarusian Module in NooJ: Texts, Dictionaries,
Grammars" in: M. González et al. (Eds.):
Formalizing Natural Languages: Applications to Natural
Language Processing and Digital Humanities, **CCIS 1758,**
https://doi.org/10.1007/978-3-031-23317-3_13

In the originally published version of the chapter 13 the affiliation of the author Anna Dolgova was indicated incorrectly. The affiliation of Anna Dolgova has been corrected as "Belarusian State University".

The updated original version of this chapter can be found at
https://doi.org/10.1007/978-3-031-23317-3_13

Author Index

Printed in the United States
by Baker & Taylor Publisher Services

Printed in the United States
by Baker & Taylor Publisher Services